THE SECRET WAR
FOR THE FALKLANDS

The SAS, MI6, and the War
Whitehall Nearly Lost

NIGEL WEST

LITTLE, BROWN AND COMPANY

A *Little, Brown* Book

First published in Great Britain in 1997
by Little, Brown and Company
Reprinted 1997 (twice)

PICTURE CREDITS

1, 2, 5, 6, 8, 9, 10, 11, 12: Associated Press/Topham;
3: Rex Features; 4: Hulton Getty; 13: Nigel West;
7, 14: Buenos Aires *Herald*; 15, 16: Imperial War Museum

The moral right of the author has been asserted.

A CIP catalogue record for this book
is available from the British Library.

ISBN 0 316 88226 7

Typeset by Palimpsest Book Production Limited,
Polmont, Stirlingshire
Printed and bound in Great Britain by
Clays Ltd, St Ives plc

Little, Brown and Company (UK)
Brettenham House
Lancaster Place
London WC2E 7EN

THE SECRET WAR
FOR THE FALKLANDS

Also by Nigel West

'Defence is very dependent on information'
Peter Carrington, *Reflect on Things Past*

'The Falklands was a war which need never have happened'
Denis Healey, *The Time of My Life*

'It is insufficient simply to garner secret information;
it has to be assimilated and correctly used'
David Owen, *Time to Declare*

Contents

CONTENTS

ACKNOWLEDGEMENTS

Because of the exceptional sensitivity of much of the information acquired while researching the book, in London, Washington DC, Argentina and Chile, I have been unable to identify sources or publicly express my gratitude for the assistance I was given, which was granted on the strict understanding that individuals would not be quoted. Accordingly, I am restricted in thanking those who have given me so much help, but I am especially grateful to Carlos Doglieli and Nicholas Tozer in Buenos Aires; Roberto Arancibia and Marcos Robledo in Santiago; and J. J. Elkin in Rio de Janeiro.

My thanks are also due to Rear-Admiral David Pulvertaft of the D-Notice Committee for his guidance, and the Controller of HMSO for permission to reproduce two Ministry of Defence documents.

LIST OF ABBREVIATIONS

AEW	Airborne Early Warning
ASIS	Australian Secret Intelligence Service
ASW	Anti-submarine Warfare
AWACS	Airborne Warning and Control System
CIA	Central Intelligence Agency (US)
CIG	Current Intelligence Group
CNI	Centro Nacional de Información (Chilean Internal Intelligence Service)
CoS	Chief of Station
DCI	Director of Central Intelligence
DEA	Drug Enforcement Agency (US)
DGSE	Direction Générale de la Sécurité Extérieure (French Secret Intelligence Service, formerly SDECE)
DiDeNa	Dirección de Inteligencia Defensa Nacional (Chilean External Intelligence Service)
DINA	Chilean Intelligence Service
DIS	Defence Intelligence Staff
DO	Directorate of [CIA] Operations
DST	Direction de la Surveillance du Territoire (French Security Service)
FBI	Federal Bureau of Investigation (US)
FECIG	Far East Current Intelligence Group
FLN	Front de Libération Nationale (Algeria)
GCHQ	Government Communications Headquarters
GIC	Groupe Interministériel de Contrôle (French government bureau)

GID	Libyan Intelligence Service
GRU	Glavnoye Razvedyvatelnoye Upravleniye (Soviet Military Intelligence Service)
INLA	Irish National Liberation Army
IRA	Irish Republican Army
J-2	Argentine Military Intelligence Service
JIC	Joint Intelligence Committee
KGB	Komitet Gosudarstvennoy Bezopasnosti (Soviet Intelligence Service)
LACIG	Latin America Current Intelligence Group
LADE	Lineas Aéreas del Estado (Argentine airline)
MI5	British Security Service
MI6	British Secret Intelligence Service
MoD	Ministry of Defence
NATO	North Atlantic Treaty Organisation
NCI	Chilean Intelligence Service
NRO	National Reconnaissance Office (US)
NSA	National Security Agency (US)
NSC	National Security Council (US)
NZSIS	New Zealand Security Intelligence Service
OFEMA	Office Français d'Exportation de Matériel Aéronautique (French government bureau)
PCP	Pilot Centre Paris (cover-name for operation by Argentine Naval Intelligence)
PFLP	Popular Front for the Liberation of Palestine
PIRA	Provisional Irish Republican Army
RFA	Royal Fleet Auxiliary
RG	Renseignements Généraux (French police)
RUC	Royal Ulster Constabulary
SAS	Special Air Service
SBS	Special Boat Section
SDECE	Service de Documentation Extérieure et de Contre-Espionnage (French Foreign Intelligence Service)
SIDE	Secretariá Inteligencia del Estado (Argentine Security Intelligence Service)
SIS	Secret Intelligence Service

SISDE   Italian Security Service
SISMI   Italian Military Intelligence Service
SUKLO   Special United Kingdom Liaison Officer (GCHQ's representative in US)
UDA   Ulster Defence Association
UNITA   União Nacional para a Independência Total de Angola (National Union for the Total Independence of Angola)
VARIG   Viação Aérea Rio Grandense (Brazilian airline)

MEMBERSHIP OF THE JIC, APRIL 1982

Joint Intelligence Committee

Chairman: Sir Patrick Wright
Deputy Chairman: Admiral Sir Roy Halliday

Colin Figures – Secret Intelligence Service
Sir Brian Tovey – Government Communications
    Headquarters
John Jones – Security Service
General Sir James Glover – Deputy Chief of the Defence
    Staff (Intelligence)
Sir Antony Duff – Cabinet Intelligence Co-ordinator
Robin O'Neill – Head of JIC Assessment Staff

Ex-officio members:
Air Marshal Michael Armitage – Director of Service
    Intelligence
Sir Michael Palliser – Cabinet Office
Alan Wolfe – Chief of Station, Central Intelligence
    Agency
Elizabeth Halliday – New Zealand Secret Intelligence
    Service
Brian Gorman – Australian Secret Intelligence
    Service

Defence Intelligence Staff

Director of Service Intelligence: Air Marshal Michael
  Armitage
Director of Management and Support of Intelligence:
  Admiral John Robertson
Director of Scientific and Technical Intelligence: Nigel
  Hughes
Director of Economic and Logistic Intelligence: Walter
  Rudkin

PREFACE

'The Argentines had only a limited number of the devastating Exocet missiles. They made desperate attempts to increase their arsenal ... We for our part were equally desperate to interdict this supply'
Margaret Thatcher, *The Downing Street Years*

The Falklands campaign of 1982 was one of the most significant military conflicts fought since the end of the Second World War. From a military perspective it was the first time the Royal Navy had been engaged by an enemy since 1945. It was also the first occasion on which sophisticated aircraft were deployed in sustained combat against surface vessels. In terms of hardware, it was a test of the world's latest air and defence systems, and a unique opportunity to push competing fighters to their limits in an environment that stretched men and aircraft alike, and in which neither side acheived air superiority.

On the ground the opposing forces were not ill-matched. The 13,000 Argentine defenders on East Falkland were well prepared and equipped with modern weapons, including the very latest night-vision goggles. When the two sides clashed, the conscripts fought well against the 10,500 British professionals ranged against them, and in some of the prolonged fire-fights inflicted serious casualties on the invaders. Above the battleground, the Argentine Air Force gained the respect of all by pressing home attacks at maximum range with conspicuous gallantry, despite heavy losses. At sea, the Royal Navy suffered a rate of attrition that was unsustainable. By the time the beach-head at San Carlos had been established on 21 May, only Her Majesty's Ships *Exeter*, *Yarmouth* and the assault carrier *Hermes* remained completely operational. All the others had suffered varying degrees of damage, and nearly half of Admiral Sandy Woodward's once impressive fleet of destroyers and frigates had been 'reduced to near-zero capability'. As the Task Force commander observed at the time, 'Frankly, if the Args could only breathe on us, we'd fall over!'[1]

The outcome of the campaign was a splendid victory for Prime Minister Margaret Thatcher, who, at the time of the Junta's occupation of Stanley, was leading an administration that had plumbed hitherto unknown depths in electoral unpopularity. The triumph was one that many experienced military minds, particularly in America, had judged almost unachievable, and the final Argentine surrender on 14 June carried her to a landslide result at the polls the following year as well as ensuring her place as a statesman of world acclaim. And yet the outcome could have been quite different, and came much closer to ignominious disaster than has ever been officially admitted. Indeed, several of those best qualified to have recorded precisely what happened have either been discouraged from writing or at least urged to minimise certain aspects of the conflict. Until quite recently, for example, the nature and scope of the American contribution had been deliberately down-played, partly for domestic reasons – to emphasise what Britain alone had accomplished – but mainly to respect American sensitivity to their administration's relationship with Latin America.

Although very little has been written about the campaign's *sub rosa* facets, they remain very compelling. Moreover, as virtually all of those who contributed have since retired, their extraordinary achievements deserve some public acknowledgement; recognition which can now be given safely, more than a dozen years after the end of hostilities, and in a time when diplomatic relations between London and Buenos Aires have been restored to the extent that the Royal Navy can resume courtesy visits to Argentine ports and troops from both countries serve alongside one another as peace-keepers on the UN Green Line in Cyprus. As for the disclosure of the identities of individual intelligence officers, the arguments in favour of prolonged discretion have diminished considerably since the collapse of the Soviet Bloc.

The story of Operation CORPORATE, the Task Force assigned to retake the Falklands, has been told by many participants – political, diplomatic and military. There is no denying the astonishing valour and sacrifice of those who underwent dreadful privations to contribute to a historic military accomplishment: the endurance of the four-man SAS 'G' Squadron patrol led by Captain Alvin Wright, for example, which spent twenty-six days concealed in shallow hides scooped out of the sodden peat of Beagle Ridge, in the most appalling weather conditions, to keep Stanley under covert observation; or the extraordinary bravery of Staff Sergeant Jim Prescott of the Royal Engineers' bomb disposal team, who perished while defusing an unexploded 1,000-pounder lodged in the air-conditioning unit of HMS *Antelope*'s Petty Officers' Mess; or the skill and courage of Lieutenant-Commander Ian Stanley, the Wessex 3 pilot of 737 Naval Air Squadron, who repeatedly risked his life to rescue thirteen soldiers trapped high on South Georgia's Fortuna Glacier after two other helicopters had crashed in the attempt (seventeen men were squeezed into an aircraft designed for five, and flown to a crash-landing on HMS *Antrim*'s afterdeck).

These are just a sample of the numerous acts of undoubted selfless conduct, the majority of them unknown to more than a handful of witnesses, that enabled CORPORATE to succeed despite a very tight schedule. But apart from the battles fought on land, sea and in the air, another dimension which has largely gone unrecorded centres on the clandestine efforts made to deny General Leopoldo Galtieri the one weapon which everyone acknowledged could have turned CORPORATE into one of the most humiliating defeats in British history.

The French-manufactured Exocet missile was, and remains, one of the most formidable weapons in the non-nuclear arsenal. Named after the *Exocoetus* flying fish, which skims over the surface of waves, its potency was demonstrated against HMS *Sheffield*, the container ship SS *Atlantic Conveyor* and HMS *Glamorgan*. Even if the warhead did not explode on impact, as happened in the first example, the Exocet's velocity and remaining volatile propellant wreaked sufficient havoc deep in the heart of the most modern warship to ensure it sustained tremendous damage, if not complete loss.

On their long, twelve-day journey from Ascension to the Total Exclusion Zone – a 200-mile radius around the islands – the Task Force commanders were consumed by two overriding preoccupations: firstly the knowledge that, unless Stanley was retaken by mid-June, logistical constraints and the weather would combine to prevent the British troops from completing their mission (although there was little talk in public about the gruelling timetable, in case the enemy found ways of delaying matters, the clock was ticking relentlessly against Woodward and his men); and secondly that the loss of either of the two carriers, *Hermes* or HMS *Invincible*, would mean elimination of the already inadequate air cover and force an immediate withdrawal. As Woodward candidly observed, 'Lose *Invincible* and the operation is severely jeopardised. Lose *Hermes* and the operation is over. One lucky torpedo, bomb or missile hit, even a simple but major accident on board, could do it.'[2] He might have said the same for the *Queen Elizabeth II*, a symbol of the country's maritime pride, or P & O's

flagship *Canberra*, crammed with troops unused to long
sea voyages.

However, the principal threat to all the ships of the
Task Force, and to many of the unprotected merchantmen upon whom the enterprise depended, came from
a single source: the air-launched Aerospatiale AM-39
Exocet, which proved precisely how deadly it could be
on the morning of Tuesday 4 May 1982.

Chapter 1

'HANDBRAKE!'

It was the moment thousands of servicemen and women had dreaded. The single cry of 'Handbrake!' sent a chill into the heart of every NATO sailor – the odds were that within a couple of minutes, if not seconds, there would be massive casualties aboard one of the most sophisticated and heavily defended weapons platforms afloat.

The most-feared word was uttered by the Air Warfare Officer (AWO) in the Operations Room behind the bridge of HMS *Glasgow*, a Type-42 guided-missile destroyer which had been in service for just four years, since March 1978. Commanded by Captain Paul Hoddinott, a former nuclear submariner who had served on *Dreadnought* and *Repulse*, HMS *Glasgow* was one of the first ships in the Total Exclusion Zone, having rushed south from Gibraltar at thirty knots as soon as the Falklands were invaded, together with *Arrow*, *Sheffield*, *Coventry*, led by *Brilliant* and accompanied by the tanker *Appleleaf*. Now, in poor weather, constant rain squalls and bad visibility, *Glasgow*, *Coventry* and *Sheffield* were acting as a forward picket line, scanning the horizon with their long-range radars for the approach of hostile aircraft. To their east, eighteen miles away, was a second line of defence for the main battle group: three frigates and the recently refitted County-class guided missile destroyer *Glamorgan*. A further layer of protection for *Hermes* and *Invincible* was provided by three fleet auxiliaries which were intended to be expendable decoys if the enemy managed to penetrate that far. Finally, both carriers were escorted by a Type-22 frigate fitted with the dual band 997/98 pulse doppler radar and a pair of the very latest six-barrel Sea Wolf point anti-missile systems which, though requiring manual reloading, were supposed to be very effective against low-flying targets at up to four miles, and able to discriminate automatically against multi-path radar reflections. In practice, the close-in Sea Wolf's computer was prone to saturation if it detected more than two contacts. In the absence of any Airborne Early Warning (AEW) aircraft, these three rather limited obstacles were all that could be placed in the path of a hostile Exocet. Only introduced in 1980, the Sea Wolf was a short-range naval weapon with a proximity fuse, guided towards the target visually by an operator with a control stick, but its disadvantage – as was soon to be discovered – was its inability to cope with multiple targets. The trials conducted before Sea Wolf's acceptance had been based on a NATO–Warsaw Pact confrontation in the North Atlantic, and apparently had not tested an alternative scenario.

The situation in which Woodward found himself was emphatically not of his choosing, but the politicians had decreed that instead of purchasing the expensive AWACS system from the United States, the RAF would develop its own Airborne Early Warning, based on the familiar Nimrod ocean surveillance aircraft. However, by 1982 the Gannet had been abandoned, the Nimrod was still on the drawing-board and NATO's northern flank continued to be protected by the trusty but obsolete Shackleton, a plane that had seen service in the Second World War but could never hope to operate in the South Atlantic, so far from a land-base. Thus Woodward, who was sometimes criticised as 'the South African admiral' because he preferred to keep his battle group closer to Africa than Latin America, was very conscious of the inadequacy of his radar cover and the vulnerability of his ships.

There had never been any doubt that, as flagship, *Hermes* would be the Argentine Air Force's principal target, but it was recognised that *Invincible* was also very attractive, for propaganda as well as operational reasons. Flying an anti-submarine Sea King off *Invincible* was HRH Prince Andrew, a pilot with 820 Naval Air Squadron. The military Junta in Buenos Aires reckoned that the value of killing the Queen's second son was incalculable, perhaps as devastating as sinking the *QEII*.

The cry of 'Handbrake!' from *Glasgow*'s AWO was quickly followed by a bearing, 'Two-three-eight', and was transmitted instantly over the UHF radio to the rest of the fleet. It was the worst possible scenario and indicated that the ship's Agave radar detection system, tuned to the transmission I-band frequency of 8–10 GHz employed by the Super Etendards, had identified the tell-tale invisible beams broadcast by the plane carrying an Exocet forty miles away. It meant that within moments a missile would be armed and despatched, allowing the Dassault Super Etendard aircraft to drop back down to sea level and head for home. Having identified and locked on to its target, the Exocet's release would make it dive low under the enemy's radar screen and, allowing for one minor adjustment in trajectory en route, would skim ten feet above the sea, controlled by an exceptionally sensitive closed-loop FM radio altimeter, and home in on the large metallic object stored in its command guidance memory. Flying subsonic at a speed of 650 knots, the missile would take 364lb of explosives into the heart of the target just above the waterline, and detonate with catastrophic consequences. Even if the missile failed to explode, its kinetic energy and remaining fuel would initiate a devastating fire midships from which no vessel could hope to survive. Thus the shouted alert 'Handbrake!' struck cold terror into the hearts of seamen, and for many would be a death warrant.

The Exocet had been manufactured by Aerospatiale since 1974 and sold to navies around the world, and of course had spawned counter-measures. The sea-launched variant had been bought by the Admiralty for the new Type-22 frigates, and the air-launched AM-39 version was considered a reliable stand-off weapon which had the advantage of being released as a 'fire-and-forget', well out of the range of most anti-aircraft missile systems. If the plane equipped with Exocet could come within forty miles of a target undetected, there was a high probability that the AM-39's search radar would engage it. Once locked on and released, there were only two alternatives for the intended recipient: shoot it down in the very few seconds when it would be visible, as it approached the hapless ship, or deceive its radar by presenting a larger target, and lure it away from the principal objective at the crucial moment when its computer made the final adjustment in trajectory. The first option – for the few ships fitted with the automated, radar-controlled Phalanx gun, which created a wall of lead through an astonishingly high rate of fire – was considered something of a last resort. Phalanx was really nothing more than a clever machine-gun loaded with special ammunition which ensured that a hit by a single round would destroy the missile, and was regarded as a last-ditch effort. The best, but rather primitive, counter-measure was to create clouds of chaff, literally millions of strands of plastic-coated aluminium and fibreglass pins, cut to the length of the Exocet's radar frequency, which mimicked the radar signature of a big target. The Exocet's relatively unsophisticated radar guidance system could not distinguish between the chaff – scattered either from onboard Protean chaff dispensers or from a helicopter – and an authentic target, particularly if the chaff was dense and the ship downfield had been given sufficient time to present its narrowest profile, bows forward to the incoming missile. There was nothing new or secret about chaff, which was actually the American codename for WINDOW, an invention that dated back to 1938 and the earliest days of radar. During the Second

World War, Bomber Command had distributed hundreds of tons of the aluminium foil over Nazi Germany in an attempt to saturate the enemy's air defences.

The modern alternative to chaff was some ingenious electronic gadgetry which acted either to jam the AM-39, or as a homing beacon broadcasting a signal to the missile which would attract it away from the main target. Unfortunately, the Task Force simply did not have any, for they were still under development, although they were later fitted to four Westland Lynx helicopters which were brought south on the Royal Fleet Auxiliary *Fort Austin* and on 19 May transferred to the carriers for permanent stand-by duty, on the deck at a moment's readiness, twenty-four hours a day. Those flying the decoy missions were told that the devices were believed to work . . . in theory.

Glasgow's crew were highly professional and, as they heard 'Handbrake!', had trained for exactly this moment. The captain put the helm hard over to offer the smallest possible profile to the missile and ordered his chaff-launchers to create the decoys that would fool the missile. There was simply no time to launch the Lynx chopper, but the counter-measures drill was executed faultlessly, the rest of the battle group being informed continuously on the range and track of the two hostile contacts.

Initially the Operations Room on *Hermes* was reluctant to believe *Glasgow*'s urgent 'Handbrake!' signal, for every precaution had been taken to avoid an Exocet attack. According to all the available information, Argentina possessed just five air-launched Exocets, and only five French Super Etendards on to which they could be fitted. Even with two additional external tanks, 132 gallons under the fuselage and 242 gallons on the port wing, these fighter-bombers had a maximum range of eight hundred miles, and would therefore require modification to allow in-flight refuelling from the Argentine Air Force's two KC-130 Hercules air-tankers if they were to engage the British battle group, which was deliberately located to the east of the islands, as far away as was practical from the Super Etendards' mainland base. Even assuming the Argentines had mastered the complexities of the Exocet avionics, and had managed to marry up an AM-39 to a serviceable Super Etendard converted for in-flight refuelling, conditions would have to be perfect for a plane to rendezvous with the tanker and be vectored towards the last known co-ordinates of the British ships by a rather elderly Lockheed Neptune maritime reconnaissance aircraft.

Because of these considerations, the urgent cry of 'Handbrake!' came as a shock, but there was no mistaking the radar return on the big UAA-1 console in *Glasgow*'s Ops Room. Three sweeps of the Agave monopulse radar in search mode illuminated positively the blips of two hostile contacts, thirty-eight miles out, on a bearing of two-three-eight, closing on the *Glasgow* at a speed of 450 knots. The radar 'painted' two bogeys incoming as they climbed at maximum speed to 2,000 feet to conduct a brief radar search. Although the Super Etendards' target acquisition sweep lasted for just three seconds, it was enough for the pulses to set off action stations on the British ships below.

In the lead aircraft Lieutenant-Commander Augusto Bedacarratz – the second-in-command of the Argentine Navy's Second Fighter and Attack Squadron – and Sub-Lieutenant Armando Mayoro threw the switches on the Exocet's navigation system to set up the pre-guidance circuits for the launch phase. Although originally based at Bahia Blanca, they had flown from the airfield at Rio Grande on Tierra del Fuego that morning and for the past hour had been guided towards the three British targets by Lieutenant-Commander Ernesto Leston and his crew of six in his ancient, twin-engined, anti-submarine SP-2H Neptune. Although the aircraft's design was of Second World War vintage, it continued to be built until 1960, and for many years held the world record for flight endurance, an astonishing fifty-five hours in the air between Perth, Western Australia and Colombus, Ohio, in 1946. As a maritime reconnaissance platform it was very slow and vulnerable, but the four planes of the *Escuadrilla de Exploración* were ideal for the purpose of keeping a radar watch on the ships of the British Task Force from a safe distance, even if they were close to the end of their working lives.

On this particular morning Leston, operating from Bahia Blanca, had spotted four blips on his long-range radar and had relayed the news to Rio Grande and, once the pilot was airborne, to Augusto Bedacarratz. For over three hours the Neptune had played a game of hide-and-seek with the Royal Navy, climbing high enough to take a bearing on the ships' radar emissions before dropping into the radar 'shadow' caused by the curvature of the earth, which left an area of dead ground in which the plane could linger out of danger. Leston had calculated that his behaviour, flying low and slow, would be interpreted by the British radar operators as a search-and-rescue mission methodically combing the sea in a grid pattern for survivors from the *General Belgrano*, the Argentine cruiser sunk the previous day. If that assumption was made, it was quite wrong, but nevertheless none of the three British vessels on radar picket duty suspected they were being monitored as they edged eastwards, or that they were being stalked by the Super Etendards which, 260 miles from the targets, had been refuelled and were making their final, lethal approach.

This was the second time the pair of fighter pilots had embarked upon their mission, for the previous morning they had waited patiently at the end of the runway at Rio Grande for the 'go' signal, but the Neptune's data had arrived too late to set up the refuelling rendezvous with the KC-130 and the flight had been cancelled, forcing the two pilots to taxi back to the hangars. The day before that, a mission assigned to the squadron commander, Captain Jorge Colombo, had been aborted because a faulty fuel valve had prevented the lead Super Etendard from taking on the precious kerosene from the tanker. Now, 400 miles away from base, Bedacarratz was flying at 500 knots as low as he dared, to avoid the two British air defence systems – the medium-range Sea Dart, and the short-range Sea Wolf – and made a second steep climb to 120 feet for the Exocet to 'see' and lock on to their targets. On his small cockpit radar screen he saw three ships, perhaps a carrier and two escorts. He made the final adjustments, activated the onboard camera to record the launch, and threw the switch that released the AM-39 from the pylon under the starboard wing, while simultaneously preparing to compensate for the sudden loss of weight. He felt the jolt of the disconnection as the missile dropped away and then, a moment later, he saw the trail of vaporised fuel from the dual-thrust booster rocket which ignited for the first 2.1 seconds of the flight before the second-stage propulsion unit took over, and he ordered Mayoro to fire his weapon. As soon as the second Exocet streaked away the pilots dived low in formation, banking left, and made a course home to the mainland. As planned, they had been in range of the feared Sea Dart, which had a formidable reputation for bringing down high-flying targets, for less than a minute.

The two missiles left a visible exhaust trail as they settled into the short flight towards their targets, now thirty miles away. Onboard the *Glasgow*, now trailing four thick clouds of chaff downwind, the Air Picture Supervisor, Leading Seaman Nevin, relayed the electronic scene across to the other ships of the battle group on the computer circuit designated Link 10. The full horror of the two incoming tracks, two very distinct amber blips on the flat screen, was shared by the rest of the fleet's radar operators and their Air Warfare Officers. Standing close by, the Electronic Warfare Supervisor ordered another chaff launch, and the eerie silence was broken by the sound of a further rocket firing into the grey sky, downwind of the stern.

Simultaneously the Sea Dart surface-to-air missile system's twin launcher on the bow was prepared for the
launch of a deadly salvo. This is the radar-guided air
defence system designed to knock out incoming aircraft
one at a time, at medium range, rather than a pair of
missiles, but, his voice characteristically calm, the Missile
Gun Director reported that the Type-909 fire control radar
wouldn't lock on to either of the tiny, intermittent targets.
The returns from both were confused by the surface
clutter created by the white crested wave-tops, so the
ADAWS-4 computer would not acquire and engage either
as a viable target even when, in growing desperation, the
automated procedure was manually overridden. Tension
in the Ops Room reached breaking point as the crew, their
faces partly concealed behind their cotton anti-flash head
masks, realised they were powerless in the face of two
incoming bogeys. The ship's only remaining armament,
the single Vickers Mark 8 4.5-inch gun on the bows,
was no protection against the AM-39 skimming across
the sea at low altitude and at just under the speed of
sound. Instinctively they started counting off the seconds
to impact and then, to huge relief, the moment passed.
They started to count again, but they were safe, the missiles
tracking straight past, at six feet above the water, across
the beam towards another target. Was it the chaff that
made them alter course, or one of the other ships, perhaps
Sheffield or *Coventry*?

On *Coventry*, the 'Handbrake!' warning had been
heeded instantly and chaff deployed with a precision
achieved after dozens of practices, but on *Sheffield*,
twenty miles away, the Ops Room had no idea of
the drama that had consumed *Glasgow* for the past
three minutes. Captain Sam Salt, at forty-two one of
the Royal Navy's most experienced submariners, who
had only taken command of his destroyer in January,
was in his day cabin after lunch, entirely oblivious to
the danger. Before being ordered to the South Atlantic

from Gibraltar, Salt and his crew had been at sea for more than four months, and now they were anxious to be home, exhausted by their long voyage. Nevertheless, they were enthusiastic members of the Task Force and fully aware of the dangers as they acted as forward 'goalkeeper' for the rest of the fleet. However, no 'action stations' had been sounded, and *Glasgow*'s warning of an attack had gone unheeded. None of the Link 10 terminals were connected to *Glasgow*'s computers, so the Ops Room was working in the standard 'Air Raid White' conditions. Due to a design fault, the powerful SCOT satellite communications circuits, which temporarily prevent the Agave radar receiver from being utilised, had been in operation, transmitting an encrypted signal over the Skynet to Fleet Headquarters in Northwood at the very moment when the ship's 965 with double AKE-2 array and 992Q radars should have spotted the two Argentine aircraft, or their missiles. Indeed, the *Sheffield* boasted good, but not the very latest, electronic warfare equipment on the market, for as well as the 992Q navigation and target designation radar, the ship was protected by a UAA-1 Abbey Hill direction-finding antenna and an omnidirectional antenna, made by the MEL Equipment Company and introduced into the Royal Navy in 1973. The UAA-1 receiver, in service since 1970, had been designed to detect radar transmissions from over the horizon and operate in a dense radar environment, providing analysis of signals across the electromagnetic spectrum and identifying all radar transmissions in the frequency band 1–18 GHz, together with directional data. In theory the UAA-1 system collects the bearing of the incoming radar from the DF antenna and the frequency and amplitude from the Omni antennae, and passes them to a processor which handles the signals in digital form and compares the frequency, pulse width and pulse repetition frequency with a library bank of analysed data. The computer undertakes an instant comparison with the data held on file and, if the incoming signal matches a hostile in the memory, the warning module is initiated automatically. Although the UAA-1 had been programmed with Soviet emissions in mind, it was linked to the Agave receiver, the unit fitted to the Super Etendards and, incidentally, to the Jaguar. Again, in theory, any Agave transmission, however brief, would start lights flashing in the Ops Room of any NATO surface vessel. But at the critical moment, there was silence on the *Sheffield*.

Because of the satellite transmission, the *Sheffield*'s Bedstead 965 air surveillance radar and the 909 target-tracking radar had been switched off. Thus the ship never had an opportunity to use her secret weapon, the Bexley 669 jammer, which would have sent an active signal to confuse the Exocet's monopulse ADAC radar, and the 667/668 noise jammer which had been designed to confuse hostile search radars of the type found on the Styx generation of Soviet missiles. The Royal Navy had planned to refit the *Sheffield* with more modern technology, replacing the Abbey Hill with the Cutlass, and improving the electronic counter-measures with the Ramses 670 deception jammers and Millpost jammers, but budget cuts had delayed the schedule so the *Sheffield* was without even an infra-red warning receiver system, then considered an essential final line of defence against hostile missile attack.

Temporarily blinded by the powerful signals transmitted by the twin SCOT antennae to the troublesome Skynet satellite, *Sheffield*'s Ops Room had taken no counter-measures. The Lynx helicopter had not been launched, and the surrounding grey skies were entirely free of chaff from the two ship-borne launchers. Moments after the Exocets had raced safely past *Glasgow*, and had been seen by look-outs on the bridge of the Type-12 frigate HMS *Yarmouth*, one struck *Sheffield* amidships, close to the water on the starboard side, ripping a hole fourteen feet wide in the hull. It penetrated the Auxiliary Machinery Space at precisely 1404 Zulu and ploughed into the Forward Engine Room, but failed to detonate. Nevertheless it ignited the fuel feeds and a tremendous fire followed, creating a choking, thick black smoke that quickly engulfed the whole of the centre of the ship and suffocated all the men in the Computer Room. The blast ripped through the galley and the Damage Control Centre, setting the combustible PVC-covered cables alight and thereby inhibiting the ship's power and communications. The sudden inferno fractured the water main, handicapping the damage-control parties, and the pressurised ventilation system acted to spread the life-threatening smoke throughout the ship, making fire-fighting next to impossible. The decks became so hot that the sailors' feet were burned through the soles of their shoes.

The second Exocet fell into the sea harmlessly some miles away, 107 seconds after launch, but *Sheffield* – the first Type-42 destroyer, commissioned just seven years earlier – was doomed. Although unable to steer, and with no water pressure for the fire hoses, the stricken vessel's Rolls-Royce Olympus gas turbines were still running and a short signal was transmitted to *Invincible*, reporting the missile attack. The frigates *Arrow* and *Yarmouth* were sent racing to the scene to assist, and *Glasgow* was ordered to remain on station in case of another attack. On board, Captain Salt tried to fight the blaze, now out of control and threatening to blow up the Sea Dart magazine, until finally the order was given, four and a half hours later, to abandon ship. Twenty men had been killed, twenty-four injured, and the Task Force had been robbed of a vital component. When finally the burning hulk capsized six days later, it was the first ship of the Royal Navy to be sunk in more than forty years.

The evolution of the Exocet can be traced to October 1967 when, more than four months after the conclusion of the Arab–Israeli conflict known as the Six-Day War, an Israeli destroyer, the *Eilat*, was attacked unexpectedly by an Egyptian patrol vessel. Originally HMS *Zealous*, and built for the Royal Navy in 1944, the ship was armed with four 4.5 guns and six 300mm anti-aircraft Bofors.

During the 1967 war itself the *Eilat* had played no significant role, but in July, during the ceasefire, it participated in a naval skirmish off the northern coast of Sinai in which two Egyptian motor-torpedo boats were sunk by accurate gunfire. Then, in October, the *Eilat* was approached by a pair of Russian-built Komar-class fast missile boats. In Russian *komar* means mosquito, and the wooden-hulled vessel was itself quite light and vulnerable, designed on the model provided by the American P-6. What made the Komar so potent was the pair of Styx surface-to-surface missiles mounted on launchers on the deck. Once locked on to a target indicated by the boat's SQUARE TIE radar, the massive nineteen-foot missile used an onboard terminal homer to guide it to the target. First spotted in the Soviet Red Banner Fleet in 1960, it was a large weapon with a wing-span of nine feet, and boasted a range of twelve nautical miles, although for accuracy it was recommended that it be fired from an optimum position at half that range.

The 2,555-ton *Eilat* was on patrol in international waters thirteen and a half miles off Port Said when the Komar sped towards it and fired two SS-N-2 missiles. The first hit the *Eilat* amidships, the huge explosion caused by the massive 1,100lb warhead putting the Parsons turbines out of action. The *Eilat* responded to the unexpected attack with its ancient Bofors, using an equally obsolete tachymetric fire-control director, but moments later the second missile finished off what was left of the ship, and forty-seven of the Israeli crew were killed. It was an incident that sparked off retaliatory shelling of Egyptian oil refineries close to the city of Suez and marked a further deterioration in the fragile peace that had existed along the Canal since June. However, apart from the political consequences, the episode represented an important landmark in sea warfare, being the first time that a relatively small surface craft had sunk a much larger, 362-foot warship with a guided missile. Suddenly the world's navies were gripped by the implications of big expensive ships with large radar profiles being transformed into easy targets for relatively tiny speedboats armed with sophisticated surface-to-surface missiles. In terms of cost, the Styx offered astonishingly good value, and defence contractors in the West began work on their own versions. As they did so, further proof emerged of the efficiency of the relatively cheap anti-ship missile, first in the 1971 Indo-Pakistani War, where the Indian Navy used Styx to great effect, and then in 1973, when the Israeli-manufactured Gabriel sank five Arab patrol vessels during the Yom Kippur War.

The Exocet was developed by Aerospatiale's tactical weapons division at Châtillon-sur-Seine, north of Dijon, in conjunction with the French government. The company produced the MM-40 in 1974. The final product, built to the French Navy's specifications by Emile Stauff – the engineer who had designed the Roland anti-aircraft and the Milan anti-tank weapons – was slightly shorter than the Styx; much narrower and more streamlined, with four cruciform wings; much faster, with a two-stage solid propellant rocket; and with almost double the range of twenty-one miles. Although the warhead was only a quarter of the weight of the Styx, the Exocet flew at Mach 0.93 and packed an impressive punch, even when it failed to detonate on impact.

The key to the Exocet's success lay in its ability to fly accurately at very low altitudes. This was achieved in part by the inertial guidance platform controlled by the ADAC radar developed by the Electronique Serge Dassault. The initial pre-launch instructions were entered into the Thomson-CSF Vega fire-control computer through the shipboard Installation de Tir Standard, assembled at the DTCN establishment at Ruelle, and the active homing head took over in the final guidance stage using a small monopulse tracking radar which, operating the X-band (8.5–125 GHz) had been borrowed from the Soviet SAM-8. More recently, the ADAC's performance had been enhanced by three highly secret devices which allowed the radar pulses to switch frequencies, with the intention of confusing any enemy jamming, a Home-On-Jam which enabled the Exocet to lock on to the source of any jamming, and a classified item codenamed LEADING EDGE which made the missile highly resistant to the standard electronic counter-measures. Steady height was achieved by the RAM 01 radio altimeter built by TRT which ensured the missile flew lower than many air defence weapons could operate. As well as the advantages of speed and low altitude, the Exocet's warhead was housed in the tail, protected from hostile fire by armour plate, making it exceptionally difficult to disable, particularly from a head-on direction.

The air-launched AM-39 variant, placed on the market in 1974, was 187lb lighter, weighing in total 1,433lb. As well as Britain and Argentina, Aerospatiale's other customers included Ecuador, Peru, Chile and Brazil. By May 1982 more than 1,800 rounds had been sold across the globe, making it an exceptionally popular and versatile weapon.

Later the same day, 4 May, a pair of young Fleet Air Arm pilots of 800 Naval Air Squadron, together with Flight Lieutenant Ed Ball, on loan from the RAF, emerged from the pre-flight briefing room on the *Hermes* and squeezed into their uncomfortable rubberised G-suits in preparation for the sortie which had been postponed earlier in the day because of adverse weather. They were carrying standard-issue Browning automatics with two clips of ammunition in improvised shoulder holsters, as well as a life preserver, search-and-rescue radio beacon, emergency rations and an oxygen regulator. Fully kitted for combat, in an all-weather suit that would protect them in the Atlantic as well as prevent them from blacking out when the aircraft was under G-pressure, they had limited movement and looked awkward as they waddled across the flight deck to the three Sea Harriers that had just undergone their final inspection by the armourers and engineers.

Although Sea Harriers had only been flown off the *Hermes* since November 1979, the pilots were supremely confident in their remarkable planes. Built by British Aerospace, the vertical take-off and landing feature more than compensated for the relatively slow top speed of 736mph. During NATO trials it had proved extraordinarily manoeuvrable and, by exploiting innovative tactics in air-to-air combat with American fighter jocks, had demonstrated that, courtesy of its unique characteristics of being able to stop dead in the air, and to fly at speeds that were well below stalling for most fixed-wing opponents, it enjoyed an exceptionally high 'kill rate' against the world's most experienced and well-trained experts in realistic dogfights. By deploying the jet nozzles to 10 per cent of the vertical, the Harrier decelerated at staggering rate, forcing a following aircraft to overtake, leaving the jump jet to take the optimum position for firing an infra-red heat-seeking missile up the enemy's tailpipe. In short, the plane was an aerodynamic phenomenon, which to date had only been sold to the US Marine Corps, and to the navies of Spain and India.[1]

Each pilot struggled to climb up the jump jet's steep cockpit access ladder but, once strapped in, they began the routine pre-flight instrument and equipment checks before seeking permission from the Flight Controller to ignite the powerful Rolls-Royce Pegasus turbofan engine. Having turned all three of the jump jets, the pilots switched their nose-mounted Ferranti Blue Fox radars to the stand-by position to warm up. Then followed the standard exchange between each pilot and the Flight Controller, who called out the ship's current heading and exact geographical co-ordinates which were entered by the airmen into the

Smiths Industries Navhars system. (In order to maintain radio silence, this was passed to the pilot on a blackboard, with a few of the aircraft accessing the new Telebrief discrete landline facility on the flight deck's periphery.) The Head-Up Display confirmed the new data had been entered and accepted, and the lead Harrier flashed its navigation lights to indicate the aircraft was ready to launch. The deck crew removed the wheel chocks from the first Harrier which taxied the short distance to the take-off point and, moments later, when cleared for launch, the pilot slid the plane's unique jet nozzle stop back to 50 degrees, made a final engine check, and then pushed the nozzle aft with the rpm set at 55 per cent. The Flight Controller gave the word and the Flight Deck Officer made his manual signal. The throttle was pushed to its full left-hand range and the brakes released. Suddenly the aircraft – seconds ago bobbing gently as the jet nozzle was moved – rushed the 500 feet to the 12-degree ski ramp on the *Hermes*' bows and leapt into the sky. Once airborne, the nozzle was adjusted for wingborne flight and the engine throttled back to 400 knots to level off at 800 feet. Within two minutes all three aircraft were in formation on a course for Goose Green, the airfield close to the tiny settlement at Darwin.

For the past three days the small strip had been kept under covert observation by a four-man SAS patrol concealed in a hide, and a number of Argentine-manufactured Pucara ground-attack aircraft were reported parked neatly on what was now known to the occupation forces as Base Aerea Militar Condor. Altogether twenty-four Pucaras of the 3rd Attack Group, under the command of Major Navarro, had been deployed to the Falklands, dispersed at Stanley, Goose Green and Pebble Island. Goose Green had already experienced one air raid, at dawn on 1 May, just as a single Pucara was taking off on what was intended to be a routine reconnaissance patrol. Instead the airstrip had been blasted by the BL-755 anti-personnel bomblets dropped by three Sea Harriers which had screamed in unexpectedly at low level from the north. The Pucara nosedived straight into a crater, its front wheel buckled, and another lethal cloud of 147 bomblets straddled a parked Pucara, setting off its ammunition and killing the pilot and the five mechanics who had been engaged in refuelling the plane. Two other Pucaras were damaged beyond repair, and two more men died an hour later in the Chinook helicopter that was evacuating them to the hospital at Port Stanley. The raid, executed in tandem with a larger Sea Harrier raid on Stanley, had been considered a success, and this further operation by three more Sea Harriers was intended to repeat it. The big difference, however, was the lack of any element of surprise. The first raids, on 1 May by nine Harriers from *Invincible* and *Hermes*, had been heralded by a Vulcan B2 long-range mission from Ascension, and the Sea Harriers had hit Port Stanley's runway just as the clean-up crews were inspecting the havoc wreaked by the lone bomber. A further Vulcan mission had been prosecuted the previous night, seventy-two hours after the first, and the Argentines naturally anticipated another follow-up raid. None had materialised, but the radar operators were on alert as they spotted three intruders approaching at low altitude from the south-west in the early afternoon. A warning was transmitted to Goose Green, where the crews of two pairs of radar-controlled 35mm Oerlikons of No. 3 Section of B Battery, 601st Anti-Aircraft Regiment, went to action stations, their all-weather Skyguard radar picking up the three targets ten miles out, over Choiseul Sound.

High above the three raiders, a Combat Air Patrol (CAP) of five Sea Harriers from HMS *Invincible*'s 801 Squadron monitored progress on their Blue Fox radars, which gave them a clear view of over twenty-one miles, head-on, and were vectored to the scene by the Air Controller in HMS *Glamorgan*'s Operations Room. Armed with the twin Aden 30mm cannon and the very latest AIM-9L Sidewinders, which could engage a target head-on and boasted an improved heat-seeking warhead that was effective at low altitude against a land background, the aircraft had been deployed to protect the ground-attack mission from sudden ambush by hostile Mirage and Dagger interceptors. According to the Air Controller scanning the horizon with a 965 radar and a Type 278 height-finder, and confirmed by the CAP umbrella, there was no sign of enemy air activity. As yet, the Argentine Air Force had demonstrated no appetite for indulging in air-to-air combat with the extraordinarily versatile subsonic fighters which were to become known as 'the black death'. Nevertheless, the mobile Westinghouse AN/TPS-43 3-D radar on Sapper Hill, overlooking Stanley, tracked the trio throughout their approach, its scanning antenna rotating every ten seconds.

Aware of the hostile radar from the distinctive short, high-pitched buzz at ten-second intervals in their headsets, the three Sea Harriers made their final approach to the target, Ed Ball peeling off left to attack from the west and drop his three parachute-retarded crater-digging bombs. As the two Fleet Air Arm pilots sped over the water, ready to release their cargo of cluster bombs, they were met by a barrage of accurate 35mm cannon-fire. The first plane, with Lieutenant-Commander Gordon Batt at the controls, released its hardware but the second, flown by a former RAF pilot, Lieutenant Nick Taylor, was hit by the heavy calibre ground-fire which engulfed his Sea Harrier in flames. It skimmed across the surf in a ball of fire and ploughed up the shoreline towards the grass strip, disintegrating as it did so. Horrified, his two companions completed their attack, damaging the two Pucaras which had been caught in the previous raid and adding two further craters to the runway.

Nick Taylor had been killed instantly, without a chance to fire his Martin-Baker ejector seat, but his body was found intact, still strapped into the cockpit, by First Lieu-tenant Carlos Esteban, who also recovered his navigation notes close by. When scrutinised by the regiment's intelligence officer, they appeared to compromise the exact current position of the Task Force's flagship. The subsequent wireless signal from the 12th Infantry Regiment to the headquarters in Stanley, which was relayed to the mainland, was intercepted by the Task Force and made depressing reading, particularly because considerable precautions had been taken to prevent this information from falling into the hands of the enemy.[2]

Every attempt had been made to keep the exact time and date of the departure of Task Force 317 from Ascension a secret, and a similar effort made over its progress on the long voyage south, but there had been limitations. These included the presence of the *Rio de la Plata*, an Argentine merchantman which had deliberately dawdled off the island to observe the Royal Navy's preparations. Her master, Captain Carlos Benchetrit – having been briefed by Argentine Naval Intelligence – sent a signal to Buenos Aires at noon on 18 April to report the Task Force steaming over the horizon, and his transmission had been picked up at Two Boats, GCHQ's permanent intercept facility on Ascension, which operated under commercial cover provided by Cable & Wireless. In addition, the assembly of the Task Force had been watched by various intelligence-gathering Elint ships, including the *Zaporozhive*, which shadowed the *Canberra*, one of six Primorye-class vessels assigned to monitor NATO movements, and a long-range Tupolev-95 Bear-D maritime reconnaissance aircraft of the Soviet Naval Air Force, operating between Cuba and Luanda in Angola. Although the huge, high-flying monster with its distinctive four turboprops and numerous Elint blister fairings and antennae was rarely seen, the pulses of its I-band BIG BULGE surface-search radar, transmitted from a large radome located under the fuselage, were quite recognisable to the ships below carrying the standard NATO-issue radar warning detectors. The assumption had been made (incorrectly, as it turned out) that Moscow had probably passed on the information acquired through its comprehensive eavesdropping on the British fleet to Buenos Aires. It was also believed, but with little supporting evidence, that Soviet nuclear submarines were on the scene too, keeping an eye on developments, but none were detected venturing close to the Task Force's protection screen. Since all the Argentine defence plans depended upon knowing when the Task Force was likely to reach the Exclusion Zone, the signal sent from Carlos Benchetrit had been eagerly awaited.

Contrary to the Royal Navy's suspicion, the Argentines were entirely dependent on their own intelligence resources, which did not include satellite imagery. Certainly the Argentine Air Force was known to maintain a receiving station at Mar Chiquita, 250 miles south of Buenos Aires, but this was connected to the LandSat system which would be of no help in monitoring the Task Force so, in the absence of any Soviet contributions, Benchetrit's tip was crucial. Another tip came from a senior Argentine intelligence officer in London who had witnessed the Task Force's departure from Portsmouth.

Contact by the Task Force with the shore and with other ships had been avoided, and inquisitive Argentine reconnaissance flights had been discouraged from approaching the fleet. Shortly after midday on the morning of 21 April, three days after the Task Force slipped away from Ascension, an Argentine Boeing 707 flown by Vicecomodoro Jorge Ricardini of the newly formed Phoenix Squadron at Palomar was intercepted and photographed by Lieutenant-Commander Simon Hargreaves's single Sea Harrier from 800 Squadron off *Hermes*, approximately 140 miles from the carriers. Flying fast and high at 40,000 feet, the reconnaissance flight had withdrawn as soon as it was illuminated by the Sea Harrier's radar, but not before it had spotted 'two light aircraft carriers and eight destroyers or frigates' and had signalled the news home. The 707, in Argentine Air Force livery, returned in the early hours of the following morning, lit with conventional anti-collision navigation lights, only to be acquired again, sixty miles from the ships, by the attack radar of an 800 Sea Harrier. The same 707 came back for a third look in daylight a few hours later, was followed inbound for 140 miles without being engaged, and succeeded in overflying the centre of the Task Force. On 23 April the 707 must have suspected that the Rules of Engagement had been altered to allow the Sea Harriers to fire, for the unarmed plane, one of thirty-five civilian aircraft requisitioned by the Argentine Air Force, flew home as soon as it detected the potentially fatal sweep of the interceptor's Blue Fox radar.[3]

Later the same evening, the Task Force commander having requested and received from Northwood permission to shoot down the persistent burglar, *Invincible*'s radar caught a fifth hostile sortie, approaching high at 350 knots from the north-east and prepared to launch a salvo of Sea Dart missiles. The intruder had found *Hermes* at the most inopportune moment, while she was in the middle of a replenishment at sea, receiving fuel from the RFA *Olmeda*. The Task Force's air defence radars locked on to the target and, just twenty seconds before firing, *Hermes* discovered that the plane was a scheduled Brazilian flight from Durban to Rio de Janeiro. A visual check by a Sea Harrier confirmed the aircraft was a civilian VARIG DC-10, complete with cabin lights, and an embarrassing international incident of huge proportions was only narrowly avoided.

Thereafter the Task Force's course was watched by a spy stern trawler, the *Narwal*, which encountered the British on 29 April and immediately reported to Argentina's Naval Intelligence Service. Once again, the transmission was monitored by the Task Force's own interception unit, which belatedly corrected the first faulty identification of the *Narwal* as a Canadian research vessel. Once the error had been spotted, and the ownership traced to the Compania Sudamerica de Pesca y Expotacion SA, the frigate HMS *Alacrity* was despatched to scare her off. The measure appeared to succeed, for the *Narwal* promptly withdrew but maintained a station at a respectful distance, just outside the range of *Alacrity*'s weapons. Aboard the 1,400-ton deep-sea freezer trawler was a naval intelligence officer, Lieutenant-Commander Gonzales Llanos, and a crew of thirty elderly Argentine fishermen, the oldest among them being in their seventies. Ten days later, on 9 May, the *Narwal* ventured too close and, seventy miles south-west of Stanley, was strafed by 30mm cannon-fire from two 800 Harriers, operating at maximum range and guided to their target by HMS *Coventry*. With one man killed, thirteen injured and the engine disabled, the ship was visited later the same evening by an SBS boarding party from *Invincible* which was winched on to the *Narwal*'s afterdeck from an 820 Sea King. Llanos was taken prisoner without a fight, and the captured cipher equipment and code books turned over to GCHQ's cryptographers. According to her log, she had been commandeered in Rio del Plata on 22 April by the Argentine Navy. She sank while under tow the following day, but not before the Argentines unexpectedly suffered three further casualties: a Puma helicopter, despatched on a rescue mission to help the *Narwal*, was shot down by a Sea Dart fired from HMS *Coventry*, killing the crew of army aviators of the 601st Combat Aviation Battalion.

It was clear from the efforts made by the *Narwal* that until the loss of Lieutenant Nick Taylor five days earlier, the Argentines had only the vaguest idea of where the Task Force was operating. The unwelcome arrival of the *Narwal* indicated that its current location had been compromised, thereby inhibiting its movement closer to the islands. Clearly there would be little opportunity to prevent the enemy from tracking the Task Force, which in turn made another Exocet attack inevitable.

Chapter 2

OPERACIÓN AZUL

This was the attack that should never have happened, and according to all the intelligence reports prepared for the Task Force as it assembled off Ascension's inhospitable coastline, 550 miles south of the equator, could not have happened. The loss of the *Sheffield* sent a detectable chill across not just the Royal Navy, but the whole of Whitehall.

Responsibility for gathering intelligence data rested with the Defence Intelligence Directorate at the Ministry of Defence, but the most up-to-date material on Argentina had been prepared by a special team put together by the Secret Intelligence Service and co-ordinated by the Joint Intelligence Committee's Current Intelligence Group for Latin America, LACIG. LACIG was headed by a senior army officer, Brigadier Adam Gurdon, on loan to the Cabinet Office from the Black Watch, and had an assessment staff led by Robin O'Neill, a diplomat recently returned from three years in Gibraltar, where he had been Deputy Governor.

Another key member was Robin Fearn, formerly the British Consul General in Islamabad before his return to London in 1979 to run the Foreign Office's Latin America Department. Although it was more than fifteen years since he had been in South America, having served in Venezuela in the early 1960s soon after joining the Foreign Office from the Dunlop Rubber Company, Fearn also chaired the FO's Falklands Emergency Committee.

The Joint Intelligence Committee consisted of the directors of the three principal collection agencies, MI5 (John Jones), SIS (Colin Figures) and GCHQ (Sir Brian Tovey), together with their counterparts representing the Ministry of Defence (and reporting to the Permanent Secretary, Sir Frank Cooper, and the Chief of the Defence Staff) and the Director-General of Intelligence, Admiral Sir Roy Halliday, acting as Deputy Chairman. They met every Thursday morning in a secure Cabinet Office room under the chairmanship of a deputy under-secretary from the Foreign Office. Depending upon the topics to be raised, other Whitehall departments, the CIA Chief of Station in London and the representatives of the New Zealand SIS and the Australian SIS are invited to participate, and its proceedings are classified.

Created in 1936 to provide some co-ordination in the collation and assessment of intelligence, the JIC had not come to life until February 1940, when the formidable Victor Cavendish-Bentinck took it from the control of the Chief of the Imperial General Staff and allowed it to develop its own small secretariat. Since his departure in 1945 all of his successors had been drawn from the Foreign Office, thereby institutionalising the JIC, which had only undergone one significant reform, in 1957, after its Chairman, Sir Patrick Dean, had played too active a role in the Suez disaster. Dean retained his post until 1960, but the JIC had been wrested from the Foreign Office and brought under the authority of the Cabinet Secretary, who allowed an Assessment Staff to develop so that the JIC could take the initiative and prepare papers on issues of interest. The JIC is also responsible for the circulation of the Red Book, the classified weekly summary of current events which senior ministers take home to read each weekend. By tradition the JIC Chairman has the right of direct access to the Prime Minister, but in 1968 a new post was created – Intelligence Co-ordinator – to accommodate Sir Dick White, a professional with unparalleled experience as the only person to have headed both MI5 and SIS, and his successors became the conduit to the Cabinet. The Co-ordinator also chaired a select group known as the Preliminary Committee, which examined the budgets of the three collection agencies before their expenditure forecasts were submitted to the Permanent Secretaries' Committee on the Intelligence Services – the key mandarins who managed the entire Whitehall machine.

The JIC structure, with the Chairman at its apex, was managed by a small secretariat and built on a series of Current Intelligence Groups, small sub-committees drawn from Whitehall which monitored events, drafted reports and made recommendations on requirements. LACIG was but one of these half-dozen geographical sub-committees, the fulcrum where resources and requirements meet and priorities are assessed. Some CIGs, such as the one dealing with Eastern Europe, are permanent fixtures, while others will be created or dissolved as needs arise. Gurdon's responsibilities, as the chairman of no fewer than four CIGs, extended to the whole of the Americas, Western Europe and Sub-Sahara Africa. Although there was little work relating to North America and Western Europe, the other two encompassed Angola, Mozambique, Nicaragua, South Africa, Namibia, Belize, El Salvador and the Caribbean. To monitor events in these widely disparate regions Gurdon had three assistants, two from the Foreign Office and Captain Jonathan Tod RN, a Gordonstoun-educated Royal Navy pilot who had flown off *Ark Royal*, *Hermes* and *Eagle*, and had commanded the frigate HMS *Brighton* before joining the Assessment Staff in 1980 to concentrate on Latin America. This post required the scrutiny of all Foreign Office telegrams, study of foreign newspapers and the monitoring of reports from the CIG's component agencies, a task he fulfilled with enthusiasm, despite having to nurse his wife, who had been injured in a riding accident.

The pressure on the Assessment Staff is considerable,

with Whitehall demanding instant responses and guidance on events around the world. The tendency to produce immediate reactions was exacerbated by Mrs Thatcher's insatiable appetite for information, and in recent years the panic button had been pressed far too often for the liking of some. On one memorable occasion Adam Gurdon was summoned from his estate in Suffolk, in the middle of a pheasant shoot, to advise on the implications of the coup which brought Flight Lieutenant Jerry Rawlings to power` in Ghana. Hardly an episode of global significance, nor one that was likely to have a great impact on British interests, but the JIC was expected to prepare a briefing before the end of the weekend.

The JIC is an organisation quite unique to Whitehall, with around two dozen members of the assessment staff attached to it, drawn almost equally from the Ministry of Defence and the Foreign Office. Of those on secondment from the MoD, about half are from the armed forces, the remainder being civil servants. Individual desk officers are assigned to particular geographical areas, and they are responsible for preparing the very first draft of a JIC report, which is then submitted to the CIG chairman who distributes it among the CIG's membership. Typically a CIG will consist of desk officers from SIS, GCHQ, the Defence Intelligence Staff (representing the MoD), the Foreign Office and the CIA, and perhaps MI5 or the Home Office if appropriate.

Once a CIG has agreed the text of a report it is submitted to the Head of the Assessment Staff who, having approved the document, will submit it to the full JIC through the secretariat. When the JIC meets, the Head of the Assessment Staff will be accompanied by the chairman of whichever CIG has a report under consideration. Having been accepted by the full JIC, the paper will be circulated as an official assessment. The speed with which this process works is remarkable, the first stage in a typical weekly cycle being a meeting held on Monday morning at which O'Neill and Gurdon would talk over the topics to be discussed by the individual CIGs, and an agenda would be prepared by the same evening with a warning notice distributed to the CIG members. Typically a CIG will meet early on a Tuesday morning and will have a report drafted by the afternoon, when it is passed to the Head of the Assessment Staff. By three o'clock the following afternoon the paper will be on the desk of the Chairman of the JIC, who will hold a briefing the same evening in preparation for the full JIC the following morning. Having received approval, the final document will be included in the Red Book, ready for distribution to ministers on Friday morning.

Compared with its foreign counterparts, the advantage of the JIC lies in its anonymity. Whereas in the United States the equivalent system is handicapped by the sponsoring agency's determination to emphasise its own role, and indulge in the kind of inter-departmental politicking that is so prevalent when rival organisations compete for limited resources, the British model depends upon consensus. Every report is unsigned, thus giving no clue to the origin of its author and allowing the full CIG to endorse it without losing ground in the bureaucratic turf war fought by aspiring mandarins anxious to enhance their budgetary interests. The disadvantage of the arrangement is that by the time the CIG chairman and the Head of the Assessment Staff have amended a paper, and rubbed off most of the sharp edges, it will have become quite a bland product. A further weakness, later highlighted by the Franks Committee, was the JIC's constitutional inability to take the initiative by drawing attention to specific concerns without first having been asked to do so by another branch of government.

When Robin O'Neill was appointed Head of the Assessment Staff at the end of June 1981 he brought a fresh mind to the Cabinet Office. During his period in Gibraltar he had been responsible for the local police, and therefore had acquired a knowledge of the Rock's tiny Special Branch.

Prior to that he had routinely handled run-of-the-mill intelligence material from the Foreign Office while serving in the Cabinet secretariat dealing with European affairs immediately after Britain's entry into the European Economic Community, and had occasionally noted interesting information not drawn from secret sources while head of the South Asia Department, at a time when Mrs Indira Gandhi precipitated a crisis in India by suspending the government. On that occasion O'Neill correctly predicted her likely response to the charges of corruption that had threatened her position, without the benefit of any formal training in the collection, analysis and exploitation of intelligence. Accordingly, it was largely his own intuition that he relied upon when dealing with the topics that arose in the autumn of 1981, including the imposition of martial law in Poland and the disintegration of the Lebanon.

Like O'Neill, Brigadier Gurdon had not received any formal intelligence training before starting his three-year attachment to the Cabinet Office in January 1982, indeed had never even seen a satellite photograph, although he did have the benefit of thirty years' military service including a spell as his regiment's Intelligence Officer in Kenya during the Mau-Mau emergency. He also knew the Intelligence Co-ordinator, Antony Duff, for whom he had a high regard, having served with him in Rhodesia where he played a key role in maintaining the ceasefire. South America, however, was a closed book to him.

While serving in MO2 – the MoD branch supervising military operations outside NATO – Gurdon devised a novel scheme for disarming the various warring guerrilla groups in Rhodesia. Instead of acting as peacekeeper, on the classic United Nations model which had failed so often, Gurdon had advocated sending experienced troops to each faction, relying on good officers to gain the trust of the men controlled by Robert Mugabe, Joshua Nkomo and the Salisbury regime backed by Bishop Muzerewa. The high-risk strategy worked, thus enabling the transition to democratic elections to take place and cementing his relationship with Duff. Gurdon had also acquired an appreciation of SIS's work, seeing the spooks operating skilfully behind the scenes, and was impressed by GCHQ's clandestine contribution, an intercept station near Government House which provided Duff's team with a running commentary on the efforts made by Ian Smith's senior military adviser, General Peter Walls, to wreck the progress towards free elections in what was to become Zimbabwe. Upon his return to London Gurdon was transferred to the Royal College for Defence Studies in Belgrave Square, and then accepted a posting to the JIC.

The original JIC assessment to predict a deterioration in relations and the possibility of Argentina's military regime resorting 'to more forcible measures swiftly and without warning' had been described first in a paper prepared back in July 1981, the first of its kind since November 1979, and given the usual wide JIC circulation. Although never released, it was described in the broadest, sanitised terms by the Franks Report:

> It reviewed developments since the last assessment in 1979, including the progress of the talks held with Argentina in that period, political and economic developments in Argentina, the progress of its sovereignty dispute with Chile about islands in the Beagle Channel and its improving relations with the United States and Brazil. The assessment reviewed the options open to the Argentine Government if they decided to resort to direct measures in the dispute. It took the view that it was likely that in the first instance Argentina would adopt diplomatic and economic measures. The latter could include the disruption of air and sea communications, of food and oil supplies and of the provision of medical treatment. There was also a distinct possibility that Argentina might occupy one of the uninhabited Dependencies, following up

its action in 1976 in establishing a presence on Southern Thule; and a risk that it might establish a military presence on the Falkland Islands themselves, remote from Port Stanley. In the Committee's view harassment or arrest of British shipping would not be a likely option unless the Argentine Government felt themselves severely provoked.

As in 1979, the assessment noted that there was no diminution in Argentina's determination eventually to extend its sovereignty over the Falkland Islands area, but that it would prefer to achieve this objective by peaceful means and would turn to forcible action only as a last resort. As before, it judged that the overriding consideration would be Argentina's perception of the Government's willingness to negotiate genuinely about, and eventually to transfer, sovereignty. It recorded evidence of impatience in Argentina at the absence of progress in negotiations and at the attitude of the Islanders. Earlier in the year Argentina had reduced the scheduled flights to the Islands and delayed a supply ship. These actions were seen as evidence that in any escalation of the dispute such measures would be likely to come first. It was thought that relatively small-scale military action could not be ruled out. The final paragraph of the assessment stated that, if Argentina concluded that there was no hope of a peaceful transfer of sovereignty, there would be a high risk of its resorting to more forcible measures against British interests, and that it might act swiftly and without warning. In such circumstances military action against British shipping or a full-scale invasion of the Falkland Islands could not be discounted.[1]

It was, in short, a very routine item, containing nothing to start ringing alarm bells, and described by one who was later to study it in detail as 'an annual review, updated by changing the names of the Junta'. In consequence

the Foreign Office drew up some contingency plans and
the Ministry of Defence compiled a document listing the
military options in the face of Argentine aggression, at the
top of which was the deployment by the Royal Navy of
either a nuclear submarine or a surface vessel, noting that
two weeks should be allowed for the passage of the first
and three for the second. As before, the 'fortress Falklands'
concept, with a large permanent garrison equipped with
an arsenal of anti-ship and anti-aircraft hardware, was
rejected on grounds of cost and practicality: at a length
of only 4,000 feet, the runway at Stanley was too short
to service modern jets, and the distances involved were
simply too daunting to contemplate. Quite simply, given
the political climate in which successive ministers had
made overtures to the Falkland Islanders to accept some
compromise over British sovereignty, such as a lease-
back arrangement, there had never been any appetite for
extending an already tight defence budget to cover every
conceivable eventuality in the South Atlantic.

The substance of the analysis completed in July 1981,
which was not to be revised until Argentine troops had
surrounded Government House on the outskirts of Stanley,
was that there were four compelling reasons why the
Falklands should be considered safe for the time being:
the dispute over the Beagle Channel made Chile a more
likely target for Argentine aggression; the local political and
economic shambles mitigated against the Junta indulging
in a potentially expensive foreign adventure; the level
of endemic inter-service rivalry made close co-operation
between the army, navy and air force – as required for
military action in the Malvinas – quite unlikely; and
finally, on a political front, the Junta had every reason
to expect that it could resolve the long-standing disagree-
ment with Britain through negotiations. The Whitehall
consensus that instant hostilities were simply not possible
was unspoken. The received wisdom was that a shooting
war only occurred after a long decline in deteriorating

relations, each party conforming to a perceptible schedule of incidents which might end in conflict but could be handled by skilful bilateral negotiation. The proposition that Argentina might jump from the bottom rung of the ladder to outright aggression – thereby winning the game of international snakes and ladders without transiting the conventional intermediate stages of commercial sanctions, withdrawal of air services and the rest – was regarded as unthinkable by the gradualists who had persuaded themselves of a progressive escalation, not a *coup de main*.

The Foreign Office in particular maintained the view that although the Junta might be composed of rogues, they would not be so stupid as to indulge in military action. In any event, until the situation really started to fall apart, the Foreign Office would keep its hand on the tiller. Internally, the JIC was itself heavily weighted in favour of the Foreign Office, with the Chairman always likely to adopt his own department's position and the JIC assessment staff unwilling to challenge the FO. Such confrontations had occurred, but only rarely, the most memorable being when James Callaghan as Prime Minister had been startled by a JIC paper on Guatemala's increasingly bellicose claims against Belize. Clearly reinforcements were required to the local garrison as a warning, but the proposal to make a public commitment by sending some RAF ground-attack Harriers to Belize City had been vetoed by the Foreign Office anxious not to jeopardise negotiations then under way in New York. Alarmed by the JIC document, Callaghan asked his Minister of Defence, Fred Mulley, for his opinion, but Mulley had forgotten to read his Red Book. Infuriated, Callaghan overruled his Foreign Secretary, David Owen – who had taken the FO view that the proposed Harrier deployment would be seen as a provocation, not a deterrent – and personally ordered an astonished duty officer at the Ministry of Defence to put the RAF on alert for a transfer to the threatened colony. A classic example of how the JIC can influence events, and of how the Foreign Office attitude is always one of extreme caution while talks are in progress, the Belize episode had a parallel in the Falklands, with the FO apparently convinced it was on the brink of a breakthrough in what the diplomats termed 'the bilaterals'.

Since the distribution of the JIC's paper of July 1981, the Latin America Current Intelligence Group had met eighteen times, but the Falklands was discussed on none of these occasions because allegedly no new information had been received to alter the report's validity. Instead, Robin O'Neill had asked SIS for information on Argentina's likely negotiating position shortly before each round of bilateral talks. Thus in January 1982 Adam Gurdon initiated a response for O'Neill in time for the meetings scheduled to be held in New York the following month, when the Foreign Office junior minister Richard Luce would meet his counterpart from Argentina, Enrique Ros, to agree a framework for a joint commission to study the Falklands problem over the following year. This arrangement, and the goodwill apparent on all sides, persuaded O'Neill's staff that further time had been bought and the situation was unlikely to escalate. It was a tragic miscalculation, and in March O'Neill called for a further assessment, for presentation to the Cabinet's Oversea and Defence Policy Committee scheduled to meet on the morning of Tuesday, 16 March, by which time it was too late to take any preventive action. Although Gurdon had started work on this new, updated report, it was never completed. Instead, on the morning of 31 March, when the invasion was virtually under way, a special paper was drawn up to assist ministers dealing with the provocation by a group of scrap-dealers who had landed in South Georgia without the necessary permission. Even at the eleventh hour, a full-scale assault was considered unlikely.

In the current conflict, General Galtieri's Junta had only decided to launch the invasion at a meeting at the President's Casa Rosada held on 25 March, allowing no time for either reinforcements to be sent south or a token force deployed as a deterrent. The nearest British ships, amounting to a fleet of twenty-five frigates, destroyers, submarines and support vessels, were exercising off Gibraltar in the annual Springtrain manoeuvres, and when the first submarines were detached to go south – the nuclear hunter-killer *Spartan* and the diesel *Oracle* – they were armed with dummy torpedoes. On 26 March *Spartan*'s captain, Commander Jim Taylor, was ordered back to the Gibraltar dockyard by Northwood to be loaded with live ordnance. An added complication had been the urgent despatch two days earlier of a submarine up to the Barents Sea, to cover a gap left by an American hunter-killer on surveillance patrol which had been withdrawn because of a medical emergency.

In the face of Argentina's aggression, Whitehall had been powerless, with Westminster kept completely in the dark about the impending war. Thus the first covert deployment of a nuclear submarine did not begin until Monday, 29 March, although every effort was made to conceal the exact number of British submarines at sea in order to promote the idea that at least one was already on station in the South Atlantic.[2] This deception, in which the *Daily Telegraph* reported that HMS *Superb* was already off the Falklands – based on a leak from a submariner at the MoD to John Miller of the newspaper's diplomatic staff – meant an uncomfortable extra five days submerged outside Faslane for *Superb*, which did not materialise until 17 April after a long, three-month patrol. Meanwhile, in the South Atlantic, HMS *Endurance* was instructed to transmit bogus signals to a non-existent submarine supposedly in her proximity, so as to reinforce the idea that *Superb* was on the prowl.

While GCHQ also turned its attention to the South Atlantic, the Foreign Office attempted to play down the developing crisis. At the regular daily press briefing – held at 3.30 p.m. by the News Department, but half an hour earlier on a Sunday – the South Georgia episode was mentioned, together with an unconfirmed report that the missile-carrying corvettes *Drummond* and *Granville* had been sent to protect the 9,000-ton naval transport *Bahia Paraiso*. However, the official line for public consumption was, as reported by John Miller on Monday morning, 29 March, that 'the reports had been blown up out of all proportion'. Miller, an experienced foreign correspondent who, coincidentally, had served in Moscow at the same time as Anthony Williams had been at the embassy, was suitably sceptical of the Foreign Office's attitude and wrote that five Argentine warships had left their bases, ostensibly to 'take part in a previously-arranged joint naval exercise with Uruguay'.

Although the LACIG saw no reason to commission an update on the July 1981 report until it was much too late, the JIC itself undertook a general review of intelligence requirements in the western hemisphere in October 1981, and the then JIC Chairman, Sir Antony Acland, asked SIS and GCHQ to concentrate on the Junta's policies and intentions. This was a prescient request, but neither SIS nor GCHQ were in any position to oblige without some long-term investment, for intelligence collection is a lengthy process that often requires much cultivation before it can produce tangible results. After the closure of Piccolo Hill on St Helena, GCHQ depended upon help from the American National Security Agency (NSA) and, short of constructing a listening post inside the embassy at Buenos Aires, there was no prospect of improving its collection of Argentine signals. Aside from Two Boats, there was only the intercept equipment aboard HMS *Endurance*, which anyway was scheduled for scrapping. Fortuitously, as the conflict developed, GCHQ discovered from Elizabeth Halliday (the New Zealand Security Intelligence Service's newly arrived representative in London) that there was an intercept site at HMNZS *Irirangi Station*, located just outside Waiouru and run by its New Zealand counterpart, the Government Communications Security Bureau. Originally established in 1942 as a Naval Wireless Station, Irirangi had been running a fairly relaxed intercept programme targeted against South America, but after the campaign began the facility went into overdrive to assist Cheltenham.[3]

For the NSA itself, collection in the region was a sensitive subject, as there were no overt intercept bases in Chile or Argentina and the State Department, terminally nervous about discovery and accusations of undiplomatic behaviour, had baulked at any expansion of the embassy facility. The official line was that the nearest NSA outpost was the Naval Security Group station on Galeta Island, off Panama, but in fact the closest was a clandestine station in Chile operating under the synthetic US government cover of a NASA tracking facility at Peldehue, thirteen miles north of Santiago, and understandably the NSA had no wish to compromise this very useful source. As for SIS, its South American stations had borne the brunt of the cuts imposed by successive short-sighted governments anxious to save cash, leaving a single officer, Mark Heathcote, to cover Argentina and report to Douglas T., the Regional Controller in London. All the other SIS stations on the continent had been closed as part of SIS's programme of austerity, a far cry from the days when SIS ran fully manned stations in Santiago, Caracas, Rio de Janeiro and Lima. In consequence, Heathcote's nearest colleagues were in the Caribbean, at Bridgetown, Barbados and Honduras. Both the CIA and the Chileans were generous with unofficial assistance, but unless headquarters at Century House was willing to dedicate more scarce resources to the station, there was little prospect of SIS developing new sources. As to whether the conflict might have been averted if more attention had been given to SIS's parlous state, there is no way of telling. The secret was kept within a very close circle until a very late stage, and anyway there can be no guarantees in the intelligence game, which makes the speculation pointless.

Neither the SIS station commander nor the defence attachés, Colonel Stephen Love RA and Captain Julian Mitchell RN, the three in the forefront of intelligence collection in Buenos Aires, had the means of monitoring Argentina's military preparations for the invasion, codenamed Operación ROSARIO (Operation ROSARY) or of making comparisons between usual routines and suspiciously abnormal behaviour. Mitchell was a weapons specialist who preferred to operate independently of his two colleagues, while Love and Heathcote were more of a team, even though the SIS officer communicated directly with Century House, whereas Love reported to Squadron-Leader Bulford of the Defence Intelligence branch designated DI4. He in turn answered to Air Vice-Marshal Michael Armitage, Director of Service Intelligence, who was subordinate to General Sir James Glover, head of the Defence Intelligence Directorate at the Ministry of Defence. Glover's predecessor as Deputy Chief of the Defence Staff (Intelligence) was a former wartime Fleet Air Arm pilot, Admiral Sir Roy Halliday, who had been appointed Director-General of Intelligence and Deputy Chairman of the JIC in 1981.

A professional soldier since 1949, when he started his National Service in the Gunners, Love had been in Buenos Aires since November 1979 and spoke reasonably good Spanish, having attended a language course at Southampton University and studied in Andalucía. His experience in the intelligence field dated back to Singapore, at the end of the Malayan Emergency, and he had served with his regiment in Hong Kong. He was a pilot, qualified on both fixed-wing and rotor aircraft and, significantly, had spent two years at the Ministry of Defence in DI2, the Far East intelligence branch, at the end of the 1973 India–Pakistan conflict. While in Whitehall he had often attended the Far East Current Intelligence Group, then headed by (Sir) Percy Cradock, assisting first Colonel Charles Corroll and later Colonel Dennis Wood, the Defence Intelligence representatives on the FECIG which, at that time, took in China (then in the throes of the Cultural Revolution), Korea, Afghanistan, Sikkim, Bhutan, Tibet, Hong Kong and Korea: all potential hotspots. Love later attended the US Field Artillery School at Fort Sill, Oklahoma, and most recently worked in an administration post at SHAPE, based at Mons. Usefully, he had known of Mark Heathcote almost since he had been a subaltern, the SIS officer's father having commanded Love's regiment.

Tall, red-headed and the heir to a baronetcy, Heathcote was recruited by SIS in 1970 from the P & O shipping line, and served first in Northern Ireland under Craig Smellie and later as station commander in Athens for three years from June 1976. In Argentina since January 1980, he had been declared to his hosts, who had assigned a liaison officer from Naval Intelligence, Hector J. Valsecchi, to be the official conduit for the exchange of information on matters of mutual interest, chiefly Eastern Bloc intelligence activity. His predecessor, Simon C.-L., had overlapped just long enough to introduce Heathcote to his assets, and had then returned to London after an unusually long tour of duty lasting five years. Although Valsecchi realised that one of Heathcote's tasks was to cultivate local sources, particularly among the 17,000 permanent British residents in Argentina, he made no attempt to monitor his activities. Indeed, Heathcote and Valsecchi developed a useful relationship and, when the time finally came for the SIS station commander to depart to London, via Montevideo, he gave a farewell lunch for his hosts at a downtown restaurant the day before his official expulsion. According to one of those present, the affair became quite emotional and even Argentina's Director

of Naval Intelligence sent his apologies, saying that only
the current regrettable circumstances had prevented him
from attending. By then, of course, Heathcote and his
diplomatic colleagues had become members of the British
Interests Section of the Swiss Embassy, and had been given
five days in which to pack their bags, leaving behind
just the newly arrived counsellor (David Joy) and three
officials with Swiss credentials, a reflection of similiar
events occurring in London. As for Anthony Williams,
the ill-fated ambassador, he was to receive a cool reception
upon his return to the Foreign Office – not so much due to
any perceived failure on his part, but rather because of the
conciliatory attitude he had adopted with the Argentines,
a position that in the rapidly changing political climate
was later to be interpreted as having been too close to
appeasement. Williams, educated at Oundle and Trinity
College, Oxford, had served in numerous trouble spots
since joining the Diplomatic Service in 1945, including
Prague, Montevideo, Moscow, Cambodia and Libya. He
took the entirely practical view that there was no point
in sabre-rattling unless there was a genuine ability and
willingness to back up threats with force. In the weeks after
the invasion, this approach proved dangerously unpopular
and was to damage his career irretrievably, even though
some sympathetic to his cause believed he had become a
convenient scapegoat for the Foreign Office.

All three men in the Williams embassy charged with the
collection of intelligence were popular with their Argentine
hosts, but none had access to any significant sources, and
later they argued that because the decision to invade had
been taken at a very late stage – actually on 25 March,
with uncharacteristic discretion – inevitably they had failed
to give the three-week warning required for Whitehall
to react. Instead of cultivating well-placed sources, they
gleaned much of their information from articles in the
increasingly bellicose newspapers such as *La Prensa*, which
had been translated by their bilingual staff, and this was

Stephen Love's source for an 'immediate' telegram headed 'The Military Threat to the Falkland Islands' which he sent to London on Wednesday, 24 March (reproduced in Appendix II). This confirmed a report from the Naval Attaché, who had disclosed earlier in the day that Argentine ships had been sent to South Georgia to confront HMS *Endurance*, which had been despatched with a party of two dozen Royal Marines from Stanley on 20 March and had arrived off Grytviken four days later. Although Love warned of the likelihood of 'an encounter' with an Argentine warship, he still had no inkling of the decision to be taken by the Junta the following day. Nevertheless, as the captain of the *Endurance* was to point out, there was plenty to be observed on the Argentine mainland if individuals had been in the right places at the right time.

Love's signal of 24 March sheds light on the contrasting attitudes adopted by Rex Hunt and Anthony Williams. While the Governor had taken quite an aggressive stance over the unauthorised activities of the Argentine scrap-metal merchants on South Georgia, and had indulged in some gunboat diplomacy in his capacity as Commander-in-Chief of the Falkland Islands by ordering *Endurance* to the scene, the Ambassador had taken a rather different view. Characteristically, he had been dismayed at the increasing level of bellicosity and had advocated a calm, measured response. Far from approving Hunt's initiative, he thought it provocative and likely to exacerbate matters to a point where Britain's military nakedness might be exposed ignominiously.

The first serious alert was sounded on 26 March by GCHQ, which noted the withdrawal of two Argentine frigates, the new French-built A-69s *Drummond* and *Granville*, from joint naval exercises with Uruguay. According to the intercepted message, Admiral Jorge Anaya had personally ordered the two ships to set a new course towards the south. In fact they were to join Task Force 40, a fleet of six other ships which was to undertake the amphibious landings, supported by Task Force 20, a further six vessels intended to provide a protective screen for the invaders. The hurried embarkation of 900 troops and their twenty American FMC Amtrac armoured personnel carriers was started in Puerto Belgrano on Friday 26 March and completed the following evening, in time to sail at midday on Sunday morning. The troops chosen were the 2nd Marine Infantry Battalion, based conveniently in the town, which only five months earlier had been exercising in Patagonia with the US Marine Corps. In addition, they were to be accompanied by a single platoon from the 25th Regiment, which had been flown up from their barracks in Colonia Sarmiento. While none of this activity was spotted, not even the participants themselves believed the prepared cover story, of an anti-submarine exercise with the Uruguayan Navy and of more seasonal manoeuvres in Patagonia, this time with teams of officer cadets.[4]

At GCHQ, the second significant alert was given with the interception of a signal transmitted to the submarine *Santa Fe*, which was ordered to land a reconnaissance squad of a dozen men from the Bzos Tacticos on the beach at Mullett Creek. The only purpose for such an assignment was an imminent invasion, and this was the intercept forwarded by a secure landline teleprinter from Cheltenham to the JIC, arriving at teatime on Wednesday, 31 March. It was recognised for precisely what it was by a retired Royal Navy officer on the Assessment Staff, who took it straight to Robin O'Neill. Visibly shaken by its implications, he passed copies immediately to the Prime Minister's Private Office at 10 Downing Street, to the Intelligence Co-ordinator and to the Cabinet Secretary, Sir Robert Armstrong. Soon afterwards a warning was relayed to the Governor, Rex Hunt, but the invasion flotilla was at sea and Operación ROSARIO had been transformed into Operación AZUL, allowing GCHQ to pick up a veritable crescendo of signals, including ship-to-ship communications as well as messages exchanged between Rear-Admiral Gualter

Allara on his flagship, the Type-42 destroyer *Santisima Trinidad*, and his Chief of Naval Operations, Vice Admiral Juan Lombardo, at Fleet Headquarters in Puerto Belgrano. Much of the traffic concerned the need to delay the assault for twenty-four hours because of inclement weather, but there were other messages too. One informed the senior army officer in command of the Malvinas land forces, General Osvaldo Garcia, that the element of surprise had been lost and the party of Royal Marines in Stanley, which now amounted to double the number originally anticipated, had been warned to expect an amphibious assault. This meant a change in plans that had to be authorised by the Junta, and there were several other unexpected developments to be reported: a Puma helicopter on the polar ship *Almirante Irizar* had broken loose in the storm and was too badly damaged to ferry troops to Goose Green and Darwin as originally intended; the prospect of armed resistance, even by eighty men, also prompted a last-minute alteration to the masterplan.

While GCHQ eavesdropped on the messages circulating between Allara on his flagship and the officer commanding the marines, Rear-Admiral Carlos Busser, who was aboard the landing ship *Cabo San Antonio*, a further channel – a clandestine link between Stanley and the mainland – was also monitored. The spy already in the town was an Argentine Air Force intelligence officer, Vicecomodoro Hector Gilobert, who knew the islands well having previously operated under the commercial cover of the local manager of LADE, Argentina's domestic airline Lineas Aéreas del Estado, which is actually a branch of the Air Force. Recently replaced, after a tour of duty on the Falklands lasting twelve months, by Roberto Gamen, Gilobert had returned unexpectedly on 31 March – ostensibly to conduct an office audit, but in reality on a mission to report on the situation and confirm the presence of the Royal Marines in their barracks at Moody Brook. Instead he signalled the unanticipated presence of the change-over troops and

Governor Hunt's order to block the runway, but he failed
to spot the precautions taken to defend Government House
until too late. Accordingly, when Lieutenant Diego Garcia
of the navy's amphibious special forces unit approached
the building, he was not expecting any opposition, least
of all from the Royal Marines. Although Garcia's briefing
had appeared comprehensive, complete with a photograph
of the Government House drawing room taken during a
reception held there, the assurances that he had received
regarding complete surprise and the British troops being
safely in their barracks proved entirely fallacious, and
in consequence he was one of the first casualties of the
conflict, requiring evacuation to hospital later the same
morning. Hit by two bullets, his life was saved because
one of them was deflected by a Swiss Army knife in the
pocket of his tunic, and he made a full recovery.

Operación AZUL (Operation BLUE) had been planned
in two phases, the first being the initial assault to seize
Government House and the airfield, the second comprising
a C-130 air-bridge to bring over the main occupation force
of the 25th Regiment from Comodoro Rivadavia. As soon
as the town was secured, General Garcia was replaced
by Brigadier-General Americo Daher of the IX Brigade
and the garrison settled down for the occupation, again
generating a large volume of wireless traffic for GCHQ to
intercept.

As the Falklands crisis began, Sir Patrick Wright was taking
over from Sir Antony Acland in London as Chairman of
the Joint Intelligence Committee. Wright was to depend
on Brigadier Gurdon, Robin O'Neill and two other key
individuals: the first was portly, balding and bespectacled
Colin Figures, a career officer appointed to SIS's top post
of Chief the previous year in succession to Sir Dickie
Franks; the second vital contributor was Sir Antony Duff,
the Cabinet's Intelligence Co-ordinator since 1980, who

had returned from a visit to Canada just days before the invasion.

Like his successor, Dickie Franks was a Sovietologist, having been the case officer who recruited and ran Greville Wynne at a time when his contact Oleg Penkovsky was offering the West an unprecedented glimpse of Moscow's arsenal of inter-continental ballistic missiles. Together, at the latter end of the Cold War, Franks and Figures influenced the culture at SIS's grim south London headquarters at Century House, enhancing an Eastern European bias. This was inevitable, for both had achieved considerable success in handling agents. Franks had supervised the cultivation of Oleg Gordievsky, a KGB First Chief Directorate officer presently stationed in Copenhagen, who for the past eight years had supplied SIS with the most fascinating secrets from the department of the Russian foreign intelligence branch that covered Scandinavia and Britain. Codenamed GT/TICKLE by the CIA, he had greatly enhanced SIS's reputation at Langley, both by the quality of his information and by his survival. The very fact that, after eight years of espionage, TICKLE remained free of suspicion was itself testament to the man himself, and to the integrity of the Service.[5] If SIS could maintain such an asset over such a prolonged period, it said much about the organisation, its methods and its personnel. Following the still-painful débâcles of the 1960s, the defection of Kim Philby and the escape from prison of George Blake, the blight that had compromised Britain's premier intelligence agency had become little more than a bad memory, largely irrelevant to the mutually beneficial exchange of classified treasures. Figures, of course, was painfully aware of the damage inflicted by Blake, and his own career had been affected, compromised because he had served in Germany with the traitor. Figures joined SIS from the army – the Worcestershire Regiment – in 1951, the year Philby was sacked, and spent three years under British Control Commission for Germany cover until his posting to Jordan in 1956 for a two-year tour at the SIS station in Amman. After a year at Broadway he was sent to Warsaw for another spell overseas as station commander, and in 1966 was transferred to Vienna. Since his return to London in 1969 he had concentrated on Eastern Europe, and had supervised Gordievsky's recruitment from the very beginning in November 1973, when the local station commander, Robert C., had signalled from Copenhagen that the Russian looked a likely prospect and had approached him to make his pitch on a badminton court early one morning.

Antony Duff, the Intelligence Co-ordinator, enjoyed a considerable knowledge of the intelligence world, despite never having been one of 'the Friends'. He had served as Chairman of the JIC upon his return from his appointment as High Commissioner in Nairobi in 1975, and had held the post until his appointment to Rhodesia in 1979. Although Duff was not told about TICKLE until after Gordievsky's exfiltration from Moscow in July 1985 – when he had switched from the Cabinet Office to be Director-General of the Security Service – he had a high regard for SIS's competence. However, like the other diplomats with whom he was to deal in the coming weeks, the JIC Chairman Patrick Wright and his predecessor Antony Acland, both Arabists by training, he had no first-hand experience of Latin America. Indeed, this weakness extended into SIS where neither Figures nor his deputy, Christopher Curwen, a Far East hand, had been in South America. Of these senior intelligence bureaucrats, all but Duff (who had joined the Foreign Office straight from the Royal Navy in 1946) had been educated at either Oxford (Acland and Wright) or Cambridge (Figures and Curwen).

The CIA was indoctrinated into TICKLE from the outset, although the true identity of the source in Copenhagen was a tightly guarded secret known only to the Deputy Director for Operations, John H. Stein, and five other senior officers. A former Chief of Station in Brussels, who had spent much of his career in Africa, Stein recognised that TICKLE represented a major breakthrough for the British. In return for Gordievsky's fortnightly delivery of crown jewels from the KGB's vaults, Figures sought and received from his direct American counterpart, the Anglophile DCI Bill Casey, the CIA's current assessment of the Argentine armed forces. It was a comprehensive overview prepared by the Operations Directorate's Latin America Division, edited by Dick Kerr of the Intelligence Directorate and delivered by the CIA's Chief of Station in London, Alan D. Wolfe. Under the supervision of his flamboyant Latin America Division Chief, Duane R. (Dewey) Clarridge and his deputy, Al Wedemeyer, a complete order-of-battle for President Galtieri's army, navy and air force was drawn up and, when overlaid with the same data volunteered by the Chileans, it was considered a highly accurate picture of the opposing team in the South Atlantic. The CIA's assessment was developed from reports submitted by the Chief of Station in Buenos Aires, 'Vinx' Harwood Blocker III, who was openly declared to his hosts but worked under diplomatic cover at the embassy, and from the Latin America arms procurement team which routinely monitored (and compiled lists of) orders for weapons made by South American regimes. Led by Casey, the CIA wasted no time in ignoring the State Department and declaring itself for the British, even at the expense of Argentina's assistance for the CIA's covert operations in Honduras. All Casey's senior staff, including his newly appointed executive assistant, the youthful Bob Gates, and the Deputy Director for Intelligence, John H. McMahon, followed his lead and gave SIS full co-operation.

Casey's undisguised admiration for everything British dated back to the Second World War, when the DCI had been posted to London in November 1943 with the Office of Strategic Services as a US Navy lieutenant. Casey remained hugely nostalgic for that part of his life, and many intelligence professionals interpreted his zeal for risky covert operations as a reflection of his enthusiasm for his experiences in wartime London. Any spare time at his desk in the Director's office in Langley was devoted to updating his war memoirs, and his disregard for Congressional oversight was not unconnected with the free-wheeling, buccaneering days of OSS adventures in Nazi-occupied territory. A regular attender at all OSS reunions, he gave his full support to Operations officers seeking to take the initiative, however foolhardy the scheme, doubtless reminded by his supervision (as Chief of OSS Secret Intelligence in Europe) of missions into Germany. But for all his distrust of the State Department and bureaucrats, he was well liked in London where he had made many friends in wartime. Casey had long admired SIS's ability to evade the restrictions of oversight, and had adopted the doctrine that no worthwhile intelligence agency could function entirely legally. Thus Wolfe knew that he would have his DCI's full backing for any request made by SIS. Known in Wall Street as a wealthy, sharp lawyer willing to cut corners, Casey was a lifelong Republican and Ronald Reagan's firmest supporter. Having run the President's election campaign against Jimmy Carter, in which a copy of the incumbent's briefing notes for a live television debate mysteriously found their way to the candidate from California, Casey became chairman of the transition team and, in January 1981, was appointed DCI, a post to which he had always aspired. Significantly, he was the first DCI also to be a member of the Cabinet, indicating that despite his age (sixty-seven), and his tendency to mumble incomprehensibly, he still enjoyed considerable political influence. At Langley his arrival was greeted with relief, the CIA having endured no fewer than four different DCIs since the loss of Dick Helms in 1973, although some had reservations about whether Casey's robust approach to intelligence collection would find acceptance on Capitol Hill.[6]

As well as relying on the CIA, Figures was to lean heavily on what was euphemistically called 'unofficial assistance' from Chile, despite the absence of any SIS station in Santiago. Hostile to their neighbours for many years – a cultural difference exacerbated by a prolonged territorial dispute over the Beagle Channel – the Chileans had maintained a careful watch on all Argentine air and naval activity, particularly in Chubut Province, the southern military district garrisoned by the 8th Infantry Regiment at Comodoro Rivadavia. The Chileans were true Anglophiles, their historical links dating back to the liberation from the Spanish by the legendary General O'Higgins. Since the arrival of Mrs Thatcher's administration in Westminster, which had ended the isolation imposed by David Owen, Britain was regarded as a loyal friend, always willing to assist Santiago however unpopular General Pinochet's regime was in international circles, and always eager to deliver controversial *matériel*. Indeed, as the Falklands crisis opened, the large British destroyer HMS *Norfolk* had just passed through the Panama Canal, the latest purchase that to date had received minimal public attention or criticism. Significantly for the Argentine Navy – which took a close interest in the *Norfolk* – it carried four single Exocets slightly above and astern a single Mark 6 twin 4.5 gun. Although Chile's armed forces were numerically inferior to Argentina's, there was general recognition that Pinochet's men could be relied upon to punch above their weight if they had the right equipment. Now that the freeze on arms sales had been relaxed, Chile was looking increasingly formidable.

During that first day of the invasion the LACIG met in the Cabinet Office and produced four separate papers, answering the predictable questions which would be raised by the War Cabinet, then still being formed by the Prime Minister. With the Chief of the Defence Staff, Sir Terence Lewin, on a routine visit to New Zealand, and the Foreign Secretary, Lord Carrington, in Israel, the Prime Minister had turned in the first instance to the Chief of the Naval Staff, Sir Henry Leach, who traced Mrs Thatcher to her

room in the Commons to give her a robust briefing
on Britain's ability to assemble a force to dislodge the
Argentine invaders. In reality, the JIC's initial appreciation
was less than supportive of Leach's line. While the first
CIG papers had covered the enemy's order-of-battle and
capabilities, in reply to the 'what are we up against?'
request, Gurdon's own military experience told him that
winkling out a determined defender would be far from
easy. Any force well dug-in would be very difficult to
remove, and the data describing some of the professional
Argentine units, such as the paratroop marines, suggested
that a Task Force confronted by them could expect serious resistance. Significantly, the CIG noted Argentina's
possession of the Exocet, and this prompted Wright's
emergency JIC sub-committee to take an interest in the
missile. How many were in circulation? Who owned them?
Would the Israelis, notorious for selling weapons to almost
anyone with the money to buy them, offer them more?

The net sum of current wisdom in London was that the
Task Force was vulnerable to Exocet attack and, on the
basis that the threat from surface-launched vessels could
be contained, the concern focused on the air-launched
variant of which fourteen had been ordered by Argentina.
According to Aerospatiale, only five missiles had been
delivered, and the European Community ban on military
co-operation with General Galtieri's Junta had severed
the links that might have allowed the Argentine Navy
to undertake the necessary work before an AM-39 could
be carried and released by a Super Etendard. Although,
most unusually, the contract had been paid in full upon
signature, it was not due for completion until September
1982, and the French were entirely confident that the
Argentine arsenal consisted of just five weapons. However,
the impossible would happen. HMS *Sheffield* would be
reduced to a burnt-out hulk, and it is obvious that the
original intelligence appreciation – that the Super Etendard
could not operate at ranges greater than 425 nautical

miles – was hopelessly wrong. Thus the advice given to the Task Force, that an operating area east of the Falklands would be safe from air-launched Exocet attack, was equally misguided. The initial assessment, undertaken by the RAF, was flawed on two grounds: firstly, that the enemy would be reluctant to deploy either of the two KC-130 Hercules tankers because they were so vulnerable. (During NATO exercises, the refuelling component of any air combat scenario had proved the most hazardous.) The second miscalculation was the assumption that the Super Etendard's fuel consumption at very low altitude would make such a mission very risky, if not impossible, for the aircraft to return to base.

These two miscalculations resulted in a complete absence of any mention of the Exocet threat when the Royal Navy's skippers were briefed at Ascension and on their way down to the Exclusion Zone. The loss of the *Sheffield* had not only demonstrated that the background intelligence was faulty, it had shown that the most recently acquired data concerning Argentine capabilities was deeply flawed too.

GCHQ's contribution to Operation CORPORATE had been significant, but in the months leading up to the crisis the conclusions reached were mistaken, particularly in respect of the Argentine troops likely to be deployed for an amphibious attack on the Falklands. The JIC had decided that the professionals of VI, VIII and XI Mountain Infantry Brigades would be the Junta's preferred choice because they were well-equipped and experienced in operating in the extreme weather conditions to be expected in the South Atlantic. Both units were identified in positions along the Chilean frontier by the interception of their communications and the acquisition of their individual radio call-signs. Once the JIC had tasked GCHQ to concentrate on these units, it was assumed that any unexpected redeployment would be noted, thereby giving London at least a fortnight's notice of any hostilities – sufficient time to despatch a nuclear submarine into the

area as a deterrent. This was precisely the scenario which
had occurred in November 1977, when there were similar
indications of aggression. A surface Task Force of the
frigates *Alacrity* and *Phoebe* had been ordered south by the
Cabinet's Oversea and Defence Committee, together with
HMS *Dreadnought* and two Fleet Auxiliaries, and the rules
of engagement for a 25-mile exclusion zone around the
Falklands had been agreed in secret. On that occasion the
operation, codenamed JOURNEYMAN, had been completed
in absolute secrecy, and the military government changed
its mind.

The unforeseen problem that materialised in April 1982
was the choice of troops from Brigadier-General Omar
Parada's II Brigade to spearhead the invasion once the
beach-head was established. They were mainly conscripts,
recruited from the sub-tropical Corrientes Province in
the north of the country, more used to guarding the
border with friendly Uruguay. The Junta had behaved
quite illogically, striking at a far from propitious moment
with the most unsuitable troops. SIS had noted that the
imminent disposal of the Antarctic patrol vessel HMS
Endurance, and her two Wasp helicopters, at the end of her
current tour – as announced in the recent Defence White
Paper as part of the cuts imposed on the Royal Navy –
left the Falklands particularly vulnerable; moreover, the
sale of HMS *Invincible* to the Australians would also
inhibit the Royal Navy's ability to respond to aggression.
Indeed, the government had even cancelled the contract
for a replacement aircraft carrier. By September Argentina
would have a full complement of Exocets and reloads, and
to launch an attack any earlier seemed folly. To mount an
invasion at the beginning of April was quite irrational,
bearing in mind the changeover of Naval Party 8901; this
was the overlap period when the local garrison of Royal
Marines effectively doubled to seventy, plus eleven sailors,
for a temporary period.

The best scenario for an invasion had been compiled by

Colonel Love, the military attaché in Buenos Aires who had monitored the increasingly bellicose noises made by the Junta with growing concern. An experienced Gunner officer who was no neophyte in the intelligence world, he had become convinced that an invasion was likely and had taken the hitherto unprecedented opportunity to travel out to Stanley, in civilian clothes and at his own expense, for five days in January to make an inspection of the defences and the terrain. At first his request to the MoD was refused, but he persisted and permission was granted on condition that his wife went too, thus making the trip a private, recreational one. His subsequent report, uncompromisingly entitled 'The Argentine Military Threat to the Falklands', dated 2 March, classified secret and addressed to the Governor, Rex Hunt (but copied to DI4 and to Robin Fearn at the Foreign Office), attempted to draw attention under the heading of 'invasion' to the likelihood of 'a straight seizure of the Islands'.

> One has to remember that the military coup is a fairly well practised art here in Argentina and it is also a fact that the Army study and admire *coup de main* operations of all sorts. Of course such a plan would carry high risks but the follow-on force would be available for early committal if things went wrong.[7]

In a reference to Argentine intelligence-gathering, Love noted that

> accurate and timely intelligence from Port Stanley itself to the mainland presents no problems to the Argentines; our own ability to give early warning would depend upon any coverage of air activity in Cordoba, home of the airborne brigade, and possibly Rio Gallegos, nearest field to the Islands. With present arrangements we could not realistically hope to get any information at all.[8]

In his conclusions the Defence Attaché observed that

it would be difficult to see any operation mounted at the present stage or in the future which did not involve the Navy – and very probably the Marines . . . An airborne or clandestinely mounted *coup de main* attempt against Port Stanley would have definite appeal to a force planning the seizure of the Islands . . . Special arrangements could enhance our chance of providing early warning from Argentina, but at present we could not realistically expect to be able to detect any moves.[9]

Although he did not mention them in the four-page report, Love was conscious of a group of Argentine 'gas workers' on the Islands, and of the presence of the LADE airline office in Stanley which possessed its own independent wireless transmitter. His document, reproduced in full in Appendix I, can be read as a blueprint for a coup, complete with a description of an assault on the airport, possibly executed by special forces infiltrated on an ostensibly routine flight by a Hercules transport, and maybe heralded by some provocative manoeuvre on one of the other dependencies. His prescience is quite remarkable, even if the surprise raid on the airport never took place. In fact a Hercules *did* make a forced landing a fortnight before the offensive, a ploy that Love had instantly interpreted as a dress rehearsal to see whether the runway could accommodate a fully-laden C-130; actually the plane was not on an intelligence mission but had experienced a genuine problem with a fuel line while on the return leg of a routine supply flight from Rio Gallegos to the Antarctic base at Thule. Nevertheless, the paper bears a striking resemblance to the plan codenamed ROSARIO drawn up by the Argentines and, taken in conjunction with the concerns expressed by Captain Nicholas Barker of HMS *Endurance* in January, shows how the evidence could read differently in London.

Love's report was submitted to the Defence Intelligence Directorate at the Ministry of Defence, but was filed with the dismissive observation scrawled in the margin that 'I suspect the Ambassador has asked this to be sent. It says nothing we do not already know.' This can either be taken to mean that the Foreign Office was already aware of the shortcomings of the intelligence picture, and of the mechanics of a takeover, or that Cordoba and Rio Gallegos had been identified as essential to any military undertaking. To this latter extent Love's assessment was misguided for, as events turned out, the Air Mobile Brigade at Cordoba never went to the Falklands, apart from one component – the 105mm guns of the 4th Air Mobile Artillery Regiment. By the same token, his singling out of Rio Gallegos was spot on.

The JIC had long recognised the weak points in the Islands' defence and acknowledged that nothing short of a deterrent at sea would prevent a determined bid to capture the colony. However, because of a lack of experience of South America at all levels of the JIC and SIS, insufficient weight had been given to the Latin preference for over-optimism and giving quite undue significance to relatively trivial incidents. For example, the announcement that HMS *Endurance* was to be scrapped was nothing more than a manifestation of Treasury parsimony, not a carefully calculated political signal. Nevertheless, in Buenos Aires the simple budget cut was understood as being indicative of something entirely different, a perceptible shift in British policy. Nor was this entirely unreasonable, for *Endurance* had a very special significance, particularly within the intelligence fraternity. Although ostensibly an ice patrol vessel, the Argentines considered her most vital function to be that of an intelligence-gathering facility. They strongly suspected that she accommodated a GCHQ section in a secure classified compartment, manned by Spanish-speaking operators working on eight-hour shifts, and the Argentine Navy had taken a special interest in her equipment during a recent courtesy visit to the submarine base Mar del Plata in January 1982. Indeed, *Endurance*'s captain, Nick Barker, had been dismayed by the attention his crew attracted on that occasion, and had noted the attempts to identify any linguists on board. To replace a worn-out patrol vessel with regular visits by Royal Navy frigates was one thing, which was the British Government's official position as declared by John Nott, but to permanently eliminate a key intelligence asset was quite a different matter, as was appreciated only by the Argentinians and those privy to *Endurance*'s true role.

Chapter 3

LACIG

As the loss of the *Sheffield* penetrated the British psyche, the implications for what hitherto had been a rather splendid, media-supported enterprise took root. The Task Force had been despatched from Portsmouth with a memorable flag-waving send-off, but with neither sufficient fuel, ammunition, nor any experience of a real war – although the SIDE officer from the Argentine Embassy in London who was watching did not know this. Realistically, with considerable doubts about the operational durability of the Type-22 frigates and, to a lesser extent, about the Type-42 destroyers, Admiral Lewin had advised his ministers that the Task Force could be expected to operate for six months, but only to be effective for about half that time.

So had it all been a diplomatic sham that was about to unravel disastrously? Certainly the men who put to sea did so with no meaningful intelligence, the public libraries in the navy towns having been plundered for maps and copies of Jane's invaluable series of publications. Such intelligence as had begun to trickle in came from improbable, unpromising sources. Through Michael Chilton, the NZSIS officer in London (who was overlapping briefly with his successor, Elizabeth Halliday), the New Zealanders had offered to share their Sigint (signals intelligence) take with GCHQ, and Brian Gorman from Australia had volunteered the services of his counterpart in Santiago, one of only two ASIS stations in the whole of South America. Perhaps most bizarrely of all, the Canadians disclosed a source of some embarrassment: an elderly Canadian in Stanley had been allowed to telephone his ambassador in Buenos Aires from a local kiosk, and this conversation had become almost a daily event. If the Argentines monitored these calls they made no effort to censor their military content, and this had given the Canadians a unique window into local morale and the military situation. The embarrassment stemmed from the fact that Canada possessed no overseas intelligence collection agency, and was banned by statute from operating spies abroad. Nevertheless, this material was shared with the British, and proved quite useful, if only because there was precious little else to rely upon.

HMS *Sheffield* continued to burn furiously until she finally capsized and sank at night, six days after the attack, assisted by some plastic explosive. The news of her loss had a devastating impact on the Task Force, which had suffered its first casualties, at Fleet Headquarters and at the Joint Intelligence Committee.

Hitherto, the war had gone reasonably well. Christopher Wreford-Brown, on his first patrol in the nuclear submarine HMS *Conqueror*, had torpedoed the Argentine cruiser *General Belgrano* two days earlier, and this had prevented the much-feared pincer movement on the Task Force. Although the former USS *Phoenix* was a Brooklyn-class cruiser of pre-Second World War vintage, having been launched in 1938, its fifteen new sixteen-inch and eight five-inch guns, re-equipped for land and naval bombardment, represented a potent threat to the British. Of particular concern was the thickness of the ship's armour, which was a full four inches on much of the hull, three inches on deck, five on the gun turrets and a massive eight inches on the conning-tower. Although her top speed was rather less than the thirty-two knots she had performed when new, she would be hard to sink in any surface engagement. Accompanied by two destroyers, the *Hipolito Bouchard* and the *Piedra Buena*, each carrying four Exocets, the three ships were perceived, correctly, as the southern component of a flanking strategy intended to close in on the Task Force from two directions simultaneously. The northern end of the tactic was the former British carrier, the 20,000-ton *Veinticinco de Mayo* with its estimated ten to fourteen Skyhawks, and possibly some Exocet-equipped Super Etendards, hitherto undetected but known to be at sea and escorted by two Type-42 destroyers: the *Santisima Trinidad*, built under British licence in Argentina and launched in 1974, and the entirely British-built *Hercules*, commissioned in July 1976 but for which Vickers had not yet been paid, plus three modern French A-69 corvettes, the *Drummond*, *Granville* and *Guerrico*. Although both HMS *Spartan* and *Splendid* had been detached to find and shadow this group, they never made contact, a cause of some concern for Admiral Woodward who, even though he had spent the past four years commanding a desk in the Ministry of Defence, was a submariner by trade. According to the Naval Intelligence Division, the *Veinticinco de Mayo* had enjoyed an interesting history. As HMS *Venerable* she was launched at Birkenhead in December 1943 and then sold to the Dutch in April 1948. In 1968 Argentina bought her as the HNMS *Karel Doorman* and, with a crew of 1,000 men, this was the last of the Colossus-class afloat. Like the *General Belgrano*, the carrier was quite ancient, but as a platform for fighter-bombers, Alouettes and anti-submarine Sea Kings, it was a powerful opponent.

Following the elimination of the *General Belgrano* by two rather antique acoustic Mk 8 torpedoes (fired in preference to the *Conqueror*'s modern, but less reliable Mk 24 wire-guided Tigerfish), the British battle group was considered by Northwood to be on schedule, and the episode effectively removed the Argentine surface fleet from the scene. But although the prospect of a two-pronged attack – with perhaps sixteen Exocets flying towards the Task Force to saturate and overwhelm the defence radars – had diminished, there was still a formidable threat from the five submarines remaining, following the loss of the *Santa Fe* (the former USS *Catfish*) in South Georgia earlier in April. According to the standard reference work, *Jane's Fighting Ships*, Argentina possessed two modern German-designed boats, the *Santa Cruz* and the *San Juan* – expected to be sufficiently quiet to be more than a match for British passive sonars – and the Type-209 *San Luis* and her sister ship *Salta*, both commissioned in 1974. In addition, there was the *Santa Fe*'s sister diesel of the same 1945 vintage, the *Santara del Estero*, formerly the USS *Chivo*. In reality, of the five only the *San Luis*, with her eight 21-inch bow torpedo tubes, was operational. The two German boats were still under construction and the *Salta* was unserviceable because of a defective propeller shaft. Although the *Santara del Estero* could not submerge, she had sailed very publicly from Mar del Plata, and then been concealed in Bahia Blanca, leaving the analysts in their huge underground concrete bunker at Northwood convinced she was at sea, stalking the Task Force, thereby ensuring that the British wasted considerable effort on entirely fruitless anti-submarine manoeuvres. As for the *San Luis*, despite her poor technical condition Commander Azcueta and his crew of thirty-one kept her at sea on patrol north of the Falklands from 11 April until mid-May, and twice attacked British ships though without success. On both occasions she was able to withdraw undetected, having fired a total of four torpedoes of which one was directed at a suspected nuclear submarine, a sonar target that was more probably 'biological'; naval jargon for a whale. With her published top speed submerged as 22 knots, she was constantly in the mind of the British Task Force commander.

Notwithstanding the concerns of the admiral for the safety of his ships, the calculations made by the planners had placed a deadline on capturing Stanley, and the date chosen was the end of June. By then the South Atlantic winter would make the ground war impossible to sustain, and the preference was for a deadline in the middle of the month. That meant completing an amphibious landing by 25 May at the latest, allowing General Moore's troops a month to establish a beach-head and time to march on Stanley. Any delay in the timetable would be fatal, for the Royal Navy simply did not possess enough ships to cope with the re-supply and, in terms of cold logistics, there was neither sufficient ammunition nor equipment to fight a prolonged campaign. South Georgia fell on 26 April and the main battle group entered the Total Exclusion Zone on 1 May. The first troops to be landed on the islands, eight four-man reconnaissance patrols from the Special Air Service Regiment's 'G' Squadron, commanded by Major Cedric Delves of the Devon and Dorsets, had been inserted covertly over the following three nights by Sea King 4s from *Hermes*, to find the enemy's positions and strengths. As for the runway at Stanley, originally built by the Argentine Air Force, it was too short for the fighters and Super Etendards, could not be extended, and had been bombed on 1 May by a single Vulcan flying from Wideawake on Ascension, one of several raids planned to deny use of the airfield to Argentine aircraft.

As for tactical intelligence, the army's Intelligence Corps, based at Ashford in Kent, had been completely taken by surprise when the Falklands were invaded. Already fully stretched by commitments in Northern Ireland, Belize and Hong Kong, a small section headed by Major D. M. Burrill was despatched to Northwood, and Colonel G. Redfern led a team to Ascension to debrief the Royal Marines evacuated from South Georgia. Another unit flew to Montevideo to question the repatriated Marines from Stanley, and an imagery interpretation cell was established on *Hermes*. Later, three Joint Forward Interrogation Teams undertook the examination of prisoners, and by the end of the campaign more than 11,000 PoWs had been processed, with 600 segregated for additional attention from the specialists of the Joint Services Interrogation Wing brought down from Ashford.

Before the land campaign could get under way, a suitable
landing area had to be selected, and the various options had
to be surveyed by seven patrols of the Special Boat Section,
the clandestine warfare specialists of the Royal Marines
led by Major Jonathon Thomson. Having agreed a site for
the amphibious assault, the troops assembled at Ascension
would be ferried the 3,500 miles across the Atlantic on the
liner *Canberra*, and disembark to engage the occupation
forces. The plan was extraordinarily risky, because all the
Task Force's components were operating at their extreme
limits and there was absolutely no margin for error.
Following the loss of the *Sheffield*, the tactics changed.
The battle group moved further eastwards, putting more
distance between the carriers and the mainland, and three
combat air patrols, comprising six Sea Harriers, were put
into the air to intercept any further daylight intruders.
However, these measures were far from satisfactory, for at
a minimum there remained five Super Etendards and three
Exocets threatening the Task Force, backed by two dozen
Mirage III and ex-Israeli Dagger 1A1 fighters, as well as
twenty-seven A-4P Skyhawk fighter-bombers. Indeed, the
first British intelligence estimate of the Argentine attack
aircraft had suggested a daunting total of 247. The results
of air combat trials fought between French Air Force
pilots flying the delta-winged Mirage IIIs, and three Sea
Harriers – a deliberately realistic exercise undertaken at
very short notice to make a useful comparison and offer
some guidance on tactics to the Task Force pilots – offered
little comfort. In the simulated dogfights all three British
pilots had been repeatedly shot down by their French
opponents. If the same kill rate was duplicated by the
Argentine pilots, the Sea Harriers could expect to be
decimated by the faster supersonic fighters. Although
the 801 Squadron pilots had dismissed the practice conclusions as typically poor performances by men who did
not measure up to their more experienced colleagues at
sea, their opinion was not shared widely, even though

it was acknowledged that the 801 pilots had achieved good results in one-to-one scraps against the more potent American supersonic F-15s. Indeed, two extended tests, conducted against F-5 'aggressors' from RAF Alconbury and the twin-engined McDonnell Douglas F-15s flown over to NAS Yeovilton from the USAF Eagle Squadron base at Bitburg in Germany, seemed to have given the 801 pilots the edge. But was the confidence shown by the men on the carriers nothing more than bravado?

Uppermost in the minds of many were the chilling results of the most recent confrontation between modern weapons systems, during the 1973 Yom Kippur War, when the Israelis lost 109 aircraft in eighteen days to anti-aircraft missiles and radar guided surface-to-air missiles. Despite the high level of sophistication of the Israeli pilots and their most advanced American fighters, they had fallen prey to the relatively undisciplined Egyptian and Syrian ground forces using Soviet-supplied equipment. The more the Israelis manoeuvred to avoid the SAM-5s, the more vulnerable they became to conventional ground-fire. If that was what the Arabs could do, what would the Argentines achieve with their batteries of modern French-made Roland and British Tiger Cat missiles, manned by professionals? In addition, of course, there were the radar-controlled twin Oerlikons, the twin 20mm Rheinmetall cannon with Israeli Elta radar, the 30mm single-barreled Hispano Suizas and the 12.7mm heavy machine-guns deployed by the two anti-aircraft regiments in the Falklands, which represented a dauntingly formidable threat to any ground-attack Harriers. The omens were not good.

As for serviceability and determination, the Argentines had provided the most eloquent proof that they could penetrate the British radar screen and pick off a surface ship. Yesterday it had been *Sheffield*. Without question, *Hermes* and *Invincible* would remain the enemy's principal targets, protected in the air by just fourteen of the versatile but unproven Sea Harriers, a total that was to be reduced imminently by the accidental loss of two Sea Harriers from the *Invincible* which disappeared after apparently having collided in poor visibility. Even after the reinforcements due on the *Atlantic Conveyor* had arrived – which were not expected for another fortnight – the number would be inadequate to patrol the 35,000 square miles of sea surrounding the battle group. When the huge container vessel chartered from Cunard did eventually deliver its valuable cargo of fourteen additional Harriers, there would still be a shortfall, because six of the aircraft would be ground-attack variants on loan from the RAF, quite unsuited to flying combat air patrols. At the very best, without any further accidents or losses to the enemy, the Task Force's air umbrella would amount to twenty-five planes once the new aircraft had been flown across, without mishap, from the *Atlantic Conveyor* to *Hermes* and *Invincible*. Quite simply, it was not enough to carry out the dual role of protecting the carriers, standing 150 miles off the east of the islands, and prosecuting a war on the ground with aircraft that could only remain over the Falklands for a bare twenty-five minutes. Lurking behind these worries was the vulnerability of the fleet of transports that stretched, unprotected, across the length of the Atlantic. The Royal Navy had chartered every ship available from the trade, and there had been no opportunity for the luxury of duplicating vital supplies. Unquestionably, the loss of one or two large cargoes of logistics would be bound to bring Operation CORPORATE to a premature conclusion. If the Argentine Naval Air Squadron could sink the most modern, heavily armed warship with ease, what chance had the unprotected merchantmen? At home, the political consequences of failure were easy to imagine. No Prime Minister could expect to survive such humiliation and the government, facing a general election before May 1984 at the very latest, could expect to be driven from office, shamed by a costly fiasco in which the politicians would be blamed for a catalogue of failures both before and during the campaign. It was no exaggeration to think it likely that military defeat at the hands of Argentina would have profound military, diplomatic and economic implications for the future of the United Kingdom.

An added complication was the unpalatable news, gleaned from Sigint, that the Argentines knew *Hermes'* precise location. Although the Air Force had invested in a sophisticated encrypted communications system manufactured by Grenell (the Racal subsidiary in South Africa), which had been regarded as exceptionally secure, the Argentine Army and Navy had proved easier to monitor, and this had led to the discovery that *Hermes* had been compromised. This discovery was particularly tragic, for the information was acquired as a result of the loss of Lieutenant Nick Taylor, a particularly gifted and popular Fleet Air Arm pilot who, together with two other Sea Harriers from 800 Squadron, had participated in the second attack on the airfield at Goose Green on the afternoon of 4 May.

The accumulating statistics from the Task Force were analysed in London by the Joint Intelligence Committee's South Atlantic Current Intelligence Group and the Defence Intelligence Directorate. Clearly measures had to be taken to prevent the deployment of the remaining Argentine Exocets, but the options were limited. An effective radar screen to catch the Super Etendards on their way to their targets was quite impractical. There was no Airborne Early Warning available, and insufficient surface pickets to provide anything like satisfactory protection. Any raid would require air-to-air refuelling, so elimination of the two Argentine KC-130 tankers looked attractive, but the chance of catching them unawares was virtually negligible. If denial of the South Atlantic airspace was impractical, there remained two options: the establishment of a clandestine early warning facility at each of the three principal mainland bases, at San Julian, Rio Gallegos and Rio

Grande, whence the Argentine Air Force were mounting offensive fighter-bomber operations, or an attempt to eliminate the remaining Exocets on the ground.

The prospect of escalating the war to involve the mainland was a potentially thorny one, but contingency plans were drawn up on the not entirely confident assumption that the War Cabinet would sanction the extension of hostilities beyond the Total Exclusion Zone if there was a reasonable chance of destroying the Exocets. Clearly the insertion of a covert team to monitor air activity at, say, Rio Gallegos, was not without risk, but it was a task well suited to the Special Forces and the Director SAS, Peter de la Billière, was enthusiastic. De la Billière had joined the regiment in 1955 and commanded 'A' Squadron in Aden and Borneo before taking over command of the regiment in 1972 in time for the campaign in Dhofar. Having won the Military Cross twice, in 1959 and 1966, and a DSO in 1976, he had been appointed Director SAS in 1978. He had supervised the highly visible Iranian Embassy siege and was keen on the idea of eliminating the Exocet threat at source.

As the problem was considered, the SAS was already en route to the South Atlantic, 'D' Squadron having embarked on the Royal Fleet Auxiliary *Fort Austin* at Ascension to liberate South Georgia. While the regiment's commander, Colonel Mike Rose, remained on the amphibious HMS *Fearless*, planning future operations from a portacabin lashed to the afterdeck, 'G' Squadron was on the RFA *Resource* with the main battle group. Once landed on the mainland, either by a diesel submarine like HMS *Oracle*, by helicopter or by parachute, the teams could establish a covert observation post, a task for which they were exceptionally well trained and well experienced, and communicate directly to Hereford via the SAS's encrypted satellite channels which were difficult to detect or intercept. In these circumstances the SAS teams could provide the Task Force with early warning of Super Etendard sorties in sufficient time for the Sea Harriers to scramble and arrange an appropriate reception committee. Having completed their mission, at the conclusion of hostilities the patrols could be exfiltrated by submarine, or perhaps could trek overland to neutral Chile.

The disadvantage of the insertion programme was the lack of a guarantee that the Sea Harriers, equipped only with the Blue Fox radar that performed so poorly over land, would be able to successfully intercept aircraft leaving mainland bases in the very limited time available. Its weapons system depended upon engagement at close range, and even the impressive Sidewinder required a visual sighting within an arc of thirty degrees of the target's tailpipe. While the SAS observation posts might give an hour's warning of the Super Etendards being airborne, they would be unable to indicate either the rendezvous point for inflight refuelling or their chosen target. In addition, there was considerable risk in leaving SAS teams in such a heavily guarded environment for a period likely to exceed two weeks. As for the troops themselves, would they be willing to take on a mission of this kind, knowing that once compromised there was absolutely no chance of rescue, the only alternatives being surrender or a near-impossible march to neutral territory? Indeed, what kind of a reception could they expect if they encountered Chilean troops before they made contact with British agents?

In addition, there was a logistical problem regarding a submarine insertion. There were three British submarines operating in the South Atlantic as part of underwater component designated CTF 324: the *Conqueror*, which had shadowed and dealt with the *General Belgrano* so efficiently, and the two despatched from Faslane, HMS *Splendid* and HMS *Spartan*. All were nuclear hunter-killers, entirely inappropriate for operations in shallow water; any venture into shallows below 300 feet was extremely hazardous and Northwood would never countenance the risk, which would multiply if one of the submarines was required to surface to receive troops trans-decking by helicopter. Unfortunately the nearest diesel boat, ideally suited for clandestine missions, was the 'O' class patrol submarine *Onyx*, which could put SBS patrols ashore without surfacing, but she would not arrive in the Total Exclusion Zone for a further three weeks.

As a first step, the JIC despatched a request to the Intelligence Cell at the SAS base at Stirling Lines, near Hereford, for consideration of an infiltration scheme. As a precaution an SAS officer, Andy H., was flown – under temporary diplomatic cover as an assistant military attaché – to the British Embassy in Santiago, in anticipation of the need to establish local caches of food and clothing for evading SAS patrols from over the frontier. H.'s mission was to reconnoitre the border, recommend routes across, and prepare replenishment dumps and a reception system to sustain the thirty or so men who might be expected to trek into neutral Chile. The ambassador, John Heath, was not informed of his true role.

The second alternative considered by the JIC's CIG was an air raid to destroy the Super Etendards and the Exocets on the ground. This, it was considered, could be accomplished in two ways. The first plan called for Vulcan bombers to fly from Wideawake, the second involved Sea Harriers off the Task Force carriers. Certainly the Vulcan was a viable option, a similar operation codenamed BLACK BUCK having been flown on 1 May to deny the Stanley runway to the Argentines. On that occasion the ageing bomber from 101 Squadron Strike Command, its nuclear bomb-bay having been converted to accommodate conventional weapons, had flown the marathon 8,000-mile, fifteen-hour round-trip supported by no fewer than eleven Victor K2 tankers, each loaded with 100,000lb of fuel. After five refuellings on the outward journey, the single plane flown by Flight-Lieutenant Martin Withers – actually a back-up for the original Vulcan from 50 Squadron that had abandoned the mission because of a pressurisation problem – had dropped twenty-one 1,000lb bombs over the target from an altitude of 10,000 feet, well out of range of the French Roland and the British Tiger Cat missiles on the ground. By the time the Argentine AN/TPS-44 radar manned by the 601st Anti-Aircraft Regiment on Sapper Hill had identified the lone intruder, the Vulcan was on its journey home, its sophisticated electronic counter-measures – including the US AN/ALQ-101 jammers carried in pods borrowed from BAe Buccaneers – having defeated the Skyguard radar which controlled the eight lethal 35mm twin-barrelled Oerlikons defending the airstrip. A photographic reconnaissance flown from *Hermes* shortly after dawn showed a series of craters fifty yards apart across the airfield, with one on the tarmac; accordingly the mission had been judged a partial success. In reality the runway was still operational, potholed only in appearance through the skilful use of camouflage by the Argentines who constructed some false craters to deceive the British cameras. However, this was not to be discovered until the surrender, and at the time it was believed that a similar exercise could be flown by a Vulcan against a mainland site, but what were the chances of hitting the target aircraft or missiles?

BLACK BUCK's objective had been to drop nearly ten tons of iron bombs from sufficient height to penetrate the runway and break up the concrete strip, and to that extent it had failed. It was later discovered that the navigational co-ordinates fed into the Vulcan's computer were inaccurate: the Argentine engineer responsible for constructing the airfield had made a mistake of exactly 1,000 metres in his calculations, so every map showing the airstrip was slightly out of alignment. In consequence, the Vulcan's bombs had landed almost exactly 1,000 metres from the centre of the runway. The mission to Stanley had called for tremendous precision, but certainly not the same required to hit ten separate, tiny targets which might anyway be dispersed to protective revetments.

Without detailed up-to-date intelligence, the RAF would be wasting its time. Furthermore, mere damage to the runway would achieve very little, for there were plenty of alternative airfields further north and if the runway was too badly damaged for the aircraft to be flown off, the Super Etendards could simply be driven on low loaders to a new location. The other consideration was the risk involved. As far as BLACK BUCK was concerned, the risks had been minimal. No fighters were based at Stanley and, by making the approach low, the Vulcan alerted the local radar to its presence only at the last moment, when it was far too late to scramble Mirages from the mainland. An attack on the mainland, however, would be harder to conceal, and fighters could be expected to retaliate very quickly even if they did not pounce on the initial approach. A further factor would be the political embarrassment if, for some reason, perhaps mechanical failure, the bomber was forced to divert to Chile or Brazil.

The prospect of a Vulcan raid looked increasingly like a rather desperate long-shot, a gesture to demonstrate that Argentina was not beyond the reach of the Royal Air Force, and a Sea Harrier raid appeared equally unattractive. Argentina's coastal air bases were well beyond their range unless the carriers moved dangerously close to the mainland, and as the Sea Harrier's maximum payload was three 1,000lb bombs, seven aircraft would be required to deliver the same cargo as a single Vulcan. This amounted to almost half the Task Force's air cover and, with no prospect of replacements for three weeks, the risk of depleting that cover was simply too great. Furthermore, once the replacements arrived, itself a risky business over such a vast distance, the entire stock of RAF and Royal Navy Harriers would be committed, leaving just four in England – two for training pilots and the other pair for testing equipment. The bottom line was about to be reached, and no unnecessary risks could be allowed to jeopardise the invaluable Harrier.

The third alternative was an assault on a mainland base by Special Forces, delivered either by parachute or in an Entebbe-style raid with troops rapidly disembarking from Hercules transports, locating and destroying the target aircraft and missiles, re-embarking and flying off into the night. At first blush, this scenario looked quite attractive, as it boasted more of a chance to identify and sabotage the key equipment. On 3 July 1976 the Israelis had achieved almost complete success with three Hercules aircraft flown undetected 2,250 miles from Tel Aviv to Uganda. Codenamed Operation JONATHAN, more than a hundred hostages – hijacked on an Air France A-300 Airbus between Athens and Paris – were rescued, and all the German and Arab terrorists (with just one exception) killed, for the loss of the American-born, Harvard-educated raid commander, Colonel Yoni Netanyahu (killed by a sniper), one other military casualty and three passengers, two of whom were shot in error. JONATHAN had achieved total surprise and the entire operation was completed in just ninety-nine minutes, without the 20 per cent losses anticipated by the planners.[1] Could a modified Entebbe plan be applied to the Argentine mainland?

The Entebbe raid, executed by the Sayaret Matkal anti-terrorist unit, had many parallels with the SAS plan, but it had been developed in less than forty-eight hours with minimal rehearsal, based on information provided by French Intelligence debriefers who had interviewed some of the first batch of released hostages upon their return to Paris on 1 July. The Israelis had set out from Lod Airport with five Hercules and refuelled at Sharm-a-Sheik in Sinai; they had then taken a route down the Red Sea, flying at an altitude of fifty feet to avoid Egyptian radar, and crossed Ethiopia and Kenya on a final approach into Uganda. As the first C-130 – containing Netanyahu and his thirty-five Sayaret Matkal commandos dressed in Ugandan uniforms, fifty-two paratroopers and three vehicles – landed on the darkened airstrip, ten men jumped off the moving aircraft to place lights on the runway to guide in the following planes. The second, with seventeen paratroopers, two armoured personnel carriers and a command jeep, landed six minutes later, as troops took possession of the terminal building where all but one of the hostages were held captive, and a minute later the third C-130 arrived with thirty Golani infantrymen, two more APCs and another jeep. When the area had been secured and two Baader-Meinhof and four PFLP terrorists shot dead, a fourth C-130 with twenty Golani infantry, a twenty-strong medical team and a refuelling crew of ten arrived to evacuate the hostages. One imaginative contribution to the element of surprise achieved by the Israelis was the use of an official-looking Mercedes limousine, complete with large Ugandan flag and escorted by two Land Rovers, the appearance of which sowed precisely the intended degree of confusion among the defenders, who believed they were witnessing another visit from the Ugandan president, General Idi Amin. Undoubtedly, both the terrorists and the Ugandans were taken completely by surprise.

The entire mission had been supervised by a Boeing 707 command plane circling overhead, and the original scheme called for the transports, which were low on fuel after their 7½-hour flight, to have their tanks topped up at Entebbe. However, midway through the operation the Kenyan authorities granted refuelling facilities to the raiders, so the five aircraft flew straight to Nairobi to meet a 707 airborne hospital. After less than twenty minutes on the ground the six planes took off, to rendezvous with a formation of A-4 fighters over the Red Sea before landing at Tel Nof Air Force Base. Altogether, a total of 106 hostages had been rescued by a force of six planes and more than 170 troops, with seven German and Palestinian terrorists killed and just three, who were believed to have been in Entebbe itself, escaping. An unknown number of Ugandan troops had also been shot, and eight Ugandan MiGs destroyed on the tarmac. In contrast, the SAS hoped to neutralise ten pilots, four planes and three missiles with an assault team of sixty-five men carried on just two C-130s.

The comparison with Entebbe was not entirely realistic, not least because of the difference in the intelligence data available. The Israelis had enjoyed the benefit of up-to-date eye-witness reports of the local situation from the freed hostages in Paris, and knew the precise locations of their objectives. In contrast the SAS had no such advantage, and were handicapped by a total lack of knowledge regarding the exact whereabouts of the aircraft and the missiles. As for the pilots, there was no confirmation of where the officers' mess could be found. Indeed, disorientated by an arrival at night at an undefined corner of the base, the distances across an unfamiliar airfield could be as much as three miles, which translated into a twenty-minute run for those soldiers who could not be carried on the Land Rovers. This was more than enough time for even the most startled defender to begin organising counter-measures.

If delivered by parachute, the troops could seize the airfield, destroy the hardware and then call in the Hercules to pick them up, a daring coup in the very best traditions of the SAS. On closer examination it became clear that even a low-level drop would give the defenders too much time to prepare themselves for the assault, and the stopwatch would be against the airborne troops from the moment they deployed their chutes. However, a surprise landing in the middle of the night by two unmarked transports, suddenly disgorging troops equipped with jeeps, mortars and missiles, could achieve success and penetrate from the ground the most hardened revetments intended to protect the Super Etendards. If the mission was undertaken earlier in the evening, there was a greater chance of catching the ten pilots in the officers' mess. Once again, the plan would depend on detailed intelligence which would necessitate the insertion of a reconnaissance party to set up a covert observation post.

While the RAF went through the motions of explaining

why a Vulcan sortie to the mainland was folly, and the admirals ruled out the deployment of the Fleet Air Arm, the SAS headquarters at Hereford mulled over the possibilities of flying in a team to raid an airfield. At the same time, the War Cabinet gave its first tentative approval to what became known as 'the mainland option'. According to the Attorney-General, Sir Michael Havers, such an operation would be legal in international law, but the Prime Minister's consultation on this topic was deliberately very limited, so as to preserve secrecy, and hardly went beyond the political members of the War Cabinet and its small secretariat, the diplomat (Sir) Robert Wade-Gery and his deputy from the MoD, Roger Facer. Indeed, the issue had been raised with her already by President Reagan, who later described a transatlantic conversation in which he had mentioned a rumour that 'the British were preparing to attack military bases on the mainland of Argentina':

> This would have substantially escalated the level of combat. Our intelligence community confirmed that preparations for such attacks were under way. I called Margaret Thatcher to say that, while we fully supported Britain's effort to take back the Falklands, we thought it would be dangerous to move the war on to the mainland of South America. Margaret heard me out, but, demonstrating the iron will for which she is famous, she stood firm. I couldn't persuade her to make a commitment not to invade, and for several days we waited for a night-time attack by British planes on the mainland – one that never came.[2]

The Intelligence Cell of 22 SAS, located in a building known as 'the Kremlin' inside the regiment's compound, began setting out the options for 'B' Squadron, the only Sabre Squadron not already deployed to Ascension or further south. The very first issue under consideration was not the delivery of the troops to the target, but the target itself. Where was it? According to the data provided by the Intelligence Corps, there were five possible options. The first was Trelew, not far from Rawson in the north, now occupied by the 2nd Bomber Group which had flown in its six ex-RAF Canberra bombers from its usual home in Parana, at the other end of the country. The second was Comodoro Rivadavia, one end of the air-bridge of Hercules transports into Stanley. The third, and the closest

Principal Argentine air and naval bases.

in distance to the Falklands, was San Julian, the wartime headquarters of the 4th Fighter Group from Mendoza, and the 6th Fighter Group from Tandil. Although still operating as a civil airport, the arrival of nearly thirty Skyhawks and a dozen Daggers had transformed the area into a military zone. The fourth option was Rio Gallegos, usually the base of the two KC-130 Hercules tankers of the 1st Air Transport Group but now accommodating eleven Mirage IIIs of the 8th Fighter Group from Mariano Moreno, Buenos Aires, and a dozen Skyhawks of the 5th Fighter Group from Villa Reynolds. The fifth and most likely target was Rio Grande in Tierra del Fuego, where a dozen Daggers had been dispersed from the 6th Fighter Group, together with ten Skyhawks of the 3rd Fighter and Attack Squadron of Bahia Blanca, originally embarked on the *Veinticinco de Mayo*. Like the Super Etendards of the Second Fighter and Attack Squadrons, these were part of Argentina's Naval Air Force centred in the port of Bahia Blanca, well out of range for all but the long-duration flights of the slow aircraft of the Anti-submarine Squadron and the Reconnaissance Squadron. The question was, which airfield was supporting the Super Etendards? The smart money was on Rio Grande, partly because of the distance to the target area but mainly because of advice from SIS: the Argentine Navy had an ancient loathing of the Air Force, a hostility grounded in politics which was reciprocated in full. Rio Gallegos had been turned over to the Air Force some years earlier, leaving Rio Grande the only Naval Air Station in the south of the country. Although far from conclusive, it was probable that the Navy's fiercely independent pilots would never have agreed to fly from an Air Force base.

Aside from despatching an agent to use the Mark 1 eyeball, there was a limited choice available in terms of imagery – the technical euphemism for overhead photography. The best pictures were taken either by a satellite in orbit, by a high-flying SR-71A Blackbird spy plane, or by a sneak flight at low level. A third option was theoretically available, since the Task Force's Harriers carried the necessary equipment for oblique photography, but no Harrier mission could be expected to go undetected and, even if the plane's range could be extended, the chances of a Harrier returning to its carrier were very slim indeed. Overflight of the four most likely mainland 'candidates' would eliminate all chance of surprise, although the Lockheed SR-71 could cover them all in a single sortie and complete the assignment entirely without risk, flying at Mach 3 at an altitude of over 80,000 feet, literally on the edge of space. The two-seater was the fastest plane in the world, and had flown from New York to London in less than three hours, breaking all records at a speed rather faster than a high-velocity bullet, with the crew wearing self-contained pressure suits that could preserve life on the moon. The SR-71 also had the advantage of being the first stealth aircraft – being constructed of special composite materials, mainly iron ferrites, under a titanium skin that absorbed radar energy and made the plane almost invisible to conventional radar.

Unquestionably, it was ideal for the task, but there was an obstacle for the British. Altogether twenty of these remarkable planes were flown by the USAF's 9th Strategic Reconnaissance Wing, based permanently at Beale, just outside Sacramento in California; of these, a pair operated from the USAF base at Mildenhall in Suffolk, usually flying routine surveillance missions up to the Soviet submarine pens at Murmansk, or down to the Eastern Mediterranean where the RAF ran two bases in Cyprus. As well as returning with imagery, the SR-71s also carried a cargo of electronic sensors used to record hostile radar pulses radiating from Warsaw Pact ground stations and missile batteries, a task essential to the development of counter-measures. Although they took care never to infringe Soviet airspace, these sorties were very sensitive and each required official British approval, which always had been forthcoming with the single exception of a veto issued in October 1973 during the Yom Kippur War, on a flight for the Israelis over the combat zone. The British government feared offending the Arabs and had banned all Blackbird flights to or from both Mildenhall and Akrotiri for this purpose, leaving the USAF to fly non-stop to the Middle East from upstate New York, a 12,000-mile round trip completed in under twelve hours. As the thirsty SR-71 requires refuelling every one and a half hours when flying at cruising speed, with two tankers deployed to each rendezvous as a fail-safe precaution, this was a logistical undertaking of considerable magnitude. But it was completed flawlessly, with the crew adhering to their code of absolute silence so that not even their families learned of what had happened.

Neither the RAF nor any other air force possessed anything that could match the SR-71 but, just as Yom Kippur had created political difficulties, the question of American assistance, perhaps with a flight from a US base in Panama, raised serious political problems, as did the sharing of satellite data, if indeed there was a suitable 'Keyhole' platform available. Such material was always highly classified, but the coverage was not limited to swathes of the globe in which the United States might be expected to have interest. Thus satellite imagery was comprehensive right across the world, with a variety of 'big birds' overflying every land mass in polar orbit. To add the southern tip of Latin America to the target list would not require the insertion of a new satellite – an undertaking that would take weeks and require the necessary political will in Washington DC – and was relatively easy, even if it would not have the 'real-time' advantage of the SR-71. The problem lay in the sharing of the product, because any low-altitude satellite would be spotted immediately, both by the Soviets and by civilian agencies, and its route across the area of conflict could not be expected to go unnoticed, which would inevitably lead to an accusation of covert collusion from Argentina. Certainly SR-71 imagery of the

Soviet Bloc was shared on a regular basis with the British, but a special flight to Argentina – an entirely practical proposition, even if it might demand up to three refuellings from KC-10Q tankers – would require formal authorisation for the National Reconnaissance Office from the National Security Council. Even if NSC approval could be assured, considerable political problems could be expected, not the least of which was the Monroe Doctrine which required the United States to side with western hemisphere interests in a conflict with Old World colonialists. Enunciated by President James Monroe in 1823, the statement remained the theoretical cornerstone of US foreign policy as it applied in America's sphere of influence, and specifically rejected European interference in the region.

Altogether, the NRO controlled four quite different types of orbiting platforms, the oldest being the WHITE CLOUD ocean reconnaissance system run for the US Navy's euphemistically-titled Space Project, which monitored the movements of surface ships across the globe. WHITE CLOUD had been operational since 1971 and the current series, completed with the launch of a final cluster in March 1980, was scheduled for replacement in December 1980, but the Atlas F booster had veered off its intended trajectory from Vandenberg Air Force Base and been destroyed seven minutes after lift-off. Although the two remaining WHITE CLOUD systems were quite ancient, six and seven years old respectively, they could plot the position of a surface vessel with tremendous accuracy from a distance of 2,000 miles. Each of the six WHITE CLOUD satellites, three in each cluster held in a parallel orbit, independently intercepted radio signals from shipping and made two passes each day, giving a total of four direction-finding fixes per day for each target, making twelve individual positions transmitted to the Navy's ground stations. Assuming that a ship was radiating some electronic signal, either a communications link or radar, WHITE CLOUD could plot its movements across the sea.

Then there was the KH-8, one of the Keyhole series
of satellites designed to improve multi-spectrum imag-
ing. This meant taking an identical picture using seven
separate electro-photographic processes, thereby achieving
astonishing accuracy, even to the chemical composition of
the objects scanned. Carried on an Agena-D spacecraft, the
array of sensors was so heavy that the first KH-8 required
a converted ICBM to launch it from Vandenberg in
California in July 1966. The most recent KH-8, numbered
1982–6, had been inserted by a Titan IIIB on 21 January
to overfly the troubled area of Libya's southern frontier
with Chad and the Sudan, but had been moved into several
new orbits until, on 3 May, it released one of its cargo of
smaller, 130lb 'ferret' satellites on a course which took it
directly over the Falklands at an altitude of just sixty-nine
miles, giving the telescopic imagery a resolution of less than
four inches. Once exposed, the film cannister was dropped
to earth by parachute and intercepted by specially adapted
Hercules planes based in Hawaii.

The KH-11 had been in continuous development since
1972, when the NRO awarded the TRW Corporation
a contract to construct a platform that could produce
imagery of an unprecedented quality of virtually any target
anywhere in the world. Proof of the satellite's extraordinary performance had been disclosed inadvertently quite
recently, in April 1980, when a collection of classified
documents was recovered from five RH-53 Sea Stallion
helicopters found at Desert One, the staging area used
during EAGLE CLAW by the US Delta Force to rescue the
Tehran embassy hostages. The clandestine base, 265 miles
south-east of the capital, had been abandoned in haste
when the extraordinarily complex mission was aborted
following the accidental collision between a helicopter and
a C-130 laden with fuel. As well as the bodies of five dead
Americans, the Ayatollah's Revolutionary Guards discovered a set of plans left behind in the chaos, complete with
maps marked with the location of safe houses, call-signs

and radio frequencies, and illustrated by KH-11 photos which were then published to embarrass the Americans. The detail of emergency landing sites in the centre of Tehran revealed in the pictures was impressively accurate, and dismayed the NRO which for years had kept a tight lid on information regarding the KH-11's capabilities. As a result, the US Air Force colonel in command of Desert One was reprimanded for his failure to ensure the destruction of all the classified material.

Eighteen months later, when it had become politically expedient to release an example of the KH-11's digital imagery, to make public the development of the Soviet Blackjack bomber, carefully obscured versions of the pictures were released to a magazine, *Aviation Week and Space Technology*, which reproduced the illustrations on 14 December 1981, showing the plane parked three weeks earlier at Ramenskoye air base, just outside Moscow. Only the aircraft were identifiable, the surrounding area having been degraded deliberately, but by then the cat was out of the bag.

As Britain and Argentina edged towards war, there were two KH-11s aloft: the third in the series, 5503, launched in February 1980; and the fourth, designated 5504, blasted into space by a Titan IIID booster rocket in September 1981. Both were in similar orbits, 97.05 and 96.99 degrees respectively, allowing them to sweep across South Africa and the Soviet Union. The KH-11's performance was so impressive that the NRO was extremely anxious to keep every aspect of it secret, its product of high resolution imagery being encrypted and transmitted in a data stream, via a communications satellite in parallel orbit, to a special dedicated facility, officially entitled the Defense Communications, Electronics, Evaluation and Testing Facility, at Fort Belvoir, Virginia, twenty miles south of Washington DC.

Thus Bob Heinemann, Chief of the CIA's Science and Technology Division, had a very wide choice of imagery to make available to the British, amounting to three separate satellites, the option of a few SR-71 flights and the US Navy's WHITE CLOUD system. Certainly the mechanics of relaying the information could not have been easier. Quite apart from the three major NSA bases in the UK – at Edzell, Menwith Hill and RAF Chicksands – the Agency provided a Special US Liaison Office in the US Embassy in London, headed since October 1980 by Dr Don C. Jackson, formerly the NSA's Deputy Director for Management Services. In Washington GCHQ operated a similar office and was represented by the SUKLO, George (Bill) M. Gapp.

As it turned out, the cloud cover over Tierra del Fuego proved impenetrable initially, so the very first imagery available for analysis was regarded as ancient history. The alternative of radar imagery was of too poor a resolution to be of any help to the planners, who could only hope that weather conditions in the region would improve sufficiently for the satellites to do their job. As for sharing the data with the British, that was a political issue to be left to the politicians, and although Bill Casey had the authority to add the Argentine sites to the NRO's target list, distribution was another matter altogether. On the political front the Secretary of Defense, Caspar Weinberger, was an enthusiastic Anglophile, but there was less certainty about the National Security Advisor, General Alexander Haig, and the US Representative at the United Nations, Mrs Jeane Kirkpatrick, who also had a seat in the Cabinet. Nevertheless, given President Reagan's very close relationship with Mrs Thatcher, no political objection was made by the United States and GCHQ was granted unrestricted access to whatever it wanted. In reality, a point-blank refusal was unthinkable, for apart from all the other considerations, the American satellite defence communications system relied upon British ground stations, located at RAF Oakhanger at Bordon in Hampshire, and the British island of Diego Garcia in the Indian Ocean.[3]

SIS also had strong allies in the CIA's Chief of Station in London, Alan Wolfe, and his deputy, Mrs Kathleen Hart. Wolfe had graduated from Columbia University in chemical engineering and joined the CIA in 1950. Since then he had served in Amman, Baghdad and Kabul, and although regarded as a rather reserved individual, he was firmly 'on side' when it came to sharing imagery and fully indoctrinated into the problem of finding and eliminating the Exocet threat. A Middle East specialist by background, he was not unfamiliar with Europe, his most recent post having been as Chief of the Western European Division at Langley until the previous summer. He had also served in Iraq at the same time as Alexis Forter, another key player in SIS's *sub rosa* war against the Argentines. With Wolfe acting as a conduit to Langley, the British intelligence community had two intelligence officers in Washington DC feeding information back to London: Neville H., the 'Security Liaison Officer' from MI5, and Anthony W., his SIS counterpart, assisted by Alan H. The Security Service and SIS operate in isolation from each other, but over the Falklands there was some overlap, with Neville H. liaising closely with his regular contacts in the Federal Bureau of Investigation over an exceptionally sensitive technical surveillance operation mounted against the Argentine Mission to the United Nations. Naturally SIS ran their own station in New York, and supervised this project which required clearance from the FBI, a tricky negotiation accomplished by Neville H.

Anthony W.'s role in Washington DC, concealed behind the traditional cover of 'Political Counsellor', was central to the hidden component in the 'special relationship', a historical link between the CIA and SIS which in some areas of co-operation came close to integration, and was only really tested twice. The first occasion was Kim Philby's tenure in the same post, actually occupying the same SIS house off MacArthur Boulevard near the Sibley Hospital reserved for the Washington DC Station Commander, which had severely strained the CIA's generosity and tolerance in 1951 following the defections of Guy Burgess and Donald Maclean. Partly to reassure the CIA, Philby had been withdrawn, thus preserving a relationship which underwent severe strain during the Suez crisis in 1956 when Maclachlan Silverwood-Cope worked hard to build bridges and restore trust in the aftermath of an unfortunate episode that both agencies found it expedient to overlook. Thereafter normal relations were resumed, apart from the discreetest of murmurs about a homosexual incident in which Maurice Oldfield was almost compromised at the end of his tour in 1964.

Following Philby's departure, the SIS station in Washington DC was considered a vital post, entrusted to senior officers who were destined for SIS directorships, of whom Maurice Oldfield (1960–64) and Christopher Curwen (1968–71) subsequently became Chief. In recent years the appointment most notably had gone to the immensely popular Christopher Phillpotts (1964–66), the oriental art specialist John da Silva (1966–68), and the raconteur John Colvin (1977–79) who had been of such assistance to the CIA during his two years in Hanoi at the height of the Vietnam War, and for whom Washington was to be his final SIS job.

The two key SIS officers now entrusted with nurturing the special relationship were Anthony W. and Alastair S., his newly appointed regional controller. Educated partly in South Africa and at Harvard, Alastair S. joined SIS from the Rifle Brigade and served in Geneva, Cairo and Kinshasa before moving to the New York station in April 1974. Five years later, in September 1979, Dickie Franks brought him back to London to take over as Regional Controller for the Western Hemisphere, supervising operations in North and Central America. His replacement in New York was Tom R., a Far East specialist who had previously served in Tokyo (where he acquired a Japanese wife), followed by Hong Kong and Beijing. Thus the two senior SIS officers in North America, liaising with the Americans, were Tom

R. and Anthony W., with Alastair S. brought in after the conflict had started to act as the Controller Western Hemisphere, replacing Douglas T.

Widowed two years earlier, Anthony W. had only recently arrived in Washington, having replaced his predecessor at the end of his three-year tour in January, when he returned to London. After leaving Cambridge in 1950 Anthony W. served in the army in Malaya during the Emergency and, like his predecessor who had joined the Colonial Service as an administrator in Kenya, went to neighbouring Tanganyika. In 1963, after ten years in Africa, he had switched to SIS and was based in London until posted to Lusaka in 1967 for three years. Apart from two years in New York from 1972, supposedly attached to the UK Mission to the United Nations, Anthony W. had concentrated on Africa and had no first-hand experience of Latin America. In contrast his ambassador, Sir Nicholas Henderson, was an unusual regular diplomat, with first-hand experience of SIS; he had been attached to SIS in 1962 as a liaison officer, and served in Santiago for three years in the late 1950s. Somewhat isolated from the crisis as it developed in the South Atlantic, both Henderson and Anthony W. were to become key figures in the effort to extract maximum help from the Americans. Indeed, Henderson startled himself by his success, as he later admitted, when Caspar Weinberger drew him to one side on the lawn of the British embassy and volunteered the use of an American aircraft carrier to the Royal Navy, should the need arise. Henderson remains convinced the offer was genuine, but he received no response when he relayed the news to the Foreign Office.[4]

Also active in liaising with the Americans was the Naval Attaché, Rear Admiral John Hervey, who operated independently from the embassy at the US Navy building at Chrystal City, close to the Pentagon. A close personal friend of the Navy Secretary, John H. Lehman, Hervey was near the end of his final two-year posting in Washington when the crisis occurred. Among his contributions to the conflict was the completion of a detailed questionnaire concerning the Argentine Navy, a task he fulfilled with the help of the recently returned US Naval Attaché to Buenos Aires, who happened to work in the same building and had volunteered to undergo a lengthy debrief.

When the SAS's Intelligence Cell considered the issue of moving the troops to the target, it was clear that this required a staging area as close as possible, but one that was entirely secure so that word of the arrival of a bunch of heavily armed desperadoes would not leak out. These criteria limited the choice to Ascension, which was still 4,000 miles away, Bermuda in the middle of the Atlantic, and Belize. Of the three, Ascension looked the most attractive, as the American base had been transformed over the past three weeks into a veritable military encampment. It offered complete security, as no civilians were allowed to land, but there was one political drawback. Ascension's Wideawake airfield was American-built and American-leased, and although the US administration had given Mrs Thatcher considerable support behind the scenes – such as Caspar Weinberger's personal authorisation for the sharing of aviation fuel on Ascension and the immediate release from NATO stocks to the Sea Harriers of a hundred of the much-needed ALM-9L missiles, the very deadliest generation of the infra-red homing Sidewinder air-to-air missiles which allowed the aircraft to engage an enemy head-on – there was a condition attached: no word of the co-operation should leak to Latin America. None did, and thousands of tons of fuel were delivered to Ascension on US tankers without any public comment.

The Americans had been willing to overlook the Vulcan mission as there was no chance of the crew falling into enemy hands, but a full-scale SAS raid was an entirely different proposition. Would the Americans agree to the

SAS working from the very limited accommodation on Ascension? To date they had agreed to transit arrangements, allowing troops to be flown in on transports and then embarking on the ships of the Task Force assembled offshore, but the political climate was volatile, particularly in Washington DC. The alternatives had distance against them, but there were some advantages too. There were already SAS troops in Belize (formerly British Honduras), based at Cooma Cairn on Mountain Pine Ridge and exercising along the disputed Guatemalan frontier, and although the airport at Belize City was civilian-run, it would be possible to accommodate a couple of Hercules and the necessary teams without attracting any attention. Similarly, the American Naval Air Station at Kindley Field, Bermuda was used as a regular staging field for aircraft destined for Belize and had plenty of room to secrete the troops until the mission was on. Discreet enquiries in Belize and Bermuda indicated that both locations could cope, although the heat in Central America in May might cause the SAS men, dressed in their Norwegian kit in preparation for the Argentine winter, some discomfort.

Still reeling from the shock of the Argentine invasion, GCHQ's Director Sir Brian Tovey, who had held the post since 1978, gathered together his own South Atlantic Group at his headquarters at Benhall, on the north-west outskirts of Cheltenham. There, interpreters more used to monitoring Spanish clandestine traffic for the illicit communications of ETA's Basque separatists – always suspected of aiding the Provisional IRA – Madrid's diplomatic circuits for hints of renewed militancy over Gibraltar, and the traffic exchanged between Guatemala City and the embassy in Chelsea, were gathered together to concentrate on Argentina's signals. Intelligence Corps reservists with a knowledge of Spanish, most of whom had served in Belize, were recalled for the duration of hostilities.

Chapter 4

PARIS

Alexis Kougoulsky Forter OBE was at the end of a remarkable career. Of White Russian extraction, he served in the Royal Air Force during the last year of the Second World War, joining SIS in 1950 to be posted to Iran twelve months later. The son of an RAF squadron-leader, and educated at St Paul's and Magdalen College, Oxford, where he won a first-class honours degree in Oriental Studies, his career had concentrated in the Middle East, where he had served in Basra, Port Said, Baghdad and Tehran. In 1966 he was transferred to Saigon, and in 1971 he undertook a two-year tour of duty in Nairobi. He had established a reputation within SIS as a fearless case officer, and was particularly admired because of the time he had spent living with Kurdish hill tribes in northern Iraq. A brilliant linguist and entertaining raconteur, who loved shooting and beagling, his long run of overseas postings was coming to a conclusion, and his appointment to Paris in April 1977 had been intended as a reward after so many arduous years in some of the world's most dangerous trouble-spots. Unexpectedly, the Falklands crisis was to give Forter an opportunity to make a final, crucial contribution before his well-earned retirement.

As the crisis developed Forter made the journey across Paris from his office in the embassy to the Boulevard Mortier to sound out Pierre Marion, the former Deputy Director-General of Air France who was entrusted with President

Mitterrand's pledge to reform SDECE (the Service de Documentation Extérieure de Contre-Espionnage). Marion had succeeded the Comte Alexandre de Marenches the previous year and, unlike his predecessor who was in poor health, he was not a SDECE bureaucrat, but rather a professional with plenty of operational experience at the sharp end in his role as one of SDECE's 'honourable correspondents'. This was no disadvantage, for the organisation – which anyway had always had an unsavoury reputation as the administration's most deniable instrument of power – had been embroiled in one scandal too many. An aeronautical engineer from Marseilles, Marion's association with SDECE dated back to 1963 when he was appointed Air France's representative in East Asia and the Pacific, his office in Tokyo becoming the clandestine organisation's unofficial regional headquarters.

To a French public that expected its secret services to conduct covert and illegal operations, SDECE represented excess on a scale that had not been seen since the bad old days of the dirty war in Algeria, when the *barbouzes* were deployed to assassinate De Gaulle's political opponents. An outsider with inside knowledge, Marion came to the famed headquarters – known as *La Piscine* because of its proximity to the municipal baths – with a mandate given by the Socialist victory in the 1981 general election to restore SDECE's status. He did so by conducting a purge of senior personnel, in which fifty officers were asked to resign for 'failing in their duty', and changing the agency's name, on 2 April, to the Direction Générale de Sécurité Extérieur (DGSE). As well as sacking De Marenches's closest directors and their deputies, Marion also supervised a complete restructuring of the entire organisation. Under Alexandre de Marenches, who had spent a lifetime in the service and had directed it for eleven years while Georges Pompidou and Valéry Giscard d'Estaing occupied the Elysée Palace, SDECE had indulged in many high-risk ventures and seen its reputation plummet.[1] A graduate of the elite Ecole

Polytechnique, Marion was untainted by SDECE's dubious history, which had been marked in 1969 by the embarrassment of the Marcovic affair, which threatened to expose an embarrassing link between the mysterious murder of Alain Delon's Yugoslav bodyguard, Stefan Marcovic (one of SDECE's honourable correspondents), and a blackmail racket involving compromising photographs of Madame Claude Pompidou.[2] Soon afterwards SDECE was rocked by the indictment of two senior officers, Colonel Paul Fournier and Roger Delouette in the United States in April 1971 on a charge of importing 96lb of heroin. De Marenches had ridden out the storms and, as he departed SDECE for the last time – still fighting a rearguard action to prevent SDECE from being implicated in the murder of police inspector Jacques Massie and his family in Marseilles the previous July – he entrusted his successor with details of the organisation's greatest secret, the recruitment of Vladimir I. Vetrov.

Codenamed ADIEU, Vetrov was the French mole inside the scientific and technical branch of the KGB's elite First Chief Directorate. Now back in Moscow, Vetrov had haemorrhaged Soviet secrets to SDECE on an unprecedented scale, his continuing performance proving that *La Piscine* no longer leaked instantly to Moscow. Finally, the flow of classified material was reversed, and ADIEU allowed SDECE to regain much of the trust it had forfeited during the long period when other Allied agencies kept their distance from the French. Even the newly elected President François Mitterrand had exploited the source, by disclosing some tantalising details of the case to President Reagan at their summit at Ottawa in 1981 in an effort to impress him with his anti-Communist and anti-Soviet credentials. Originally recruited the previous year by Marcel Chalet's domestic security agency, the Direction de la Surveillance du Territoire (DST), Vetrov had served in the KGB's Paris *rezidentura* in the 1960s, and returned as the senior Line X specialist, concentrating on the acquisition of embargoed strategic *matériel* in the high-technology field. Over the past fourteen months ADIEU had supplied the DST, and latterly SDECE, with thousands of top-secret Directorate T documents exposing a previously unsuspected network of agents, businessmen and clandestine operators who had been assembled by the KGB to modernise the ancient Soviet electronics industry. Single-handed, Vetrov gave SDECE that most essential of commodities in the intelligence community, a reliable source, and as such he represented an invaluable bargaining chip with which to re-establish relationships that had long since been compromised.[3] As for Anglo-French relations, President Mitterrand had promised, perhaps mindful of France's overseas possessions, that there should be full co-operation, and this had extended to encouraging Francophone Senegal to allow the RAF to land at Dakar en route to Ascension, a vital link in the air route from England. On the President's instructions, Marion had offered Forter total support, and SIS had taken up the offer with enthusiasm.

Fluent in French, Forter made his mark early with Marion and entrusted him with some snippets from SIS – actually donated by Oleg Gordievsky – to demonstrate that information from ADIEU would be reciprocated. However, on this occasion the Soviets were not the issue, nor were Marion's other current preoccupations, with the guerrilla war in Chad and with terrorism in Paris sponsored by the Syrians. Instead, the purpose of Forter's visit was to ensure the DGSE's co-operation in dealing with the Falklands crisis. Already France had supported Britain's case in the UN Security Council and had voted in favour of Resolution 502, the binding directive requiring Argentina to remove its troops from the islands forthwith. France, which had established the first colony on the Falklands in 1764 before ceding it to the Spanish three years later, had also played a key role in persuading the EEC to impose a six-week ban on trade with Argentina. The sanctions, effective on 7 April, were to be considered again on

17 May, but in the meantime France had undertaken to sever all trade links with Buenos Aires. This was a significant step, for Aerospatiale was halfway through the very lucrative Exocet and Super Etendard contract signed in 1979 and, most unusually, paid for in full, up front.

As Forter confirmed, the state-owned Aerospatiale company had supplied sea-launched MM-40 missiles to the Argentine Navy and was due to equip a total of fourteen Super Etendards, sold by Dassault-Breuget for $160m, with fifteen of the AM-39 variant, deliveries to be completed by September 1982. Argentina had been obliged to buy the French equipment even though the original choice was to renew the popular Skyhawks bought in 1973, because of the Kennedy Amendment which prohibited American defence sales to countries with poor human rights records. Accordingly Argentina's sales enquiry was rejected, leaving the market to the French as the only other manufacturer of conventionally-launched carrier-borne aircraft since, ironically, the British Aerospace Sea Harrier had been turned down. Already a team of fifty men, including ten A-4 pilots from the 2nd Fighter and Attack Squadron at Bahia Blanca, each with a minimum of 1,000 hours on jets, had attended a specialist language course lasting two months at Rochefort, followed by conversion training at Landivisian, near Brest in Brittany, with experience of deck landing for the squadron's Landing Signals Officers on the *Clemenceau* operating off Toulon.

The first batch of five AM-39s and planes was delivered to Argentina on 17 November, and a technical team from Aerospatiale was scheduled to arrive on 12 April to begin work on the first five Super Etendards. That visit was cancelled, in compliance with the EEC embargo, but the very first group of Dassault technicians – eight specialists led by Hervé Colin – who had accompanied the first consignment, were still at the Base Espora headquarters preparing the aircraft for operations. Significantly, Marion invited Forter to visit Bordeaux and see for himself that the second batch of aircraft remained in France. He also asserted that although the Super Etendards were intended to fly off the *Veinticinco de Mayo*, which had put to sea from Puerto Belgrano on 28 March, the carrier's steam catapult had malfunctioned, so the planes already delivered would have to be land-based for the foreseeable future.

Forter's preliminary report to his Chief, Colin Figures, indicated that apart from the surface-to-surface MM-40s, the Argentine Navy had possession of five AM-39s, together with ten Super Etendards and ten pilots who had undertaken the Aerospatiale conversion course. This information was confirmed independently by an especially useful source, Lloyd's of London, which had provided the insurance cover for the shipments. According to the French, the detailed work required to marry the missiles to the wing pylons had not commenced, and literally hundreds of tests would be required before the avionics of both systems were fully integrated. At first glance, considering the need to test-fire the missile, the risk of an air-launched attack on the Task Force seemed as unlikely as the JIC had initially suggested, but Pierre Marion disclosed to Forter some disturbing news concerning the Argentine Military Commission in the Avenue Marceau. According to his information, a naval officer named Captain Carlos Corti, who enjoyed diplomatic status, had transformed his office into the headquarters of Subconfraer for the purpose of procuring Exocets.

It was convenience, not coincidence, that Corti's company was accommodated in the same building as the Office Français d'Exportation de Matériel Aéronautique (OFEMA), the French government bureau which supervised defence sales abroad. Corti, of course, was a highly respected overseas customer, having made a huge investment in the Exocet, and he ran a small organisation that consisted of himself, his deputy Julio I. Lavezzo, and two clerks. Altogether the Argentine Navy's order for the MM-40 amounted to forty-eight missiles, equipping ten ships with forty launchers, with eight reloads as spares. To date, sixteen MM-40s had been supplied and four ships had been fitted with two launchers each. The remainder of the order, a further ten ships, were to be installed on four MIKO-360 destroyers and six MIKO-140 frigates still under construction in Germany. In addition, Corti was responsible for supervising the Naval Aviation contract for fourteen Super Etendards and ten AM-39s, of which five of each had been delivered already.

Despite his status as a good Aerospatiale client, Corti himself was the subject of intensive surveillance under-taken by no fewer than four different organisations that had opened files on his activities. Firstly there was the Renseignements Généraux (RG), answering to the Ministry of the Interior, which had arranged an official telephone intercept on Corti's office and home telephones. Tran-scripts were prepared on a daily basis at the intercept centre at the Caserne de Latour-Maubourg, on the Avenue de Tourville, run by the Groupement Interministériel de Contrôle (GIC), and delivered by despatch riders to the RG and the internal security service, the Direction de la Surveillance du Territoire.

The DST had a special interest in Corti because of an unhappy episode in Franco-Argentine relations three years earlier, when a pair of French nuns vanished in Buenos Aires, two more names to join the *despareceidos*, 'the disappeared', among the many hundreds of victims of Argentina's *guerra sucia*, 'the dirty war'. The French authorities made no progress in their search for Sisters Alice Domon and Renée-Leonie Duquet, a matter of considerable controversy in France, but evidence emerged of a clandestine operation conducted in Paris by Argentine Naval Intelligence, which had established an office with the cover title of Pilot Centre Paris (PCP) under the direction of a certain Captain Alfredo Astiz. The PCP, originally led by Jorge Acosta, codenamed TIGER, was exclusively staffed by naval intelligence personnel, among whom was Jorge Perren, codenamed PUMA. In fact the PCP's purpose was to infiltrate and report on the activities of Argentine expatriates who had fled to Europe after the military coup of 1976, many of them suspected members of the notorious 'Montoneros'. Astiz, who had already attracted some controversy during the dirty war, when he worked at the Naval Mechanical School in Buenos Aires – used as an interrogation centre by Naval Intelligence for the questioning and torturing of prisoners – had been implicated in several abductions and been sent to Paris to keep the exiles under surveillance. This was not an easy task, for the Montoneros were well funded, backed with an estimated $100m. In one kidnapping incident alone, the right-wing Montoneros extorted $60m from one of Argentina's leading industrialists for the safe release of the Born brothers, so the organisation was considered a formidable opponent throughout the eleven years of terrorism. Although Astiz left France before attracting the attention of the DST, he was compromised by Elena Holmberg, the 47-year-old cultural attaché at the Argentine embassy in Paris who had flown home to Buenos Aires in December 1978 with a dossier regarding the PCP's illicit operations. Ominously, Holmberg was abducted in broad daylight by three gunmen whose car pulled across hers as she drove to her home a few blocks from the Foreign Ministry. Her body was found on 11 January 1979 in the Rio Lujan, fifty miles north of Buenos Aires. According to the police investigation she had been drowned, and her murder, so soon after her return, served to heighten the DST interest in Argentine missions in France.[4]

Quite by chance, Subconfraer and OFEMA shared the same switchboard, thus allowing the DGSE to share in monitoring Corti's activities without the knowledge of the RG, DST or the GIC. The overt reason for the DGSE's interest was twofold: Carlos Corti, a former press spokesman for the military Junta, who was a legitimate target because of his very close relationship with the regime in Buenos Aires, and the Falklands conflict. But these were only recent pretexts. The principal reason was that Aerospatiale was headed by General Jacques Mitterrand, the new President's brother. The President had given his personal assurance to Mrs Thatcher that the Argentines would receive no military assistance from his government, and the DGSE's task was to ensure that there was no possibility of the Elysée Palace experiencing any embarrassment. Marion explained none of this, but Forter was dismayed to learn that Corti was on the brink of buying four AM-39s at the highly inflated price of $6.3m from an American arms dealer, Marcus S. Stone. The normal cost of an Exocet was around $450,000, so apparently Corti was willing to pay more than double the market value, an indication of how keen the Argentines were to break the EEC's embargo. Although Marion could not give Forter transcripts of the intercepted telephone conversations, it was clear that the sale was to be brokered outside the EEC, with the cash going to a bank in the Netherlands where an account had been opened by Stone's partner, an arms dealer named Souty. However, as the level of surveillance on Stone and Corti was stepped up, the deal started to fall apart. Stone, operating from an office in Los Angeles, had persuaded Corti to transfer the full purchase price to Amsterdam, but recovery of the funds proved difficult when no Exocets materialised. Apparently undeterred by this experience, or by his inability to find either Stone or Souty, Corti responded to pressure from Buenos Aires and simply redoubled his efforts to find some black market missiles.

Marion's explanation for the level of desperation manifested by Corti fascinated SIS in London and appeared to offer an opportunity to intervene. The original Argentine order for the Exocets had been delayed by Aerospatiale so as to accommodate a rather larger request from Baghdad. Since the outbreak of the Iran–Iraq War in September 1980, Saddam Hussein had become France's best customer, spending more than $700m on Exocet, Roland and sixty Mirages delivered in January 1981, not to mention the Osiraq atomic reactor at Tuwaitha which the Israelis subsequently destroyed in a daring air-raid in June 1981. Ostensibly neutral in the conflict, and subject to the UN's arms embargo, both President Giscard d'Estaing and his Socialist successor leaned in Iraq's favour, to the extent of cancelling an Iranian contract for three missile boats and airlifting weapons and spares direct to Baghdad. In comparison, Argentina's status was of little consequence, so Corti was not given any choice in the matter, but offered in compensation a free test missile and free delivery of the missiles by air in January, instead of by sea in November. Never having anticipated AZUL, Corti obligingly agreed to extend the delivery period, thereby allowing the Iraqis to acquire a hundred missiles, but creating a crisis when the Navy fliers at Ospera demanded their AM-39s. Now caught by the EEC sanctions, Corti approached the Libyans in the hope that Iraq might agree to release the missiles originally intended for Argentina. After a nail-biting delay, the Libyans relayed Baghdad's refusal but offered a consignment of weapons instead, which was accepted and delivered by a chartered Boeing 707 soon thereafter. Nevertheless, Corti was left with the problem of finding a source to complete the order the French had been paid for.

Forter's telegram to Century House included a summary of the DGSE's willingness to co-operate with the British, together with two vital items of information: Carlos Corti's direct private telephone line in Paris, which would be passed on to GCHQ so that all his long-distance calls via satellite could be intercepted, and Marion's disclosure that according to the Aerospatiale team still in Argentina, the Super Etendards had been transferred from Base Espora to Rio Grande.

While the technicians at Cheltenham made the necessary preparations to monitor Corti's transatlantic calls, the news that the Second Fighter and Attack Squadron had been dispersed to Tierra del Fuego transformed the situation, for whereas most of the Argentine mainland bases were impossible propositions in terms of frontal assault, two sites were within easy distance of the Chilean frontier: Rio Gallegos, at the mouth of the river Gallegos, was a bare fifty kilometres from Chile and the terminus of the El Turbio railway; if the SAS could make it across the border, they could find refuge in the Chilean town of Puerto Natales. Likewise Rio Grande, on the island of Tierra del Fuego, was only a short distance from neutral Chile. Suddenly the idea of an SAS raid looked less like a suicide mission. The Argentines, however, had taken precautions which had gone undetected.

The possibility of an attack on the mainland had always been considered seriously by the Argentine Navy, and immediately after the sinking of the *General Belgrano* four Marine Infantry Battalions were sent to Rio Grande to defend the strip between the coast and the runway. In addition, the army established an anti-aircraft unit beside the base and maintained regular helicopter patrols along the shoreline. One of these patrols, a Huey helicopter of the 601st Combat Aviation Battalion, crashed with the loss of all eleven crew early in the morning of 30 April, close to Comodoro Rivadavia. While the Argentines had prepared contingency plans to cope with a landing of saboteurs from a submarine, they had not appreciated the absence of any Royal Navy diesel submarines in the South Atlantic, nor had they contemplated the kind of airborne raid the SAS were planning.

Chapter 5

BUENOS AIRES

Vinx Blocker was a worried man. His CIA station was one of the largest in the Latin America Division, employing nearly a quarter of the Americans in the embassy, yet he had not foreseen the invasion. Indeed, he had been out at Langley when the CRITIC cable came in from David Edger, his deputy in Buenos Aires, and he had jumped on the first plane south. Born in Martinique, the son of a State Department diplomat, Blocker was built like a football player and was thoroughly professional in his chosen career. Fluent in Spanish, he knew his way around Latin America, having served under the legendary David Atlee Phillips in Santo Domingo in 1966, and his station on the embassy's third floor ran numerous sources in the Argentine military, yet none had tipped off the CIA to Operación AZUL. Indeed, the CIA had not received any forewarning from the satellite directly overhead at an altitude of 400 kilometres, designated 1980–85A, which covered the area just before the invasion. At exactly 1700 local time 1980–10A had overflown the scene, but nobody was watching. Perhaps most embarrassing for the CIA, the US Chief of Naval Operations, Admiral Tom Haywood, had been scheduled to start a routine goodwill tour of Argentine naval facilities on the morning of the invasion, and was given the news of the landings by Admiral Anaya himself. Furious, Haywood flew to Brazil on the first available flight.

Blocker had been posted to Buenos Aires in 1980, and established a good rapport with his two principal contacts, General 'Freddie' Sotera, head of the J-2 military intelligence service based at the army headquarters, and General 'Belusa' Martinez, chief of the Secretariat Inteligencia del Estado, the feared security service (best known by its acronym SIDE) which was conveniently located in a large office at 10 Plaza de Mayo, virtually adjacent to the Casa Rosada. The tallest building on Buenos Aires's central square, it dominated the President's palace and was distinguished externally only by the numerous radio antennae on the roof. Staffed mainly by military personnel seconded from the services, SIDE had a reputation for omnipotence, based largely on the quality of its political gossip acquired through a sophisticated telephone intercept facility provided by the CIA. SIDE's wiretapping programme was easily the most comprehensive in Latin America, although it tended to malfunction in heavy rain because the city's rats had developed a taste for the cable insulation. Apart from this minor disadvantage in the winter, the coverage was very efficient, so much so that the technician in charge recruited his own renegade gang of kidnappers from inside the police, thus enabling him to identify wealthy victims and manipulate the official response to each abduction.

Blocker's main task in Argentina, apart from liaising with the local apparatus, was to mount operations against the Soviets – who maintained a large KGB *rezidentura* under Arnold I. Mossolov at the embassy on Rodriguez Pena Street – the Cubans, the Chinese, the East Germans, the Nicaraguans and the Czechs, who ran a significant electronic intelligence-gathering facility in their embassy on Villanueva Street. As for being declared to other services, Blocker only maintained relations with Mark Heathcote and kept his distance from the French. Having previously served as Chief of Station in Guatemala, where he assisted SIS during the Belize crisis before the British established a station commander in Guatemala City, he was held in high regard at Century House.

Apart from attempting to penetrate the CIA's traditional foes in Buenos Aires, the Latin America Division at Langley was keen to have Blocker cultivate Sotera for help in Central America, the main regional hotspot where a huge covert action programme was attracting unfavourable attention. Argentina had long enjoyed a special relationship with the Nicaraguans, Guatemalans, Panamanians and Hondurans, offering scholarships to selected cadets at the military academy in Buenos Aires, and had exceptionally good contacts in these countries. Here American and Argentine interests coincided, with the CIA willing to underwrite the cost of camps in Honduras to train anti-Sandinista Contra rebels. Indeed, when General Galtieri had been entertained in Washington DC the previous November, he had expressed his support for the American effort to combat Castro's subversion in the region, perhaps partly influenced by the prospect of a promised consignment of twenty-four UH-60 Blackhawk helicopters. On that occasion he gave not the slightest hint of a scheme to seize the Malvinas, and the Americans took the view that the British ambassador, Anthony Williams, had placed too great an emphasis on the growing tension in South Georgia. The prevailing attitude was that 'not even the Argentines would be stupid enough to move against the Falklands. Some incursion into Chile was far more likely.'

The American preoccupation with Soviet and Cuban activities in Central America had a very direct parallel with the missile crisis of October 1962, when Nikita Khrushchev had poured military hardware into the Caribbean and taken the preliminary steps to the deployment of ICBMs ninety miles from Miami. Certainly Bill Casey's Deputy DCI, Admiral Bobby R. Inman, saw history repeating itself and made Nicaragua a priority target. The crisis started back in 1979, when Anastasio Somoza's regime in Managua was deposed by Marxist Sandinista rebels, who wasted no time in taking delivery of huge consignments of Soviet military hardware. Inman, a former Director of the Office of Naval Intelligence and Director of the NSA, had monitored this escalation until 9 March 1982, when he participated in a public presentation of photographic reconnaissance material which was very reminiscent of the U-2 briefings given shortly before the US had imposed a quarantine on Cuba twenty years earlier. A technocrat with a long background in intelligence, Inman had introduced a photo-interpreter, John T. Hughes, who gave a compelling lecture illustrated with imagery of T-54 and T-55 tanks, MiG-17 fighters, and significant construction work to extend the facilities and runways at four major military airfields. According to Inman, fifty Nicaraguan pilots were presently undergoing advance flight training in Bulgaria and when they returned home, perhaps with MiG-21s, the Warsaw Pact would be posing a threat as far away as Costa Rica and the Panama Canal. From everything Inman said, it was clear that the focus of his Latin America Division was concentrated on Central America, not South America.

Blocker's CIA station in the new bunker-like embassy on Cervino Street was but one component in the large effort to collect intelligence and report from Buenos Aires, with a special effort to anticipate any decline in relations with Chile. Responsibility for dealing with President Galtieri fell on the ambassador, Harry Schlaudemann, one of Washington's most experienced career diplomats, who had previously served as the Assistant Secretary for Latin America and had known Blocker since they were both in the Dominican Republic in the mid-1960s. Few knew the continent, its politics and personalities as well, and he was assisted by a strong team including two colonels, one the head of the US Military Assistance Group, the other – Bob Olsen – a military attaché who had spent nine years in the country and had married an Argentine. Both officers had served in Argentina before and had developed a wide range of contacts in the military, but neither had learned anything about AZUL. In fact, the only clue was picked up by a young CIA officer directed to improve the station's reporting of the military, who had overheard a drunk in the officers' mess boasting about some practice amphibious landings. At the time his tale was dismissed as another example of the CIA neophyte's well-recognised tendency to exaggeration, but in retrospect the CoS conceded that perhaps there might have been something in what the ambitious young man had said. Certainly Schlaudemann was sufficiently close to the Junta to pick up the nuances, but there were none to be detected, even though the ambassador had long acknowledged with distaste that the military was more interested in finding a way of restoring its tarnished reputation and clinging to power than anything more noble or practical, such as taking the stern measures necessary to rescue the economy. 'They were anxious to avoid Nuremberg-style trials so they made sure everyone was implicated somehow in "the dirty war".'

Intelligence picked up by two other agencies in the embassy was also routed through the CIA: the Drug Enforcement Agency had maintained a local representative since 1976, when evidence emerged of cocaine shipments passing through Buenos Aires to the United States, and successive FBI officers, under the Bureau's standard legal attaché cover, had been permanent fixtures since the Second World War, long before the CIA was established, when J. Edgar Hoover exercised proprietorial rights over all foreign intelligence collection in Latin America. The DEA's office, located directly beneath the CIA station in the embassy, covered Uruguay as well, but often ran operations into other countries, including Bolivia, where the DEA's country attachés were not made welcome by a host country which had long succumbed to a cocaine economy.

In addition to the CIA station and the attachés, the embassy also accommodated a further intelligence resource, a highly secret intercept facility managed by the National Security

Agency. The existence of the NSA's listening post, a clear breach of diplomatic protocol, was a closely guarded secret, although the Argentine authorities doubted that the impressive antenna array on the roof was entirely dedicated to exchanging messages with Washington DC. Their assumption was quite correct, for whereas the Chileans took a more relaxed view of the NSA's collection activities and were grateful for the occasional reciprocity in the form of tips about Soviet submarines in the southern Pacific, the Argentines would have opposed any attempt to monitor their domestic communications. From the very outset of the crisis, the NSA's covert site produced the most impressive data, and was the source of the CIA station's cable to Langley revealing that the invasion had got under way.

Once the landings had started, an inexorable machine was set in motion. Blocker rushed back to his post to discover that two of his best sources were out of touch . . . on the Falklands. His deputy David Edger had been working overtime to set up a communications link between SIS's local sources and his own organisation, a move authorised by the DDO at Langley in anticipation of Heathcote's imminent transfer to Montevideo with the rest of the British embassy staff. As for Schlaudemann, his every suggestion of a compromise fell victim to the Junta's system of veto. Any single member could scotch a proposal to resolve the crisis by compromise, but Admiral Jorge Anaya, the principal hawk, proved quite intransigent, even though his navy was not to be visible at sea after the sinking of the *General Belgrano* and was to play a minimal role in the rest of the drama.

From the intelligence standpoint, as seen from General Sotera's impressive headquarters, the crisis had gone into a sharp, almost irrecoverable decline immediately after the invasion, which had been planned on three entirely flawed assumptions: that the British would not fight for the Malvinas, that the Americans would remain neutral, and that the Soviets would veto any critical resolution in the Security Council. This had been the opinion of the politicians, without reference to the few intelligence officers who had a detailed knowledge of Britain, or even of those who had studied the British Army. Indeed, the first intelligence appreciation of the British response to the invasion was not commissioned by J-2 until 5 April, when Major Carlos Doglieli was brought back from staff college to predict what was likely to happen on the military front. A knowledgeable student of British military history, Doglieli took just five days to research his detailed report, entitled *Informe de Inteligencia Especial Nro 7/82*, which identified the units he thought would be sent to the South Atlantic, and he delivered his final and very prescient draft on 19 April. It was signed by General Sotero on 21 April, distributed to the General Staff the following day, and flown to the Islands by Doglieli personally on 23 April. This document represented the first professional appreciation of the military response, a task that should have been undertaken two months earlier, in February, when AZUL first began to take shape. Amounting to ninety-three pages, it included descriptions of the SAS and SBS, and made very depressing reading for those authorised to peruse it. Certainly Doglieli himself, with his passion for British military music and his encyclopaedic grasp of British military performance, tactics and doctrine, never had any doubts about the outcome, nor shirked what he saw as his unpopular responsibility to tell the disagreeable truth to anyone who would listen.

Of course, neither SIDE nor J-2 had ever given any serious thought to a war with Britain, still less to one with a large part of NATO. SIDE maintained an entirely satisfactory relationship with SIS, and several SIDE officers had undergone training in advanced surveillance techniques in London. As for J-2, the principal enemy had always been Chile, a preoccupation that demanded the deployment of the army's elite troops of two mountain brigades and the airborne brigade along the Andes. Likewise, SIDE had long considered the Chilean DINA to be the main adversary, and maintained a close watch on the Chilean service attachés operating from the embassy, which was also the target of the intercept stations run by the army's electronic warfare wing at City Ball, thirty-five miles north of the capital. However, both agencies were powerless to prevent surveillance of airfields in the south, particularly since half the population in the region was of Chilean origin. Whilst the navy's electronic intelligence organisation at Rio Gallegos could meet the demand for tactical interception, it was no match for the big ears employed by GCHQ and the NSA. Indeed, it was a common assumption that all three encrypted duplex circuits to the islands (transmitted over equipment purchased from the Israelis) to Buenos Aires, Comodoro Rivadavia and Bahia Blanca, were the subject of hostile interception and decryption. The only uncertainty was whether the NSA was achieving 'real-time' access, and how quickly the raw data reached the British Task Force.

Without doubt the Chileans remained an irritant, with all the news from the Cristobal site being entirely negative: the Chilean Navy had vanished from Valparaiso and, more ominously, had imposed radio silence, while the Chilean Army's radio traffic had escalated to a point which suggested an Israeli-style unannounced general mobilisation and a concentration of forces uncomfortably close to Mendoza province. It was also considered significant that electronic jamming from Chile had been reported from the south. Even if Chile failed to intervene, the threat had to be taken seriously, which meant retaining Argentina's best troops close to the border as a deterrent.

Just as the sinking of the *Sheffield* had transformed the British attitude to the conflict, J-2 recognised that Britain's astonishing lack of any Airborne Early Warning made the Task Force terribly vulnerable to the Exocets. The Nimrod had been designed as a maritime surveillance platform and although 206 Squadron was known to be flying missions down to the Exclusion Zone, in planes hastily converted for airborne refuelling, it was really nothing more than a toothless tiger, because its unarmed aircraft and ancient Searchwater radar were never intended for use in an AEW role. As for the old Shackletons, they had no airborne refuelling capability either, leaving the British Task Force entirely reliant upon inadequate surface radars. This was a weakness to be exploited, but Captain Jorge Colombo's four Super Etendards were in danger of being disadvantaged not just by a lack of missiles, but by a shortage of a vital item which was readily available on the open market, the long-range fuel drop tank. As soon as Colombo submitted his request for the additional accessories, Naval Intelligence undertook the task of finding a source, and approached a retired naval officer resident in Miami who had assisted with procurement in the past. The big 375-gallon tanks were of critical importance, particularly for the Mirages which, even with two tanks fitted, could only stay over the Islands for twelve minutes at high altitude, a figure that could be halved for the lower heights at which the Harriers could be found. Without the tanks, the British would be handed air superiority. This time, of course, the usual doors were closed to Argentina but, in what was later to be interpreted as a rehearsal for the main performance, a mysterious intermediary emerged who revealed the existence of an available stock in the People's Republic of China. Money was passed to Florida and allegedly was relayed to Beijing, but no drop tanks ever emerged and by the time it was realised a rather crude deception had been executed, Naval Intelligence had written off the funds.

As yet, Argentina had found few friends to rescue the country from the three dreadful miscalculations which haunted J-2's analysts, and most were less than helpful. The Brazilians had suppressed their innate hostility to their southern neighbours and offered to supply maritime reconnaissance aircraft, while the Libyans delivered an entire cargo of 60mm mortars and some useful French-made Matra Magic 530 air-to-air missiles for the Mirage IIIs. Ecuador had sold a quantity of rather old 35mm ammunition, while Peru had produced ten French M-5Ps, the fighter-bomber version of the Mirage III, and also handed over some SAM-7s, the Soviet-made system bought the previous year at the height of the conflict with Ecuador. Perhaps most surprisingly, the West Germans turned a Nelsonian eye to the arrival on the islands of an engineer to replace a defective part of the Roland battery's fire control director. While the French, who were partners in the development of the partnership's surface-to-air system, had rigidly enforced the EEC embargo, it seemed that this particular German had an old score to settle with the RAF which, he alleged, had bombed his family during the Second World War. He slipped into Argentina unobserved and remained on the Islands for just forty-eight hours, long enough to restore the Roland's effectiveness. His request to be present in the fire control cabin when the battery was next engaged was politely refused, but his employers were supplied with copies of the tapes recording the Roland's performance in authentic combat, always useful to boost sales. Only the Soviet assistance – of Cosmos satellite imagery of the Task Force – was declined, the suspicion being that too many strings would be found attached. Although the Soviet Union was one of Argentina's best customers for agricultural produce, buying millions of tons of grain annually, the relationship ended there, much to the past disappointment of the cosmopolitan *rezident* and his wily ambassador, Sergei Striganov, who clearly relished the prospect of detaching Argentina from the influence of the West.[1]

When Mossolov served previously in Costa Rica he cultivated the Argentine ambassador, Rudolfo Baltierrez, who had returned home to become General Galtieri's influential press secretary, but this potentially useful connection was jeopardised by a misunderstanding over what Baltierrez mistakenly interpreted as an offer to sell weapons. The link was severed, leaving the KGB impotent while the GRU attempted to re-establish a back-channel to the Commander of the Air Force, Brigadier Lami-Dozo, through the Soviet military attaché. This also failed, creating a chill in relations that extended to Moscow where the Argentine military attaché, Brigadier Rodolfo Etchegoyen, was left completely isolated, with neither contact with his Soviet hosts nor access to their Elint and imagery of the South Atlantic.[2] This initially had been provided by an Elint ocean surveillance system based on Cosmos 1337, launched in February 1982, which was intended to work in conjunction with two older satellites, 1286 and 1306, but evidently this coverage was considered insufficient because in the days that followed there was a veritable flurry of Cosmos launchings: Cosmos 1345 (radar) and the large 1346 (communications) on 31 March, two days before the landings; 1347 (photo) on 2 April, and between 15 April and 23 April, satellites 1350 and 1353 from Plesetsk, with 1352 and 1368 from Tyuratam; on 29 April, Cosmos 1355 was put into orbit to maintain ocean surveillance over the South Atlantic, and soon afterwards 1356 to 1369 were launched, providing near comprehensive cover, apparently for Soviet consumption only. Cosmos 1372 boasted a nuclear-powered radar, and the 1371 collected radio signals which were relayed to earth stations via the Molniya satellite.[3] In addition, the manned military Salyut-7 space station deployed its own smaller satellite to assist the communications link to Moscow. The last Cosmos of the campaign was 1372, launched from Tyuratam on 2 June, at an inclination of 64.9 degrees, which had a duration of just seventy-one days. This activity was quite unusual and, when combined with the two early warning Cosmos 1348, launched on 7 April (to replace 1172) and 1367 on 20 May, was unprecedented, eloquent proof of huge Soviet interest in the conflict.[4]

The Soviet bid to capitalise on the war collapsed into the

kind of recriminations that characterised the Kremlin's dys-
functional foreign policy under the ailing Leonid Brezhnev,
with the Ministry of Foreign Affairs split between those
willing to take the risk of offending Britain, and the
opportunists advocating neutrality and an abstention in
the United Nations Security Council vote. Britain's ringside
view of this debate was provided by SIS's mole in the
KGB, Oleg Gordievsky, who was a witness to the erratic
behaviour of his own *rezident*, Arkadi Gouk, the top
professional who had consistently misread the situation
in London. The net result of the indecision was the
sudden arrival in Buenos Aires of a team of intelligence
professionals, under TASS, Novosti and *Pravda* cover,
purportedly to improve the standard of reporting from
the scene.

Immediately following the loss of the *Sheffield*, the
J-2 cell made the Exocet a priority. The procurement
programme in Paris, stalled because of the EEC embargo,
was to be boosted, and a special effort was to be made
via a most mysterious but ostensibly neutral channel,
through Lima.

Although Peru, like Brazil, had publicly declared recognition of Argentine sovereignty over the Islands, President
Fernando Belaunde Terry had gained the respect of everyone, particularly at the United Nations, by taking the
initiative and attempting to mediate a peaceful settlement.
However, even while the negotiations were continuing,
the Peruvians lodged a request with the French authorities
for an immediate delivery of the air-launched AM-39,
which supposedly was intended to be fitted to some
British-supplied Sea King helicopters. While the Peruvian
involvement on the diplomatic front was welcomed by all
parties, the demand for an accelerated delivery schedule
from Aerospatiale was greeted with dismay in Paris and
London, for few had any doubt about the intended ulti-
mate destination of these Exocets. Although the end-user
certificate would identify the Peruvian Navy, it was quickly

obvious that this was a further ingenious scheme to improve the Argentine inventory, so the French procrastinated. When the Peruvians increased the pressure, offering to send a ship immediately to collect the hardware, the French baulked, asserting that there was a serious danger of British sabotage, and perhaps an attempt to sink any vessel taking on a cargo of Exocets in Europe. The issue of the Peruvian Exocet contract was considered so crucial that it was the subject of a telephone conversation between Mrs Thatcher and President Mitterrand on Saturday, 29 May.

Prevaricating with the Peruvians proved easier than expected because of an unexpected problem that arose over the method of payment. Whereas the Argentines had paid Aerospatiale in full and in advance, the Peruvian order required evidence of funding; the documentation offered by the Peruvians was distinctly odd and raised several questions, in particular over the letter of credit supplied by the Banco Central Riserva in Lima. According to the official records, the bank document was supported by a deposit of $200m supplied by a local bank, the Banco Andino, a wholly-owned subsidiary of the Banco Ambrosiano – which had been Italy's largest private bank – based in Milan and headed by an influential Italian financier, Roberto Calvi. This was extraordinary, for Calvi was one of the figures who dominated the headlines during the scandal of the Banco Ambrosiano collapse that had rocked the political establishment the previous year, bringing down Arlando Forlani's Christian Democrat government. Although the Banco Ambrosiano was now in the hands of administrators appointed by the Bank of Italy, the Banco Andino apparently had escaped unscathed, having been supported by a declared loan underwriting agreement worth $250m made by the Vatican's Instituto per di Religione, the IOR (Institute for Religious Works), and by capital supplied by a local bank, the Banco de la Nación. Although there was no direct link between the

Banco Central Riserva in Lima and Argentina's desire to buy Exocets, Calvi himself had strong Argentine connections through his associate Licio Gelli, who had personally negotiated the Banco Andino's loans. Gelli, on the run in Uruguay and Argentina since April 1981, had been a close friend of Juan Perón, and accompanied the dictator when he returned home from exile in Spain in 1973. Since then he had held the honorary post of economic adviser to the Argentine embassy in Rome and, significantly, he was also a very close friend of Carlos Corti, head of the Argentine Naval Purchasing Commission in Paris, who was married to Gelli's niece, Sabrina.

The Peruvian angle was an entirely unexpected development and sent SIS officers in Rome, led by Norman McMillan, to research the background to Gelli's involvement, with the intention of providing the French with enough circumstantial evidence to undermine the claim that the Exocets were destined for Lima, not Buenos Aires. Calvi, appointed Chief Executive of the Banco Ambrosiano in 1970, since then had overseen the dramatic expansion of what had been a small provincial Catholic bank, set up in Milan at the beginning of the century, into an enormous international institution with branches across Italy and representative offices in the Caribbean. The bank's success was based in part on its partnership with the IOR, channelling the Vatican's investments into South America. In one of many complicated deals, the IOR took a large stake in one of the Banco Ambrosiano's companies registered in Luxembourg, in which the Sicilian financier Michele Sindona was a significant shareholder, thereby establishing a business relationship between three friends: Roberto Calvi, Sindona and Archbishop Paul Marcinkus of the IOR. When Sindona was exposed as a fraudster in 1980, following the collapse of his Banca Unione and the Banca Privata Italiana, he was convicted and imprisoned in the United States on charges connected to the closure of the Franklin National Bank, prompting a crisis of confidence in the Banco Ambrosiano which was left with no assets except a commitment from the IOR in the form of a 'letter of comfort' acknowledging some responsibility for Calvi's indebtedness. Calvi himself was arrested and sentenced to four years' imprisonment, but released pending an appeal after only four months, and was now living at his apartment in Rome, still running his doomed bank. Behind the scenes he was working furiously to save himself and Ambrosiano, calling in favours from his vast list of contacts in the political world, the international business community and, most dangerously, the Italian underworld.

Calvi's involvement in the Peruvian Exocet contract was enough to persuade the French to procrastinate, using the doubts surrounding the Banco Andino as an excuse. Certainly the bank was unusual, for although it was theoretically headquartered on the top four floors of the impressive new Edificio Alide building in the Paseo de la Republica in Lima, all the board meetings were held in Switzerland or Luxembourg. Indeed, the chairman was Filippo Leoni, then Ambrosiano's joint general manager, who was based in Milan, his deputy having been Giacomo Botta, latterly in charge of Ambrosiano's foreign department, also in Milan. Andino had only opened for business in October 1979 but expanded rapidly, apparently with the support of the Peruvian government, which had used the Banco Ambrosiano to finance the purchase of Augusta/Bell helicopters and Italian frigates some years earlier, and of Peru's minister of finance, Silva Rueta, who was among Calvi's acquaintances. Within a year of its inauguration, Andino had taken over some of Ambrosiano's debt portfolio in Panama and Liechtenstein, and had declared assets of $890m. In reality much of the business was nothing more than a complex series of internal transactions, mainly back-to-back loans, moving deposits from Ambrosiano's subsidiary in Managua, where Calvi's friend President Anastasio Somoza had been removed from power and

replaced by a revolutionary Sandinista regime. As we shall
see, the fate of the Banco Andino and that of Roberto Calvi
was to become inextricably linked to Argentina's fortunes
in the Falklands.

Chapter 6

SANTIAGO

Although he had never served as an intelligence officer, General Pinochet had a strong academic background at the Army Staff College as an expert in international politics, and held the profession in high regard. Since Chile had endured border disputes with her neighbour to the north, Peru, as well as with Argentina, he was determined not to be trapped into a conflict on two fronts. A devotee of Napoleon, with a marble bust of his hero always close to his desk, Pinochet was not surprised to learn on 30 April that Argentina had embarked on an invasion of the Falklands. The only curiosity was that the intelligence report submitted to him that same morning had been dated 3 March. Where had it been for the past three weeks?

Chile's intelligence structure had been riven by inter-service rivalries since the December 1978 crisis with Argentina, which occurred only five months after Pinochet conducted a purge of the Air Force and sent an entire generation of twelve senior officers into retirement, leaving just two generals in the Air Force. Since then the Army had dominated the intelligence scene, not just running the G-2 military intelligence branch but effectively controlling the two civilian agencies, the CNI and the DiDeNa. Headed by General Humberto Gordon, in 1978 the CNI had taken over the security responsibilities of the feared DINA, the organisation run by General Manuel Contreras and his deputy, Brigadier Pedro Espinosa, that was so closely associated with the era of political repression in which some 2,000 political activists had disappeared. The DINA had been closed down because of the implication of Contreras and Espinosa in the murder of Orlando Letelier and Ronni Moffitt in Washington in September 1976. A bomb placed on the rear axle of Letelier's Chevrolet Malibu had blown up, killing the former Cabinet minister and his American assistant. Letelier had lived in the United States since the 1973 coup and had campaigned against the military Junta, becoming enough of a nuisance to the regime for DINA to target him for assassination, which had been carried out by a former CIA contract agent. The Carter administration had been incensed once the DINA connection was confirmed, particularly when the Justice Department's applications for the extradition of those responsible was rejected in Santiago. In acknowledgement of American sensibilities, and of pressure from the Chilean Navy, which had been particularly outraged by the assassination, the Navy and Air Force had withdrawn all their personnel from DINA in 1977, and this proved to be the catalyst for the organisation's dissolution.[1]

The headquarters at 74 Avenida Vicuen McKenna, and the adjacent houses at the end of the cul-de-sac of Belgrado Street, had been restored to civilian use and the entire apparatus dismantled to be replaced by the Centro Nacional de Información (CNI), which was deliberately denied an overseas collection role although it continued to maintain a watch abroad on diplomats suspected of being unsympathetic to the military government, and to keep troublesome exiles under surveillance. External strategic intelligence had been placed in the hands of a new body, the Dirección de Inteligencia Defensa Nacional (DiDeNa) which employed a combination of civilians and military personnel to study external strategic issues. The three military branches reported directly to Pinochet, who chaired a monthly meeting of all five organisations, while the CNI reported to a co-ordinating unit, the Ministry

for the Presidency, where Santiago Sinclair supervised
the activities of the CNI and the DiDeNa, which was
headed by Brigadier de la Fuente. In addition to these
intelligence agencies, both the criminal police and the
paramilitary Carabineiros operated their own independent
services, further contributing to the duplication of effort
which characterised Chile's ubiquitous security structure.

When the proposition that Argentina would invade the
Falklands was first made on 1 March at the monthly meeting chaired by Pinochet, it was rejected by the Chief of the
Defence Staff, Admiral Ronald McIntyre. His scepticism
was not shared by Balliol-educated naval reservist Emilio
Meneses, who was the analyst at the DiDeNa assigned to
dealing with Argentine affairs. He had taken just three days
to prepare a compelling scenario in which he outlined the
circumstances, which he considered imminent, of an attack
on the Falklands. Disbelieved by Brigadier de la Fuente,
the report had been delayed and was not circulated to the
Ministry of Foreign Affairs – where the Deputy Minister,
Ernesto Videla, ran the sensitive Argentine department –
until 27 March, and did not reach General Pinochet's desk
for a further three days. In the opinion of Meneses, an
attack was likely in March or April 1982, and if not, was
certain in September or October.

Located on the sixth and seventh floors of an old
bank building at 720 Avenida de Libertador Bernardo
O'Higgins, with an unmarked entrance on Juan A. Rios
Street, the DiDeNa shared offices in the same block with
the rest of the Chilean intelligence community, with the
exception of the CNI which operated from an elegant
mansion at 557 Avenida Republica, once the university's
School of Sociology. Although the order from the Defence
Staff was for military business to be conducted as usual,
the invasion ensured that the lights burned late into the
night at the establishment known to insiders simply as
'720 Almeira', and it was here that advice concerning
Chile's military strategy was developed. Over the following

two weeks, two visitors from the British Embassy became familiar faces in the building: the ambassador himself, John Heath, and the naval attaché, Captain Michael Johns RN. A career diplomat, Heath spoke Spanish and, having served in Mexico, was sent in February 1980 to re-establish relations with Santiago at ambassadorial level after five years of frost in Anglo-Chilean relations. Harold Wilson's Labour administration had reduced Britain's representation to consular cover in 1975 in protest at the military regime's human rights record, and had imposed an embargo on all future defence sales, a particularly damaging sanction when the country was under threat and anxious to acquire spare parts for the Air Force's British-bought equipment, Hawker Hunter fighters and Rolls-Royce Avon aero-engines. Similarly, the US had imposed the Kennedy Amendment to prevent American supplies reaching Santiago, so Heath's success in restoring the procurement link proved enormously popular with the regime. Formerly the British Consul-General in Chicago, Heath had broken off his studies at Oxford to serve on the staff of the 11th Armoured Division in France, Belgium and Germany before joining the Foreign Office in 1950. Although inevitably he had bumped into 'the Friends' (as SIS is known) in various postings, including Maurice Oldfield when they both worked in Singapore, he had no intelligence connections, and there was no SIS station in the embassy. Indeed, the Foreign Office had taken a very conscious decision to keep SIS out of Santiago so as to avoid any accusation that the embassy was collecting intelligence about the military government, thereby risking a local misunderstanding. Reopening the SIS station – closed after David Spedding's departure in September 1974 – might have been misinterpreted by the Chileans, so Heath and Johns were largely on their own, the nearest SIS station being in Buenos Aires.

As for Johns, a Royal Navy engineering officer without much Spanish, his role in the coming crisis would be limited, but he had the advantage of liaising with counterparts who were predisposed to be helpful. This willingness to assist manifested itself at an early stage when the RFA *Tidepool*, recently sold to the Chilean Navy, was released upon delivery and, thanks to American influence in Panama, allowed to steam back through the Canal into the Atlantic to join the Task Force.

In visiting the plush offices of the Director of Naval Intelligence, Captain Monsalves, the objective of the two Britons was to remind the Chileans of a coincidence of interests that gave both countries good reasons to collaborate. Perhaps somewhat mollified by the scepticism expressed at the Meneses report, Monsalves received his British visitors with much diplomacy. Certainly he neglected to mention the significant figure of seventy-seven, the number of Royal Marines and sailors who had just surrendered on the Falklands. By coincidence, this was the precise number of men who had perished during the celebrated siege at La Concepción in 1882, when they resisted 3,000 Peruvians, fighting to the very last man, a celebrated episode in Chile's proud military history.

Certainly Chile had long regarded her larger, richer neighbour as representing a permanent threat, especially 'down south' where the military concentration in Punta Arenas was invariably the focus of tension. Since 1978, when the last crisis had been settled with an uneasy level of co-existence, all the armed forces had been dedicated to monitoring their opponent's operations and, uniquely, the local command on 'the big island' answered directly to the Defence Staff instead of to the military district. This was a recognition of the very tense relationship between the two countries, and a general acceptance that any future hostilities were bound to be concentrated in the area of the long-standing territorial dispute. Through years of observation and analysis a pattern had emerged, and the Chilean G-2 reckoned that any attempt by Argentina to mobilise would be spotted instantly. Unfortunately, it would take seventy-two hours to determine whether Argentina proposed to launch an offensive west against Chile, or east against the British. That this was a serious preoccupation was emphasised by the discomforting geographical fact that the Chilean fleet's headquarters at Valparaiso was just fifteen minutes' flying time from Argentina. Perhaps in recognition of the lessons learned at Pearl Harbor, the A-2 ('Anchor two') Naval Intelligence Division had taken the lead in developing Chile's quite sophisticated signals-interception capability. This coverage was spread in an arc from the secret site on San Felix – the inhospitable dormant volcano midway between the mainland and Easter Island in the Pacific, where Bolivian and Peruvian communications were monitored – across to Dawson Island, off Tierra del Fuego, which had gained notoriety some years earlier as a prison camp, and down to Chile's permanent weather station in Antarctica.

Naturally Britain, desperately short of reliable intelligence about Argentina, and a country which had enjoyed a long and close relationship with Chile from the days when the country's liberator, General Bernardo O'Higgins, had lived in Richmond Hill, London, wanted access to Chile's crop of raw Sigint from Argentina's air bases and weather reports from the Pacific. But there were two other important objectives: the first was to persuade the Chilean Navy to put to sea, thereby increasing pressure on Argentina's southern sea flank, and the second was to create sufficient activity along the land frontier to keep troops tied down on the mainland which might otherwise be sent to reinforce the Islands. Actually Chile needed little persuading for her Navy, so Anglophile that it celebrated Trafalgar Day rather more enthusiastically than the Royal Navy, had already anticipated a scenario in which Argentine ships might take refuge from the Royal Navy in the Chilean territorial waters of the Magellan Straits. If neutrality was to be maintained, the Navy would have to exercise control over any vessels seeking asylum, and ensure there was no hot pursuit by the British. However, A-2 was very much aware of Chile's overriding national interest in ensuring that Britain continued to maintain sovereignty over the Falklands. Every Chilean had a grasp of Argentina's rejection of the adjudication, made by the British Crown under the terms of the 1884 treaty, in which Chile had been given possession of the three strategic islands at the entrance to the Beagle Channel. The crisis of 1978, when both countries were just six hours away from full-scale war, was resolved temporarily by the Pope, whose intervention had been prompted by the deliberate leak in Washington DC of the Argentine Junta's intentions. Thus the CIA averted aggression, but relations between the two protagonists remained extremely tense thereafter. Indeed, claims and counter-claims of espionage along the length of the frontier were commonplace, and exchanges of prisoners on a scale only rivalled by the Berlin Wall were not infrequent. Thus the invasion of the Falklands was not viewed in isolation in Santiago, but rather as another chapter in a very uneasy peace. Uppermost in the minds of the Chileans was the strategic importance of the Falklands, which offered the best natural harbour south of Bahia Blanca.

In 1978, when the Argentine fleet had sailed on 4 December with the intention of seizing the disputed Chilean islands, the amphibious forces had endured more than two weeks at sea, constantly battered by the Atlantic which, even in mid-summer, was a harrowing experience for all but the most seasoned sailors. If Port Stanley fell to Argentina, it was widely recognised that the threat to Chilean interests would escalate dramatically. Indeed, any doubt on this issue had been dispelled by General Galtieri himself, in a broadcast made on the morning of the invasion, in which he referred to the occupation as but 'the first step to recovering Argentina's territory', words that could only be open to a single interpretation in Santiago. In short, the prevailing political view was that as long as Britain retained the Falklands, Chile should be reasonably secure. If, on the other hand, Britain lost the war, Chile could expect to be next, and on that occasion Argentina would have the overwhelming advantage of a secure anchorage from which to threaten Antarctica. However, the current Chilean analysis of the strategic situation in the South Atlantic immediately after the invasion was especially discouraging, for none believed that the Argentines could be dislodged from the Falklands without the three-to-one numerical superiority dictated by conventional military doctrine. Fully aware (and indeed beneficiaries) of Britain's military cutbacks, the Chileans could not imagine that the Falklands would be retaken, much as this was the earnestly desired conclusion.

Ambassador Heath's objectives while visiting the Chilean DNI were far from his daily diplomatic routine, but these sensitive tasks fell to him because he was handicapped by the lack of a local SIS officer. Although the splendid residence alone was physically rather larger than the American premises, the size of the staff had been reduced considerably in recent years. Coverage of Chile on the intelligence front fell to Mark Heathcote, two hours away by commercial flight from Buenos Aires. As well as reminding A-2 of Britain's community of interests with Chile, Heath had a very particular request for the immediate deployment of Chile's two Oberon-class diesel submarines down south, in as public a way as possible so that it should not escape the notice of the Argentines. Usually based at the big naval yards at Talcauhuano, 280 miles south of Valparaiso, the submarines operated independently of the main fleet and their deployment would be likely to cause consternation in Buenos Aires. Ideally, from the British perspective, the Chileans should allow their submarines to be spotted by Argentina to demonstrate their potential, but remain suitably distant from the Exclusion Zone to prevent detection and engagement by the Royal Navy.

John Heath was also anxious to create a fast communication channel for intelligence collected by Chilean military intelligence, G-2, and the air intelligence branch, designated D-2. Both organisations were dedicated primarily to monitoring Argentine military activity, and over the years had gained unrivalled experience at watching and analysing their neighbour's potentially hostile troop movements. Supported by a string of signal intercept stations along the border, enhanced by surveillance flights close to their neighbour's airspace, Chile's military and air intelligence analysts were reputed to know the exact current location of every Argentine in uniform. Now this order-of-battle data took on a special significance that transcended the rather academic nature of the work, for Britain possessed only minimal information regarding what the Task Force could expect when it reached the Islands.

In recognition of the vital part Chile was being asked to play, albeit behind the scenes and with only the barest resources, the ambassador made a startling suggestion: the Royal Air Force would be willing to make a loan of the appropriate equipment, including three Canberra PR-9s from 18 Group, No. 1 Photographic Reconnaissance Unit, based at RAF Wyton, fitted with oblique cameras to overlook Argentina from Chilean airspace, and two Sigint Hercules for the collection of technical data. Flying fast at altitudes of over 60,000 feet, the twin-engined, two-seater Canberras had been operational since 1958 and had often evaded Soviet interceptors while patrolling beside Warsaw Pact airspace.[2] Despite their age, the specially converted aircraft with longer wings for high-altitude flight were still extremely effective, and the Argentine Air Force would be powerless to prevent their use.

The details of this offer remain obscure, but it is known that two Hercules aircraft, fitted with airborne refuelling probes, were spotted by independent observers at Belize, San Felix and Punta Arenas. The tiny island in the Pacific was, of course, a closed military facility with no civilian inhabitants or visitors, but Punta Arenas shared the airport with the three domestic Chilean airlines, so special security measures were enforced to prevent passengers from seeing any military activity. All airliners were required to close their cabin window shutters on arrival and departure, and opaque covers were placed on all airside windows in the airport building. Nevertheless, those sufficiently interested noticed that the Chilean Air Force's inventory of Hercules aircraft had doubled without explanation or any announced purchases, and that the additional planes had been painted in the European camouflage convention of grey-green, not the American-style Vietnam colour scheme of tan with two shades of green. Curiously, the additional C-130s bore the identification label 'Fuerza Aérea de Chile' on the fuselage but with the second word misspelled 'Aera', and without the accent on the first 'e'. According to personnel stationed at Punta Arenas during the conflict, senior officers were told not to be offended while on the base if rather Anglo-Saxon-looking personnel, with English accents and wearing name badges identifying them as 'Gonzales' and 'Garcia', failed to salute properly.

Perhaps coincidentally, Chile retained possession of three Canberras after the war – serial numbers 341, 342 and 343, which were officially sold in October 1982 – and subsequently received a total of nine Hawker Hunters and thirty spare engines on exceptionally advantageous terms. This generosity may or may not have been a reflection of the accuracy of the intelligence material supplied by Chile to Britain. Either way, the news proved encouraging. According to the Chilean assessment of the Argentine Air Force, the total number of attack aircraft was around 130, slightly more than half the figure originally suggested by the RAF.

From the moment the *Sheffield* was sunk, the Argentine Naval Air Service realised that it possessed the means to win the war. All the training against a Type-42 destroyer, calculated to be their toughest opponent, had paid off, but their success had made Jorge Colombo's 2nd Attack and Fighter Squadron, and the air base at Rio Grande, a priority target.

By one of those extraordinary coincidences of war, the unit selected to defend Rio Grande was commanded by Miguel Pita, a man almost uniquely well qualified in Argentina to anticipate likely British tactics and prepare the most appropriate counter-measures. A staunch Anglophile, and former naval attaché in La Paz, Pita had deployed his men of the 1st Marine Brigade from Bahia Blanca within the first week of the invasion, the heavy equipment being moved by sea and landed at the shingle beach of Santo Domingo, with 2,600 troops following by air from the Naval Air Station Espora. They had expected to be sent to the Islands, but after the loss of the *General Belgrano* it was considered impossible to move them by sea, and the fully-stretched air bridge of C-130s and Fokker F27s and F-28s was already fully committed to logistic support for the existing garrison. Thus, more by accident than design, some of Argentina's best troops were on hand to prepare an in-depth defence of the airfield when the Super Etendards arrived on 21 April.

Pita thought he knew what to expect because, ironically, he had been trained by the British in clandestine tactics, and in 1962 spent three months at Fort Monckton, SIS's secret facility outside Gosport in Hampshire, on a course taught by a former SOE agent who had made a speciality of destroying bridges in Nazi-occupied France. During the period Pita spent on the English south coast, training in unconventional warfare with a selection of other specially chosen overseas candidates, he concentrated on night-time infiltration from the sea in rubber boats and the sabotage of railways with plastic explosives. The course had been run regularly since the end of the Second World War for Allied and other countries which, in the event of being overrun by Communists, could be expected to develop a stay-behind resistance organisation. Sponsored by NATO,

SIS had supervised covert networks in Italy, Switzerland, Austria and Sweden and provided the necessary *matériel* to be hidden in skilfully constructed caches. The highest level of secrecy was maintained, so that it was not until the early 1990s that the first details emerged, initially in Italy and then in Belgium, of the existence of an independent resistance organisation variously codenamed GLADIO, in Italy, and P-26 in Switzerland. In a series of official reports into the networks, which were deliberately concealed from politicians and military staffs, the network organisers described the training facilities made available by NATO; Effrem Cattalan and Colonel Albert Bachman of P-26, and Colonel Schwebach of Belgian Intelligence, reluctantly confirmed the level of assistance given by Allied special forces. Much of GLADIO's training in England was conducted at Fort Monckton, where Pita developed his talents as a clandestine operator.[3]

When Pita, an exceptionally experienced intelligence officer, was presented with the challenge of ensuring the security of Colombo's aircraft, he knew exactly what to expect from SIS, the SAS and the SBS: he was convinced British saboteurs would be landed on the nearest shore with the objective of infiltrating the airfield and destroying the aircraft and missiles. Knowing what to expect gave him a tremendous advantage, or so he believed, and he took his precautions around Rio Grande accordingly.

Since a high proportion of the town's population of 25,000 inhabitants were of Chilean origin, Pita acknowledged that there were few opportunities for deception and that the dispersal of the Super Etendards to safe revetments or camouflaged sites on the exposed airfield would be difficult to achieve in daylight. Instead, as a precaution introduced after 1 May, the planes were moved at night into the town and concealed in car parks, guarded by the Marine Logistics Battalion which was headquartered there, but these awkward and time-consuming exercises did not amount to a guarantee of safety for the aircraft.

Aware that his activities were also likely to be the subject of satellite reconnaissance, Pita established two perimeters around the base and sowed what appeared to be a very extensive minefield to cover the approaches to the most vulnerable points. For the benefit of the overhead surveillance, Pita pretended that the minefield extended much further than it really did, and to ensure the message was received by the enemy he arranged for the local radio and television channels, which were routinely monitored by the Chileans, to broadcast warnings about the mines. In addition, he deployed the 2nd Battalion around the base and located the motorised 1st Battalion just to the south. The 3rd Battalion, equipped with twelve Panhard armoured cars, was located at the Estancia Jose Menendez, eight kilometres from the airfield by a good tarmaced road, as a mobile support unit ready to move to any zone in response to an emergency. To keep his troops on their toes, Pita ordered constant daily patrols to cover an area from Cavo Penia in the south to a line just north of the town, and live firing every night. However, convinced by his own experience that the threat would come from the sea, he rotated only a single platoon inside the airfield's inner perimeter, to guard the hardened bunker built during the 1977 Chilean crisis, never having contemplated the prospect of an airborne assault directly into the base.

From the end of April, when the threat of attack seemed most likely, Pita had produced a classic defensive ring around the airfield, complete with an integrated air defence box measuring three kilometres east to west and six north to south, at the heart of which was the AN/TPS-43 radar dug in above the beach at Cavo Domingo. Protected as a strongpoint, the site had a strategic importance, both as an early-warning system with a range of 300 kilometres – more than enough to alert the control tower of an imminent raid – and as a target for an attack by Shrike missiles which home in on the energy radiated by such sites. Although the Westinghouse equipment was a powerful deterrent to an airborne attack, it could by the same token be expected to attract hostile aircraft carrying the dreaded Shrike, which locked on to the sources of radar transmissions and literally followed the beams right into their control centres. There was no defence against the Shrike except the termination of transmissions, but Pita did have the advantage of two radar pickets on constant patrol offshore which could be expected to overlap the AN/TPS-43 cover and give greater protection to the coastal flank. This additional radar screen was provided by the two Sumner-class destroyers, the *Hipolito Bouchard* and the *Piedra Buena,* which previously had served as escorts for the *General Belgrano.* The remainder of the air defence box consisted of the 40mm Oerlikons which were a permanent feature at the base, now reinforced by four Air Force 30mm Rheinmetall-202 units and six Bofors operated by the Navy.

Assisted by the highly efficient French-made RASIT land surveillance radar, and the tough regime of constant patrols, Pita had no other method of detecting the infiltrators he expected daily. He had taken all the security measures that were reasonable, but he had no reliable source of information regarding British intentions. Indeed, apart from the maritime surveillance operation run by the Air Force, Argentina's resources were limited to the mysterious 601st Intelligence Battalion, the military intelligence unit which was operating in Montevideo to monitor British activity at their embassy. Known as a 'dirty tricks' organisation capable of mounting clandestine operations, the 601st had despatched several teams to Uruguay to keep a watch on Stephen Love who, unlike Mark Heathcote who had flown home upon his expulsion, did not return to London until the end of May, rightly believing that he still had a role to play because he was officially accredited to the embassy in Montevideo and had visited the capital once a month from Buenos Aires before the invasion. His presence, together with some of his counter-surveillance measures – which included changing the CD plates on his car for a Dutch registration number – persuaded the 601st that he was a potentially dangerous adversary. In reality, he remained excluded from the campaign's inner loop of decision-making and was obliged to rely on the BBC World Service for much of his information regarding the conduct of the war. Upon his return to England, his principal contribution was to use his accumulated knowledge of the enemy by advising GCHQ on the likely locations of military sites on the islands, which the Argentine forces habitually referred to by operational names with a historical significance.

Thus the scene was set for one of the most remarkable confrontations in military history, the British Task Force gambling on edging cautiously closer to the Falklands, with Colombo's men at Rio Grande praying earnestly for an improvement in the weather that would allow them to sink one of the carriers. Simultaneously, the SAS was putting the final touches to an audacious plan to eliminate the Exocet threat once and for all. Remarkably, the scheme hatched at Hereford bore little resemblance to the scenario drawn up with such care by Miguel Pita.

Chapter 7

STIRLING LINES

The intelligence cell at the headquarters of 22 SAS was buzzing. The Director SAS, Brigadier Peter de la Billière, had called for a strike at the enemy's heart, and now he had been given an opportunity to plan and execute the operation.[1] Some of 'G' Squadron was already with the Task Force, with Colonel Mike Rose on HMS *Fearless*, the remainder being aboard the Royal Fleet Auxiliary *Resource*. As for 'D' Squadron, it had recently returned from Bessbrook in South Armagh, where its tour of duty had been marked with another significant success – the detection by men of the Mobility Troop of an assassination attempt by the South Belfast UDA on the life of Bernadette McAliskey, formerly Bernadette Devlin MP. A senior figure in the Trotskyite Irish Republican Socialist Party – the political wing of the Irish Nationalist Liberation Army – and a prominent member of the H-Blocks Committee, she had been at the centre of a political dispute which had split the INLA, and therefore had acquired plenty of enemies on both sides of the sectarian divide. Having been alerted to the possibility of an attack on her home at Derrylaughlan near the Republican town of Coalisland by the RUC Special Branch section designated E3B, which concentrated on the loyalist paramilitaries, a team conducting a close target reconnaissance was on hand to apprehend the gunmen early on the morning of 16 January 1981.[2] Despite the advance warning from an informer – probably Brian

Nelson, the mole inside the UDA run by British military intelligence – Bernadette and her husband Michael were seriously wounded by the hooded terrorists who smashed open the front door of their cottage with a sledgehammer and shot the couple at close range, hitting them fifteen times altogether before the SAS patrol could emerge from their concealment and respond. They intervened just as the trio were returning to their Vauxhall Avenger and took them into custody without firing a shot. They then summoned help with a flare which brought units of the local garrison, the Argyll and Sutherland Highlanders, rushing to the scene by road. The first-aid administered by the SAS men (wearing Parachute Regiment uniforms) to the McAliskeys undoubtedly saved their lives, and they were flown by an army helicopter to Musgrave Park Hospital in Belfast for surgery. All three UDA men, Andrew Watson, Thomas Graham and Raymond Smallwoods, were handed over to the Argylls and were later convicted of attempted murder and sentenced to life, fifteen years' and twenty years' imprisonment respectively. The episode did little to reduce Bernadette McAliskey's hostility to the army, but the capture of the UDA's team was a considerable accomplishment for the Squadron which, of course, declined to acknowledge its participation publicly. The RUC was particularly pleased at the prospect of interrogating the three, who were already suspects in several other assassinations, including that of Ronnie Bunting in October 1980.[3]

Back from Northern Ireland, the whole of 'D' Squadron was despatched to the South Atlantic aboard the RFA *Fort Austin*, to undertake Operation PARAQUAT, the recapture of South Georgia. This secondary action, considered an essential prelude to the assault on the Falklands, had been co-ordinated by HMS *Antrim*, which accommodated the Headquarters Squadron and 17 and 19 Troop, supported by 16 Troop on *Endeavour* and 18 Troop on *Plymouth*, while PARAQUAT preoccupied 'D' Squadron until it could complete its mission and join the destroyer HMS *Brilliant* to link up with the Task Force on 28 April. With 'A' Squadron in Northern Ireland, and some of 'G' Squadron in Belize, only 'B' Squadron was left.

Led by Major John Moss, a Parachute Sapper officer from 9 Squadron, Royal Engineers, who had previously served one tour as a troop commander in Dhofar and Northern Ireland before returning to the regiment a year earlier, 'B' Squadron provided some of the key anti-terrorist personnel who, with 'G' Squadron's Mobility Troop, comprised the famed Special Projects Team which had ended the Iranian embassy siege with such spectacular results in April 1980. The Squadron's 6 (Boat) Troop had just returned from a training exercise conducted with the SBS in the north of Scotland and was in preparation for FLINTLOCK, the annual NATO war-games in Germany, when the emergency began. Abandoning plans for deployment in Germany, the Squadron embarked on an intensive training programme to practise the seizure of an enemy-held airfield.

According to De la Billière's plan, codenamed Operation MIKADO, the entire Squadron would be loaded on to two C-130 Hercules transports which would crash-land on Rio Grande's runway. The objective was to seek out and destroy the five Super Etendards parked on the tarmac, and disable the three remaining air-launched Exocets known to be in the Argentine arsenal before disappearing into the night. Whilst superficially attractive, MIKADO demanded high-quality information of the kind that was not available from SIS. Mark Heathcote, for example, had never visited Rio Grande and so was not consulted, and the days when the Foreign Office maintained a consul in the town were long gone.

According to the latest intelligence, which was minimal, the easiest part of MIKADO would be getting the attackers on to the ground, landing two Hercules on the 10,000-foot runway before hitting the hangars and the officers' mess. Thereafter, the difficulties would escalate. Rio Grande itself is on Tierra del Fuego, about as remote from anywhere as one is likely to find in the world, more than 1,000 miles from Buenos Aires, covering an area 130 miles long and 60 miles wide at its narrowest; it is covered with desolate tundra and divided almost equally between Argentina, with the provincial capital at Ushuaia, the most southerly town on the globe, and Chile. On the Chilean side is the single garrisoned settlement of Porvenir, with a short airstrip used mainly by oil exploration companies, about 100 miles from Rio Grande. Directly east of Porvenir, across the Straits Estrecho, is the Chilean port of Punta Arenas, 1,400 miles south of Santiago. On the assumption that the Chileans would give the SAS a friendly welcome, and the two C-130s survived the landing and subsequent fire-fight, the plan called for a flight into Chile. If not, and on the assumption that the Argentines would not pursue 'B' Squadron on to Chilean soil, their task was to march fifty miles due west, at night and without the benefit of any navigational aids, across entirely featureless swampy terrain to neutral territory. If the journey could be completed in darkness, there were no aircraft at Rio Grande capable of night attack. Thereafter the choices were limited. Apart from Punta Arenas, itself on the long peninsula of Pen Brunswick in the region known as Magellan's Antarctica, there was no other air base for hundreds of miles. In these circumstances, and in the extreme weather conditions with the onset of the Antarctic winter, hostile action by the enemy would not be the sole preoccupation for the men of 'B' Squadron who survived the inevitable fire-fight on Rio Grande's runway. The planners calculated that by approaching the base from the west, the Argentine radar would only detect the planes at a range of thirty miles, which translated into a six-minute warning for the defenders. Would the men on the ground be sufficiently alert to respond to the unexpected arrival of the heavily armed men of 'B' Squadron, 22 SAS?

The prospect of a long hike over the frozen, windswept wasteland of peat bog under adverse conditions was

1 HMS *Phoebe*, part of Operation JOURNEYMAN, the top-secret deployment of a task force to the South Atlantic in November 1977 to deter an anticipated Argentine invasion. The crew were sworn to secrecy and the Royal Navy pretended the Exocet-armed frigate had accompanied HMS *Alacrity*, the RFA *Resource* and the tanker *Olwen* to Belize. In reality the modernised Type-21 anti-submarine vessel was using its newly installed satellite communications equipment to link *Dreadnought* to the Admiralty.

2 HMS *Dreadnought*, the nuclear hunter-killer which was an essential component of Operation JOURNEYMAN. The crew were appalled when James Callaghan asserted in the Commons that their deployment had been leaked deliberately in Buenos Aires by SIS, although they suspected they had been detected by the RFA *Cherry Leaf* during an unauthorised exercise conducted during the operation.

3 The Aerospatiale air-launched AM-39 Exocet. As the Task Force sailed from Ascension, the Royal Navy did not realise that the Argentines had mastered the missile's complicated avionics and possessed five of the deadly weapons, a threat that was only appreciated after the loss of HMS *Sheffield*.

4 The SAS storm the Iranian embassy in London, May 1980 thereby establishing their reputation for ruthless efficiency and impressing the Prime Minister, Margaret Thatcher, who met PAGODA Troop later the same day. When the threat of air-launched Exocets was fully appreciated the SAS offered an apparently attractive solution to the Task Force: to destroy the missiles and their aircraft on the ground in Argentina.

5 Two members of the SAS Special Projects Team in balaclavas firing tear-gas into the embassy, moments before the rest of 'B' Squadron's 6 Troop abseiled down the front of the building and smashed their way in with sledge-hammers. 'B' Squadron, however, were less keen to raid the Argentine airfield at Rio Grande when the War Cabinet refused permission for the attack to be launched overland from Chile.

6 Sir Peter de la Billière, the Director SAS who sacked Major John Moss of 'B' Squadron on the eve of Operation MIKADO when he voiced his men's reservations about the wisdom of crash-landing two C-130s on the runway at Rio Grande. The General was infuriated by the squadron's reluctance to undertake what he perceived as a daring master-stroke which would safeguard the Task Force, while the troops considered the scheme to be nothing more than a suicide mission.

7 The sheepish Fleet Air Arm crew of the Sea King helicopter abandoned in Chile after Operation MIKADO's reconnaissance mission had been aborted. The crew are pictured at the British embassy in Santiago. The SAS team avoided capture by the Carabineiros and were exfiltrated later.

8 Sir Antony Duff, the Intelligence Co-ordinator to the Cabinet throughout the Falklands campaign, and a key member of the Joint Intelligence Committee, whose experience as a submariner during the Second World War proved invaluable.

9 HMS *Endurance*, the ice patrol ship which represented Britain's only intelligence collection asset in the South Atlantic. The government's decision to scrap her in a cost-cutting exercise baffled the Junta, which misinterpreted the news and dismayed GCHQ.

10 HMS *Sheffield*, having been hit amidships by a single Exocet that failed to explode. The subsequent fire made the deck too hot to stand on and eventually destroyed the ship. The ship had been caught unawares because of a basic design fault, and the unexpected loss of this sophisticated guided-missile destroyer from an air-launched weapon made Whitehall re-evaluate the Task Force's entire strategy, and led to the risky ventures to deny the Junta further air-launched Exocets.

11 The disgraced Italian banker Roberto Calvi. His partner, Licio Gelli, was related by marriage to Carlos Corti, the Argentine Naval Intelligence officer in Paris who headed the Junta's illicit Exocet procurement programme. Calvi planned to finance the secret purchases with letters of credit issued by the Banco Andino in Lima, but the scheme was foiled

12 Blackfriars Bridge, where Calvi's body was found hanging a few days after the Argentine surrender in the Falklands. His final deal, to finance the purchase of Exocets on the weapons 'grey market', was frustrated by SIS. The subsequent police investigation concluded that Calvi had committed suicide, but a second inquest returned an open verdict.

13 The anonymous offices of OFEMA in the Avenue Marceau, Paris, which also accommodated the Paris branch of Argentine Naval Intelligence, whose officers attempted to acquire more Exocets. Their increasingly desperate efforts were monitored by three French security agencies, as well as SIS and GCHQ, and ended in an elaborate sting which cost millions but yielded no missiles.

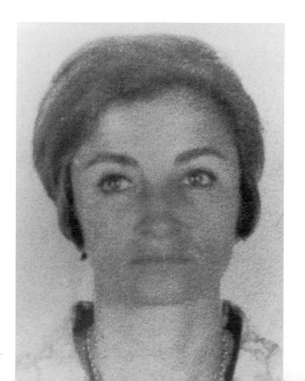

14 Elena Holmberg, the Argentine diplomat who tried to blow the whistle on the clandestine intelligence operation conducted in Paris. She was murdered in Buenos Aires. Her unsolved death alerted the French to the extension of the 'dirty war' to Europe and ensured that the 'Pilot Centre Paris' was the subject of continuous surveillance.

15 The converted trailer used to fire surface-launched Exocets at British warships that ventured too close to Port Stanley. Of the four missiles flown into the Falklands, one hit HMS *Glamorgan*. A masterpiece of improvisation, the power was supplied by a vintage 1939 Siemens searchlight generator originally built for the Luftwaffe.

16 Two Exocet launch tubes mounted on a flatbed truck, ready for deployment at night along the coast to deter British warships from bombarding Argentine infantry positions. The final surrender came before the last missile could be launched, and the vehicle was discovered by astonished British paratroops.

itself neither unduly worrying nor unexpected. Because no one in the regiment had any first-hand experience of the terrain, De la Billière had drafted in the son of an old friend, Sir Cosmo Haskard, who had served as Governor of the Falklands for six years in the 1960s. Surprised to be transferred at a moment's notice from Sandhurst to Stirling Lines, Officer-Cadet Haskard gave a detailed description of what the SAS could anticipate in the South Atlantic. The regiment prides itself on physical fitness and stamina, and every soldier undergoes what is arguably the most demanding test of endurance required of any military unit in the world: the notorious six forced marches across the perilous Brecon Beacons, undertaken in darkness at speed, with increasingly heavy back-packs over distances of up to forty kilometres. On the final, most arduous course the men carry Bergens packed with bricks weighing 65lb as well as food, water and a rifle without a sling, and during the week will have climbed the equivalent of Everest. Only a tiny proportion of the applicants get through the selection process, with injuries commonplace and death from exposure or injury a not infrequent occurrence. (Three years earlier, in February 1979, Major Mike Kealy, a newly appointed squadron commander who had won a DSO with 'G' Squadron in Oman, died of exhaustion in a typically atrocious blizzard on the Black Mountains.) Having swum the River Wye and passed the Navigation, Point to Point, Sketch Map and Endurance tests, the few left would be flown to Belize for six weeks of jungle training. Having coped with SAS selection, Tierra del Fuego seemed entirely manageable.

The men of 'B' Squadron spent a week flying in and out of RAF bases in Wales and the north of Scotland, simulating the surprise attack that was intended to replicate the success achieved by the Israelis at Entebbe in 1976. The training was so realistic that on one occasion half the Squadron nearly perished when the pilot, on his final approach to a blacked-out airfield in the Highlands, descended into a thick mist and completely lost sight of the runway. The plane plunged towards the ground, terrifying all aboard, and made as hard a landing as possible without ripping the airframe apart, leaving the passengers distinctly queasy. On each approach the RAF, acting the role of defenders, reported exactly when the approaching planes had been detected on radar. For the very few who knew, or suspected they knew MIKADO's intended target, the RAF's debriefs were not encouraging.

Although, when they guessed their target was on the Argentine mainland, some of the soldiers initially expressed scepticism that the mission would be given approval, the quality of equipment distributed to them made them realise that MIKADO was in earnest. Suddenly expense was no object, and weapons promised for months – such as the XM 203 'over-and-under' Armalite, with a 40mm grenade-launcher attached to the underside of the rifle's stock – unexpectedly materialised, but more than one soldier compared the operation with Arnhem:

> They say history repeats itself, and it seemed the Head Shed were about to prove it. Back in the Briefing Room at the Kremlin in Hereford, they had outlined a plan to crash two C-130s containing a heavily-armed B Squadron on to the runway . . . with the aim of bringing the Falklands War to a rapid conclusion. It occurred to me they were making the same mistake as Monty when he sent the Paras into Arnhem in an attempt to short-circuit World War II. As in the case of Arnhem, the Head Shed wouldn't believe the intelligence reports presented to them.[4]

Both aircraft were to make a very low-level approach on the Argentine mainland and disembark the troops before the defenders could assess what was happening. The kind of raid that the SAS's founder, David Stirling, would have been proud of, it was precisely what the SAS were created to accomplish, the destruction of hostile aircraft on the ground. In addition, a not-too-dissimilar operation, a night raid on the Argentine airstrip on Pebble Island by 'D' Squadron, was being planned simultaneously. That raid was executed on the night of 14/15 May by forty-five men, supported by a pair of artillery spotters, with only one minor casualty, leaving the wrecks of all ten planes present.

According to the plan, three of 'B' Squadron's Troops would fan out across the base at Rio Grande to locate and sabotage the hardware, while the Boat Troop would identify the officers' mess and kill everyone inside. Even if some of the aircraft had been dispersed, or if the missiles were concealed, at least the 2nd Escuadrilla de Ataque would lose most, if not all, of its qualified Super Etendard pilots. As a preliminary, an advance team of volunteers drawn from different Troops, and led by Captain Andrew M. of 6 Troop, would be inserted into Argentina by Sea King to reconnoitre the target from close range, confirm the presence of the distinctive French aircraft and assess the strength and state of readiness of the defence forces. This was just the kind of clandestine surveillance, conducted from skilfully concealed hides, at which the SAS had excelled in Northern Ireland. A former teacher from Manchester, with a Master's degree in mathematics before he joined the Royal Hampshires, Captain M. was an unconventional SAS officer, but he was popular with his men. If his team saw an opportunity to destroy the aircraft, they were to be equipped to do the job themselves. If not, they were to call in the main raiding party. Naturally, there was considerable competition to be included in this advance party, particularly among the younger members of the Squadron, but some of the older hands were more cautious. Indeed, by the time Jake W., a senior staff sergeant from a Highland regiment who had seen action in Aden, Borneo and Dhofar, had explained his doubts about the operation's viability to the officer who was young enough to be his son, Captain M. apparently turned pale. Nevertheless, he did not pull out.

Paradoxically, the final infiltration by Sea King helicopter was likely to prove the least hazardous. First the nine men had to be flown via Ascension to the Task Force for a parachute drop with their equipment into the sea. Once aboard *Invincible*, the last phase of the operation could begin, with a covert helicopter flight at night into Argentina, approaching the coast from the south and making a final dash into hostile territory from the west. Only a Sea King stripped of all but the essentials and operating at extreme range could undertake such a mission, so it was proposed that once the aircrew had dropped the SAS patrol at the Estancia Las Violetas the helicopter would fly back into Chile and land in neutral territory, the crew claiming a navigational error. In reality the two helicopter pilots would be assisted on the final leg by the prominent landmark of the lighthouse at Cap Domingo, and en route back to Chile would be guided by the civilian navigation beacon transmitted on the 290 azimuth by the airport at Chabunco.

As 'B' Squadron's training progressed, doubts were expressed about the wisdom of the Director's plan, but nevertheless, despite some serious misgivings, Captain M. and his hand-picked team were delivered safely to *Invincible*. A short period of rest followed while the Director SAS obtained the War Cabinet's consent to insert the patrol and make a final study of the latest poor-quality, cloud-obscured aerial photographs of the area around Rio Grande supplied by the Americans. One of these pictures had shown a farmhouse rather closer to the landing zone than Captain M. anticipated, and when he broached the issue with the rest of his party at the final briefing the weapons specialist, 'Nasty' Neil H. from the Royal Marines, produced a Welrod silenced handgun, made famous during the Second World War by SOE, and offered a drastic solution. Appalled, Captain M. stormed out of the meeting.

At last all the preparations were completed, and a Sea King 4 of 846 Naval Air Squadron, serial number ZA 290, was stripped down and fitted with the extra fuel tanks that would extend its range for the low-level circuitous flight to the mainland, which took place on the night of 17/18 May. The pilot was a marine, Lieutenant Richard Hutchings, his co-pilot Lieutenant Alan Bennett, and the winchman was Peter Imrie, on a one-way flight to the South American continent, having been brought as close as possible by the *Invincible* which had steamed west under cover of darkness at full speed, without radar, escorted by HMS *Brilliant*.

Coincidentally, the date chosen was Argentine Navy Day, when the opposition might be expected to have relaxed their guard following a day of celebrations. Fully laden with the team of nine SAS men dressed in their Norwegian Arctic warfare gear, including three exceptionally experienced NCOs – Neil H., the weapons expert, Mick G. from the Gordon Highlanders, and Sergeant Danny 'the Rat' S. – the Sea King attempted a horizontal take-off from the flight deck and, dangerously overloaded with fuel, weapons, satellite communications equipment and Bergens packed with food, only narrowly avoided plunging into the sea as the rotors gradually achieved lift. As soon as the helicopter was clear, *Invincible* and *Brilliant* turned east towards the Exclusion Zone and a few hours later put on a fireworks display of high-intensity Lepus flares dropped from a pair of Harriers as a decoy to distract the enemy's attention. In addition, the *Invincible* launched a dawn raid on Port Stanley and had six 1,000lb bombs dropped, to demonstrate that the ship was still in the vicinity.

The remainder of the Sea King's flight across the bitterly cold Atlantic was uneventful but, as the helicopter approached the target area, twenty kilometres north of Rio Grande, the Omega radar warning receiver alerted the pilot to a lock-on by a hostile radar. Then his co-pilot reported a flare fired some distance away, towards the coast. After a

quick consultation with Captain M., it was agreed that the
mission should continue, but as they landed by the isolated
estancia a second flare was seen much closer. The patrol
was already scrambling out of the sliding side door, with
Taff U., Pete C. and Stude C. on the ground when, after
an agonising few moments of crisis management, Captain
M. announced that he was aborting the mission which, in
his judgment, had been compromised. The whole scheme
had depended upon surprise, and his principal task was
to avoid discovery and maintain a covert hide from which
the Rio Grande base could be kept under surveillance. The
prospect of being chased across the pampas by well-armed
Argentine troops was not part of the plan, and the merest
hint of a raid could transform a brilliant *coup de main* into
a costly fiasco. Accordingly Captain M. shook his head and
called out to the two NCOs already on the ground, 'I'm
sorry, it's Chile after all.' Uncomprehending, Gwynne E.
made the memorable reply: 'Chilly! It's fucking freezing.'

The mission's fallback was to return to neutral territory,
the Sea King having insufficient fuel to attempt the return
journey of more than 500 miles to the Task Force, so
Hutchings flew the helicopter on the 290-degree course to
Chile, dropping the SAS team off in the empty wilderness
before flying on towards a dirt track ten miles east of Punta
Arenas on the last remaining drops of fuel. While the SAS
team set up a bivouac and Mick G. sent a 'mission aborted'
signal to Hereford, the three aircrew set fire to their aircraft
to destroy any incriminating evidence of their clandestine
assignment and moved off on foot in what they hoped was
the direction of Punta Arenas.

At this stage Moss recognised that the element of surprise
had been lost and requested a return to the original plan,
the infiltration overland from Chile, but this was vetoed.
So too was his proposal to insert a second advance party.
The order from above was to proceed regardless, as the
raid was still viable. Accordingly, John Moss gathered the
forty-five members of 'B' Squadron together in the Interest

Room early in the morning for a final pep-talk before they departed, and explained the crucial importance of destroying the Exocets. It was 'only "B" Squadron, 22 SAS,' he announced, 'that can prevent the Task Force from sustaining hundreds of casualties.' He was determined to proceed, with or without help from the advance reconnaissance team. 'Blind or not, we're going in. Our country is at war and we're needed.'

Moss's speech went down well with most of those present, but a few old hands recognised that the project amounted to suicide. As one NCO commented, 'Give me a blindfolded tightrope walk in a force-10 gale any time.' This was not to be an Entebbe raid against poorly armed, ill-disciplined tribesmen in khaki who could be expected to panic at the first sound of gunfire. The Argentine troops guarding the base would be well-organised and equipped with much the same kind of weaponry as their opponents. The first to voice his concern was Sergeant Jake W. of 6 (Boat) Troop, one of the regiment's most highly respected, longest-serving NCOs, who sought out Moss and voiced his concerns. Although the full plan was known even at that late stage to only very few men in the regiment, Jake W. had participated in the planning of Captain M.'s mission, and had gleaned enough from the training over the past weeks to realise the full implications. How was the Squadron to reach the target? Even with half-loads the Hercules aircraft would not have enough fuel to divert to anywhere else so, once over the Argentine mainland, the SAS would be committed. There would not be enough time to circle and find Rio Grande, and if there was even the slightest error in navigating the first approach, the planes were likely to be shot out of the sky as they came round for a second attempt. The C-130 was renowned for its ability to take punishment and remain airborne, but this surely would be too great a test. Indeed, if one Hercules was destroyed, which meant the loss of half the Squadron, the other could not abort and would have to carry on. In his judgment this amounted to needless and deliberate sacrifice, and Moss accepted his reasons for withdrawing. Although he did not say so, the same thoughts had occurred to him. How could you mount a raid of this kind based on a black-and-white map published in 1939 and photocopies of the current edition of *The Times Atlas*? As for satellite imagery, the cloud cover had obscured the target so there was no real certainty that the Super Etendards were on the field at Rio Grande. Indeed, about the only useful satellite intelligence had been the radar signatures of the control tower unit and the new AN/TPS-43 installed on the coast, neither of which was particularly encouraging. In contemplating failure, what would be the consequences? A huge boost to Argentine propaganda and a tremendous blow to morale for the Task Force, and in percentage terms the prospects of success, if they were obliged to stick to the unsatisfactory plan, looked to Moss to be the equivalent of a subaltern's life expectancy on the Somme.

A few moments later, with only minutes to go before the coaches were due to arrive, Moss told De la Billière about Jake W.'s resignation, and expressed the view that the raid was not viable. Privately, he thought the RAF would baulk at the prospect of such a risky undertaking, but he could not understand why the safer route overland from Chile had been denied to them. For his part De la Billière was infuriated to learn of Moss's doubts at the eleventh hour, especially as he had fought so hard in London to obtain the War Cabinet's approval for a scheme which 'B' Squadron previously had assured him was feasible. Without argument, De la Billière told Moss he would not be going on the mission, and replaced him with Rose's second-in-command, Ian Crooke. Dismayed because he had always intended to go on the raid, despite his reservations, Moss drove to his home in Hereford and told his wife that De la Billière had sacked him. Within six months, a period he spent on leave and undertaking odd jobs around the base, Moss returned to his regiment. He had requested an interview with the regiment's new CO, Colonel Neville Howard, but as the situation remained unchanged – which Moss accepted, particularly because his men were still in the South Atlantic – none took place.

De la Billière has described this episode with a degree of understatement in his autobiography, *Looking for Trouble*, without explaining the background to this extraordinary turn of events:

> I was dismayed to find that the attitude of this unit seemed lukewarm. I was also puzzled, because I had never known such a lack of enthusiasm; throughout my career the SAS had invariably reacted like hounds to a fox the moment they scented conflict. The trouble, I found, lay in the squadron commander, who himself did not believe in the proposed operation. To my mind there was only one thing to be done, and that was to remove him immediately. Clearly this was a regimental matter, and the decision should have been taken by the Commanding Officer; but as he was not present, I had to act myself. At midnight one night I dismissed the man from his post, and in his place appointed Ian Crooke, a first-class leader. By morning the attitude of the squadron had changed entirely, and they were ready to go ... To remove an officer from his command in the middle of a war is not an action which anyone would take lightly. I was not worried about the impact on the individual; tough as it was on him, I had to do what I thought was right for all the people whose lives were going to be at stake. The more worrying question was, how would the squadron fare under a new leader?[5]

The dread RTU, 'return to unit', is regarded by all SAS personnel as a punishment, unless it is one of those rare occasions when a volunteer opts to leave by choice. Moss had accepted Jake W.'s withdrawal, but he was not RTU'd;

instead he was allowed to serve out the remainder of his eighteen months' service in the regiment. However, when word spread others felt they should do the same to show 'Jakey' support, knowing that he had protested to save lives. A minority took the view that he was too close to retirement to participate in such a high-risk venture. An eyewitness, Harry G., recalled the scene:

So well respected was Jakey that the news came like a thunderbolt to us all. Groups stopped to discuss the situation. One was addressed by a senior sergeant.

'I think Jakey's right and we should support him by offering to resign also.'

Bob T. spoke up angrily. 'What you're suggesting is mutiny. I'll have none of it.'[6]

Far from being mindless killers, as the SAS are invariably portrayed in the media, its personnel have a very highly developed sense of self-preservation, and a very realistic approach to soldiering based on continuous self-assessment and criticism, which led to the adverse comment on the merits of the raid. Others regarded this dissension as close to mutiny, and there was a lively discussion as the news circulated while the men of 6 Troop and 8 Troop queued to draw their weapons from the armoury and climb on to the coaches for the drive to RAF Brize Norton before the long flight to Wideawake. Whilst a few were acquainting themselves with the new satellite communications sets, kindly donated by the Green Berets at Fort Bragg, North Carolina and flown over to London on Concorde, most were preoccupied with the crisis in confidence that had struck the camp, with the majority supporting Jake W. and Moss.

Already demoralised by the loss of these two men, 'B' Squadron's Boat and Air Troops arrived on Ascension to hear the grim news that a disaster had hit their colleagues in 'D' Squadron. A Sea King had been cross-decking men

in relays from HMS *Hermes* to the *Intrepid*, in preparation
for an attack on Darwin and Goose Green, when a large
sea bird, possibly an albatross or a giant petrel, had been
sucked into the helicopter's engine intake. The aircraft had
plunged into the sea between the two ships but, with none
of those on board wearing immersion suits, the bitterly
cold temperature had taken its toll in a very short time.
This was to have been the last flight of the evening, and
on board were some of 19 Troop who had participated
in the Pebble Island raid, plus a few from 'G' Squadron.
Ten men in various stages of shock and hypothermia had
been plucked from the water but twenty others, including
two Squadron sergeant-majors, Carpenter and Gallagher,
and six sergeants (Philip Currass, Sid Davidson, J. Arthy,
Paddy O'Connor, W. J. Hughes and P. Jones), had died.
This was the regiment's biggest single loss since the end of
the Second World War, and as the scale of the tragedy was
absorbed by 'B' Squadron, Ian Crooke received a signal
from Hereford that MIKADO, the raid on Rio Grande,
had been postponed, apparently because an Argentine
radar picket had been discovered off the coast, thereby
extending the radar cover and making the approach of
a pair of Hercules more susceptible to detection. Further
postponements followed until the two Troops were flown
to the Task Force and parachuted in as replacements for
those lost in the Sea King accident.

Meanwhile in Punta Arenas the wreckage of the helicopter, with only the tail assembly intact, had been discovered
by the Carabineiros, having been alerted by a local woods-
man. Although he had heard the helicopter overhead, and
had later seen the flames when the aircrew set it alight, he
had been distracted by a row with his wife and had failed
to report the incident for several hours. The Carabineiros
sent a message to Punta Arenas and the astonished British
Ambassador in Santiago, John Heath, was informed of a
possible crash while the Carabineiros buried the evidence.
He had not been told of the plan to attack Rio Grande and

was anxious to receive instructions from London. A few hours later the airmen emerged on Route 5 and, reassured by the Chilean registration plates on the passing vehicles, surrendered to the Carabineiros. All three insisted that they had been blown off course and had suffered navigational problems while flying a reconnaissance mission, and after some interviews with sceptical Chilean officials they were flown to Santiago on a military transport and received by the consul, John Cummins, who arranged local accommodation for them. The ambassador had politely rejected the President's suggestion that the trio should stay overnight in his official residence, but he agreed to hold a brief press conference on 26 May at the British embassy. The Chileans were particularly anxious to exhibit the airmen, so as to maintain their pretence of neutrality and reassure the Argentinians that the episode had been an authentic helicopter crash, and nothing more sinister which might imply Chilean complicity. Reluctantly, the ambassador agreed, and a short statement was read by Lieutenant Hutchings:

> We were on sea patrol when we experienced engine failure due to adverse weather. It was not possible to return to our ship in these conditions. We therefore took refuge in the nearest neutral country.

While the Spanish translation was issued to the assembled media, the RAF personnel were escorted out of the building's rear entrance and driven to the airport for a scheduled flight to Madrid. Upon their return to Yeovilton they received a short leave, but were soon back with 846 Squadron. After the hostilities all three were decorated.[7]

As soon as they saw their contact, Andy H., they explained how Captain M.'s mission had been compromised, which was the detailed news the SAS had received from the team. Andy H. renewed his discreet efforts to find the missing patrol and, as luck would have it, was eating a meal in a small remote café when two of its members marched in, armed to the teeth. Amid many recriminations, all the team were flown to Santiago where they were hidden in local safe-houses until the hostilities were concluded.

Meanwhile, in Rio Grande, Miguel Pita had been alerted to the approach of the unidentified helicopter that had flown into Argentine airspace from Chile at low altitude, constantly dodging behind hills and dropping into radar dead ground. This was not exactly what Pita and his marines had been expecting, but he was convinced that this incursion represented either the preliminary to a major raid or was itself the evidence of an infiltration by saboteurs. Although the helicopter was seen to return to Chile and disappear, Pita knew that it had either delivered an SAS party or, more likely, had planted a navigation beacon with which to guide the bombers in to the target. Accordingly, 1,200 marines spent three days conducting an intensive search of the entire area, sweeping twenty-five kilometres north of the base and concentrating on the two sites, the Estancia Las Violetas and Sección Miranda, identified by the radar plot as the most likely helicopter landing areas. Two amphibious armoured personnel carriers took troops into the more inaccessible areas, but no trace was found of the intruders, leaving Pita convinced that the SAS had managed to exfiltrate themselves overland. Despite this episode, no reinforcements were drafted into the base, and the prospect of an airborne assault was never considered.

The explanation for the flares spotted by the Sea King pilot, which convinced Captain M. that his mission had been compromised, has been difficult to determine, but there are two possibilities. Although Pita's men never fired on the helicopter, there had been live firing that same night, and perhaps the flares were connected with that exercise. An alternative is the evidence of Captain Washington Barcena, in command of the *Hipolito Bouchard*, who recalls a radar contact in heavy fog on the relevant night.

He had opened up with all his weapons, including his 5-inch guns, but had seen nothing more.

The failure of Captain M.'s mission on 17/18 May made no impact on the Task Force, because the exact nature of the mission was unknown to all except a handful directly involved in *Invincible*'s risky dash to the west under cover of darkness, but the pressure began to mount three nights later as the first landings in San Carlos Water were undertaken, bringing much of the Task Force closer to the islands. The vulnerability of the surface vessels, and particularly the merchantmen, was demonstrated on the afternoon of Tuesday 25 May, when two Super Etendards, flown by Lieutenant-Commander Roberto Curilovic and Lieutenant Julio Barazza, executed a flawless airborne refuelling and approached the Task Force from the north. Having positively identified the location of the Task Force at a hundred miles north-east of Stanley, the two pilots were determined to find either *Hermes* or *Invincible*, and had been warned by their squadron commander, Jorge Colombo, not to bother returning unless they had registered a kill. As Colombo knew, there were only three AM-39s remaining, and each one had to count until the reloads he had requested could be delivered. He also recognised that with the British establishing a beach-head at San Carlos, the war had reached a critical stage. A serious naval loss now could leave the recently landed ground troops stranded and facing a harsh Falklands winter which they could not expect to survive, 8,000 miles from home and 7,000 miles from Gibraltar, the nearest British naval dockyard.

Curilovic and Barazza had been vectored to their Hercules tanker faultlessly, 185 miles north-east of Puerto Deseado, and an hour later – approaching unexpectedly from the north-west – had identified a large radar return on their first 'pop-up'. Both Exocets were launched and

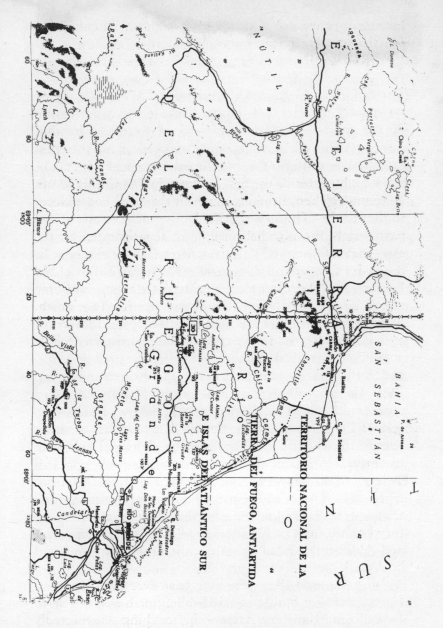

Map showing the eastern coast of Tierra del Fuego. The Estancia Las Violetas can be seen north-west of Rio Grande.

the two airmen dropped down to sea-level and headed for home, the missiles tracking towards the same huge ship. The first warning came from the Type-42 destroyer *Exeter*, recently arrived from her guardship patrol in the Caribbean off Belize, which broadcast an air-raid alert. Then the Type-21 frigate *Ambuscade*, the most northerly surface vessel of the Task Force, spotted the two planes and prompted *Hermes* and *Invincible*, just two miles away, to scramble their decoy Lynx helicopters, packed with chaff and secret electronic wizardry. Finally *Brilliant* picked up the intruders, and all the counter-measures were deployed to deceive the incoming missiles.

Although the pilots believed they had fired at an aircraft carrier, the ship was in fact the SS *Atlantic Conveyor*, a massive 18,000-ton roll-on roll-off container ship chartered from Cunard which had been brought into the middle of the Task Force from the comparative safety of the end of the line of auxiliaries, in preparation for a final dash by night to unload her valuable supplies at the San Carlos landing area. Seconds after the two AM-39s had been launched the Agave radar receiver on HMS *Alacrity* sounded, and the cry of 'Handbrake!' was transmitted across the carrier group, followed moments later by a further warning, 'Ashtray!' to indicate positive identification of an Exocet in flight. All the ships responded instantly, releasing chaff and manoeuvring away from the bearing of the AM-39s, but the *Atlantic Conveyor* had neither chaff nor electronic counter-measures, so that when the first weapon initiated its mid-flight adjustment in trajectory, narrowly missing the *Ambuscade*, its radar locked on to the massive return offered by the container ship's hull. One missile penetrated the hull on the starboard side and detonated, causing a massive fire; the other continued until its fuel was exhausted and fell harmlessly into the sea. On board the *Atlantic Conveyor* the fire spread rapidly, encouraged by secondary explosions caused by the fully-fuelled four-ton trucks packed on one of the decks.

Twelve men were killed, including the master, Ian North, who drowned after he had given the order to abandon ship and had waited until the remainder of his crew left the vessel.

The news of the loss was quickly reported in London, where only relatively few understood its full significance. The Argentines had now expended four of their five AM-39s, so the threat had been reduced to only a single missile. However, it was acknowledged that if the *Atlantic Conveyor* had been selected deliberately this represented a very dangerous change in tactics, for while the radar pickets like the Type-42s were bound to be regarded as expendable so long as they fulfilled the function of a defensive screen, the merchantmen and their cargoes were irreplaceable. Certainly the *Atlantic Conveyor* held a considerable strategic significance, for although she had already cross-decked her fourteen Harriers six days earlier, her holds had contained 18 Squadron's three Chinooks, which represented the Task Force's almost entire heavy lift capability, plus a Lynx and five Wessex helicopters for 848 Squadron. In addition, 11 Field Squadron of the Royal Engineers lost all their stores, including the steel matting that would allow the Harriers to operate from land. Without the equipment, the Harriers would have to continue flying from the two carriers, thereby either placing the ships at risk or limiting the time the planes could fly over the combat zone. However, it was the destruction of the Chinooks, which can carry up to twelve tons of cargo or eighty troops at a time, which was particularly grave, because without them the ground forces would be obliged to walk the forty arduous miles over East Falkland's very worst terrain from San Carlos to engage the enemy at Stanley.[8] Such a delay in a very tight timetable might make all the difference, so the planners looked at alternative methods of moving the soldiers into combat. Their recommendation, a bold seaborne flanking movement to Fitzroy Bay, was to lead to the major setback of the campaign, the loss of the *Sir Tristram* and the *Sir Galahad* on 7 June to bombs dropped by the Argentine Air Force. Fifty-one soldiers trapped aboard the *Sir Galahad* also died, with forty-six injured, making the incident the worst single military loss of the campaign for the British. However, in the meantime, some very special measures were being taken in London to ensure that no further air-launched Exocets reached Jorge Colombo in Rio Grande.

Chapter 8

HEATHROW

The meeting in the Post House Hotel at Heathrow on Sunday, 23 May was brief, and a direct consequence of SIS's determination to tip the balance of the war in the South Atlantic in the Royal Navy's favour. Those present were Alan Rudgwick, Tony Divall and his new case officer, a man who called himself Tony Baynham, and their objective was to deny the Argentines any AM-39 reloads. Their declared target was the Naval Purchasing Commission in Paris, and Carlos Corti in particular. Before this first encounter with his new agent, Baynham had studied Divall's rather large personal file, which had made quite extraordinary reading even for someone of his own military background, with experience of the SAS in the Middle East and well used to handling unusual characters operating on the fringes of legality.

Born in Kent, Divall served in the Royal Marines during the Second World War, and after being demobbed in 1946 he heard through the Royal Marines Association of a British organisation in Germany, known as 'T Force', that was recruiting ex-commandos to hunt suspected Nazi war criminals. Having been interviewed at an office in Victoria by men in civilian clothes, he was offered an assignment of unknown duration with the Control Commission for Germany at a unit based at a villa in the centre of the spa town of Bad Salzuflen, in the British Zone between Dusseldorf and Emden. Divall accepted the post and soon after his arrival he learned that he was now part of the British Secret Intelligence Service. This was to be the start of his career as an SIS officer, graduating from the station's communications department to running agents from the Berlin station, located in a requisitioned mansion on the Rheinbaden-Allee. Soon Divall developed a talent for arranging clandestine exfiltrations across the Soviet Zone and supervising an underground 'railroad' codenamed JUNK, which allowed a two-way traffic of human cargo into Russia. Consignments of gold Swiss watches, much valued by the Soviets, went eastwards, in exchange for people and illegal roubles moving in the opposite direction. Divall supervised five networks, run independently, which were managed by Emil Gruschow, a jeweller with a shop on the Kürfurstendamm; Karl Schaffer, a professional smuggler; Jankiel Zamroczynski, a money-changer; and a travel agent named Korngold. One of his principal men in Berlin was a respected jeweller, Mandel Goldfinger, who operated a ring of smugglers that stretched from Switzerland, where the watches were purchased legitimately, to Germany and the main railway line to Brest-Livotsk, the first large city in the Soviet Union. Based on railwaymen anxious to supplement their income, up to a hundred watches at a time were concealed in ingenious hiding places on trains to avoid the four separate searches conducted along the route, and generated a steady flow of the banned roubles down the pipeline to the West. SIS used the valuable cash to construct an extensive network in the Baltic states, managed from the SIS station in Stockholm. Its agents – dropped on to the beaches after a short clandestine trip across the Baltic, and all volunteers from the NTS organisation of Ukrainian nationalists – needed a plentiful supply of Soviet currency, which SIS believed was put to good use.

Divall's career as an SIS professional sustained a setback in 1955 with the appointment of George Blake to the Berlin station, then relocated in a discreet but secure compound neighbouring the Olympic Stadium. Although Blake was not to confess to his duplicity for a further six years, the station's productivity underwent a marked change during his four-year tour of duty between January 1955 and the summer of 1959. Several operations were compromised in 1956, including the tunnel that had been dug under the border to a conduit carrying the landline cables between the Soviet military headquarters and Moscow. Codenamed PRINCE, the joint CIA/SIS project had provided a wealth of raw intelligence, but the tunnel had to be abandoned when the Soviets discovered it in April 1956, eighteen months after it had come on-line. At the time the Soviet success – which they exploited by holding a press conference underground, in the main shaft surrounded by US manufactured recording equipment – was written off by Allied analysts as sheer bad luck, the result of an unavoidable inquisitive border guard stumbling over something that had made him suspicious. There was no reason to suspect betrayal, or to question the loyalty of George Blake, a trusted senior SIS officer who had been involved in PRINCE from the very earliest planning stage. Only after Blake confessed in April 1961 to his espionage for the KGB, which dated back to his release from Korea in April 1953, did SIS's management realise the devastating scale of his betrayal.

While the Berlin station was experiencing some inexplicable disappointments, Divall had found a new interest: motor-racing. By chance he had bought a sports car from the local Peugeot distributor and learned that the company was an SIS front headed by Dusko Popov, a Yugoslav playboy and former wartime double agent. Like many of SIS's other commercial enterprises, this was used as a conduit for passing currency across the Soviet zone of occupation to help pay for the networks of agents later to be betrayed by George Blake. However, before Blake was exposed as a traitor Divall was posted to London by his station commander, Peter Lunn, in anticipation of another overseas assignment. The offer that emerged, after several months attached to a training unit, was a posting to the

Singapore station, which Divall considered so unattractive that it served to persuade him to resign. No sooner had he done so than he was invited by the legendary SIS handler Harold Shergold to help run Boris Nelk, an important Estonian agent who had recently returned from the Soviet Union via Sweden. Divall agreed to delay his departure to run the case with Ryder Latham, and spent a further two months at a safe-house in Dawson Place, Queensway, preparing the spy for a new mission to Estonia. Together they flew to Helsinki for a rendezvous with Alphons Rebane, an Estonian émigré handling SIS's local operations who followed on a later flight accompanied by Shergold, and then set out across the Gulf of Finland in a fast motorboat for a point on the coast near Juminda. No sooner had the agent clambered into a dinghy for the final stage of his journey back into the Soviet Union than two patrol vessels arrived on the scene and opened fire. Divall only narrowly escaped into international waters, and upon his return was informed that the Estonian was suspected of working as a double agent for the KGB.

Appalled by how close he had come to being sacrificed, Divall confirmed his resignation, on the understanding that he would maintain a loose contact with SIS in the future. This he was able to do easily, because his new career in motor-racing was to be sponsored by Walter Hagen & Co., a German firm based in Krefeld and run by a former British Army officer, Colonel Freddie Archer, and a former Yugoslavian submariner, Eugn Sostaric, who had enjoyed a colourful war as an MI5 double agent operating under the codename METEOR. Although ostensibly an automobile distributor and public relations company, organising promotional events for the Standard Motor Company and its best-selling model, the Vanguard, Walter Hagen & Co. was really a cover for SIS operations into Yugoslavia in support of the Monarchist movement. Divall reported to Guy Bratt at the SIS station in Brussels, who also acted for GINGERBREAD, an SIS network covering most of Germany, Austria, Switzerland and Holland. GINGERBREAD's purpose was to operate as a stay-behind organisation in the event of the Soviets over-running Europe, but when the British embassy in Brussels was burgled and a safe in the SIS station compromised, control of the operation was switched to Vienna. After a year Divall moved to Hamburg and through an acquaintance participated in a very lucrative business transaction, the sale of war-surplus German weapons to buyers representing the FLN rebels in Algeria. At that time Hamburg had become the centre of gun-running to North Africa, and through contact with the entrepreneurs working at the law's periphery he participated in what was subsequently revealed to be the German end of a Chinese procurement programme for its embryonic nuclear industry. Everything that Divall learned he passed on to his current grateful SIS case officer, Peter Lunn.

Between 1961 and 1965 Divall concentrated on an organisation based in Hong Kong, gathering information for SIS's local station concerning China's acquisition of high technology. His agent was a German, Heinz Becker, who knew nothing of Divall's undercover role and – having settled in Hong Kong following tax problems in Hamburg – was running Farbeck, an import–export company in Macao supplying isotopes and semi-conductors to the Chinese in Canton. Although the Chinese expressed an interest in the purchase of heavy water, no deliveries were made, and a couple of Barr & Stroud high-speed cameras, also required for atomic tests, were seized in Hamburg before they could reach China. Thereafter Divall became more widely recognised as an arms dealer, specialising in the sale of surplus stock to African purchasers, particularly in the Congo and Biafra and later – with the financial support of the Verona brothers, Catholic missionaries – to the Anya-Nya rebels in southern Sudan who were based in Uganda.

In 1971 Divall, by now a well-established and valued SIS

source, participated in a plot financed by a wealthy Libyan exile, Umar al-Shalhi, to overthrow Colonel Muammar Qaddafi. By the time Divall learned of the scheme, twenty-five mercenaries had been hired in Toulon and a German-built coastal patrol boat, the *Conquistador XIII*, had been purchased to land an assault team on the coast near Tripoli. Their objective was the main prison, known as the Tripoli Hilton, in which the young British-trained Qaddafi had incarcerated 150 supporters of the ex-King Idris, whom he had deposed in a bloodless coup in September 1969 while the King was on holiday in Turkey. Since then a counter-coup, masterminded from Fort Lamy in Chad by the King's nephew, had been thwarted in February 1970 by poor security and the intervention of Qaddafi's ubiquitous intelligence agency, the General Investigation Division (GID).

Equipped with weapons bought from Omnipol, the obliging Czech national arms company, the men were to slip ashore at night in six inflatable dinghies and blow a hole in the gaol's perimeter wall, allowing the prisoners to escape and help in seizing the capital. The operation was timed to coincide with a revolt in Benghazi and Tripoli, allowing the mercenaries to disappear in their Zodiacs, but in March 1971 – once SIS had been alerted to the plan – the Italian authorities had impounded the *Conquistador XIII* in Trieste on a pretext, before the weapons could be collected from Ploce in Yugoslavia. Apparently both the CIA and SIS had concluded that the West's interests were not served by allowing the raid to proceed, thus forcing the organisers to abandon the project, even though SDECE characteristically had turned a blind eye to the recruitment of the mercenaries in France. Thus the elaborate arrangements made for the procurement of the necessary hardware – complete with an end-user certificate made out to a dealer in Chad, with transport by sea from Ploce to Douala in Cameroon – were abandoned, and Divall's discreet role in the affair remained undetected, even when details emerged in *The Hilton Assignment*, a sanitised account of the affair written by the journalists Patrick Seale and Maureen McConville, with several of the key names changed, which was published in 1973.[1]

Divall's SIS handler during this period was Donald G., who joined SIS at the end of the war. He had served in Paris, Warsaw and Singapore, and by coincidence had known Vinx Blocker when they both served in Santo Domingo in the early 1960s, in the days when SIS ran a network of stations across South America and the Caribbean which was comprehensive enough to rival the CIA's local organisation. Together, Donald G. and Divall had made a formidable team and scored some impressive successes, not least against the Provisional IRA which became a significant priority in April 1970 following the discovery of 500 pistols and 180,000 rounds of ammunition at Dublin airport. The Gardai's Special Branch had intercepted a consignment of weapons worth £30,000 imported from Vienna by a well-known Belfast republican, John Kelly, through a naturalised Irishman of Belgian extraction with a strong background in Flemish nationalism, Albert Luykx; but the episode revealed the apparent complicity of senior members of the Fianna Fáil party, including Charles Haughey, the Minister of Finance, and Neil Blaney, the Minister of Agriculture, who were sacked by the Taoiseach, Jack Lynch. The affair was the source of much embarrassment to the Irish authorities, not least because of the close involvement of an Irish intelligence officer, Captain James Kelly, who had been assigned by Colonel Michael Hefferon – the long-serving Director of Eire's military intelligence branch, G-2 – the task of monitoring the deteriorating situation in Ulster. A senior and experienced officer, Kelly had worked for G-2 continuously since 1960, apart from two years abroad as a United Nations observer on the Israeli border with Syria. On Hefferon's instructions he had undertaken several missions to Belfast to make contact with the Republican movement and to prepare contingency plans for the possibility of a breakdown of civil order. This led him to take the initiative in acquiring enough weapons to train militant members of the minority community in the North, should the necessity arise.[2]

This consignment, the very first purchased abroad by Irish nationalists during the most recent troubles, had been negotiated with Otto Schluter in Hamburg, who arranged for the weapons to be flown into Dublin by Aer Turas, a Dublin-based freight company headed by an ex-RAF pilot, John Squire. Despite the apparent political sponsorship of the transaction, and the official endorsement of G-2's Captain Kelly, the local Special Branch led by Detective Superintendent Fleming intervened and arrested all the participants. At the subsequent trial, held in September 1970, it emerged that Jack Lynch's administration had attempted to distance itself from the activities of the two ministers; the Irish intelligence personnel were described as retired, Kelly having left G-2 a few days before the arms were intended to arrive in Dublin, and Colonel Hefferon conveniently having been replaced as G-2's Director by Colonel Patrick Delaney a few days earlier, having held the post since October 1962. Particularly awkward was the disclosure that the air cargo route had been adopted because a previous attempt by John and James Kelly – to the Dublin docks on the *City of Dublin* – had failed. On that occasion 500 rifles destined for Dundalk had been refused the necessary advance customs clearance, so the scheme – in which the cargo was described as 'mild steel' imported by Welux Limited – was abandoned at the very last moment, leaving just forty bullet-proof vests as the non-lethal cargo. Although the prosecution failed to convict any of the defendants, it was clear from the evidence that the IRA had succeeded in establishing a link with arms dealers on the Continent. John Kelly had served six years of an eight-year sentence in Belfast prison for illegal possession of weapons back in 1956, and had attempted to escape from the Crumlin Road Prison in 1960. His supplier in Hamburg, Otto Schluter, had narrowly escaped a car bomb at the height of the Algerian civil war when SDECE identified him as a source of weapons for the FLN.[3]

The entire affair, which became a *cause célèbre* in the Republic, proved hugely embarrassing for what was left of Jack Lynch's administration, some of his most trusted ministers having been implicated. The Special Branch had intervened in the most timely fashion and the subsequent investigation was assisted by well-informed anonymous letters which kept the local newspapers apprised of the latest developments. The controversy also cast an unwelcome spotlight on G-2's clandestine operations north of the border, the existence of a hitherto unacknowledged covert Special Branch unit working under the personal direction and control of the Secretary of the Justice Department, and the willingness of senior politicians to resort to subterfuge to help the militants in Londonderry and Belfast.

By the end of the trial there had been days of cross-examination, in which Captain Kelly's G-2 colleagues, emerging for the first time from their traditional anonymity and secrecy, contradicted the evidence of government ministers to support Kelly's version of events, namely that the entire project had been officially sanctioned at the highest level. As the evidence mounted of a G-2 deniable operation that had gone horribly wrong, the ineptness of the subsequent cover-up became apparent, ensuring that the jury acquitted all the defendants within an hour of beginning their deliberations. In particular, the Minister of Defence James Gibbons, the prosecution's principal witness, saw his testimony compared unfavourably with a rather different version of events concerning the government's participation which he had given previously to the Dáil. The political fall-out that followed helped to blight Charles Haughey's career, effectively neutered G-2, and ensured Special Branch's primacy. It also provided an example of Southern interference in the affairs of the

Six Counties which made other politicians, sympathetic to republicanism, shy of tangling with the terrorists.[4]

For the first time, SIS was instructed to commence major operations against the Irish extremists, a responsibility hitherto confined to the Security Service in Northern Ireland and the Metropolitan Police Special Branch, neither of which was capable of dealing with the current campaign that was marked in February 1971 by the death of the first British soldier in Belfast, Corporal Robert Bankier of the Royal Green Jackets. Initially SIS concentrated on the Provisional leadership, a tightly knit group all known to the British authorities and led by John Stevenson, a railwayman from North London who had served in the RAF and had received an eight-year prison sentence in England for his part in a raid on an Officer Cadet Corps arms store at Felsted School in Essex in July 1953. While in prison Stevenson learned Gaelic and changed his name to Sean MacStiofain.[5] Another key figure was Joe Cahill, Chief of Staff and former Commander of the IRA's Belfast Brigade, who was sentenced to death in 1942 for the murder of an RUC constable but reprieved to serve only seven and a half years in prison. He had been interned in 1957 and 1971, and became leader of the Belfast Provisionals after the arrest of Billy McKee. When he fled south to escape arrest his place was taken by Seamus Twomey, formerly the manager of a betting shop. Cahill was closely associated with Ruairi O'Braidaigh, the President of Sinn Fein who had escaped from internment at the Curragh in 1958 and led the raid on the Hazelbroucke Barracks, a REME training centre at Arborfield in Berkshire, in August 1953. O'Braidaigh escaped to Ireland after the raid, but the police discovered where the weapons were hidden and three of his companions were arrested and sentenced to life imprisonment.

The first British operation, conducted in London, concentrated on John Kelly, who was lured to a rendezvous with 'ex-Captain Malcolm Randall', supposedly a disgruntled former British Army officer of Arab extraction. Randall met Kelly at Oxford Circus tube station and tried to interest him in buying weapons and his training expertise, but Kelly disengaged after a further meeting in Dublin in which G-2 took a close interest. Convinced Kelly had been tipped off, SIS withdrew 'Randall' and continued with the 'dangles', the coat-trailing exercise intended to entrap senior Republicans and exhaust their funds.

Another of SIS's principal targets was David O'Connell, one of the founders of the IRA's Provisional wing who had been seriously wounded and spent six years in Crumlin Road Prison during the IRA's campaign in 1962. At the age of twenty the young schoolteacher from Donegal had been appointed the IRA's Director of Operations, having proved himself during the January 1957 raid on the RUC barracks at Brookeborough, County Fermanagh. On that occasion two of the IRA gunmen had been wounded, and later died, and O'Connell himself had fled across the border, only to be imprisoned for six months on a charge of refusing to answer questions, a crime under the 1939 Offences Against the State Act. Subsequently O'Connell, now marked with the scars of seven sten-gun bullets on his stomach and missing a knuckle on his right hand, was implicated in an attempt to smuggle weapons from Czechoslovakia to Ireland in October 1971 when a chartered Belgian DC-6 on a flight from Prague – loaded with four tons of bazookas, mortars and grenades packed into 116 wooden crates – was impounded at Schipol Airport.

After Kelly's conviction in September 1970 O'Connell undertook a fund-raising tour of the United States, and spread the word of his interest in buying weapons. This had led to an approach from an American who walked into the headquarters of Sinn Fein above a shop at 2a Kevin Street and offered to supply guns and ammunition to the Provisionals for the remarkably low commission of £500. At the time the Provisionals were reliant on a very poor stockpile, most of the IRA's armoury having been sold a few years earlier to a group of Welsh nationalists. In consequence the movement was handicapped by possession of a wide variety of weapons, but with various batches of ammunition of different calibres and quality. The American, who called himself Freeman, proposed a tempting deal which promised to turn the ill-equipped PIRA in Londonderry into more than a match for the British Army.

Once the cargo had been delivered to Amsterdam it was to be stored in a warehouse rented by a helpful businessman from Cork, and then escorted on the final leg of the journey by boat to Shannon by O'Connell and his young mini-skirted companion, Maria McGuire, who spoke fluent French, German and Spanish. The daughter of a civil servant in the Ministry of Agriculture, McGuire lived with her parents in the Dublin suburb of Churchtown. After graduating from University College, Dublin, she spent three years in Spain, and for a brief period was married to an Englishman in Madrid. Upon her return to Ireland she became an actress and joined the Provisionals, becoming entranced first by Ruairi O'Braidaigh's brother Sean and then by O'Connell.

The plane's pilot, Jean Honweghen, and an American arms dealer based in Luxembourg, Ernst Koenig, were taken into custody on 16 October, but O'Connell and McGuire disappeared, abandoning their rented car at Amsterdam's Central railway station. Pursued by the police, who had found the pair registered in the same hotel room, they travelled to Brussels before catching a train to Rouen and finally Le Havre. When they eventually returned to Ireland, on a scheduled flight from Le Bourget to Cork, O'Connell was questioned briefly by Special Branch officers and released. Later he was elected Vice-President of Sinn Fein.[6]

Financed by American supporters, O'Connell had purchased the weapons from Koenig and produced a forged Department of Trade import certificate identifying the buyer as Wendamond Limited, a company registered in London. In fact SIS had become aware of the transaction as soon as Koenig approached the Czech state arms company, Omnipol, because its representative in Vienna, George Strakaty, had been an SIS source for many years. Run by an SIS case officer, Strakaty had defected from Prague and tried to start a new life in Canada, but later returned to Europe to re-establish a relationship with SIS through Divall. He had been contacted by an arms-dealing acquaintance, Harry Briggs, and as soon as O'Connell opened serious negotiations with Omnipol SIS had tipped off the Dutch authorities. The plane, chartered from Pomair in Ostend, was subsequently released, but the arms remained in Holland. Undaunted by this setback, O'Connell had persevered. But so had SIS.

Early in 1973 Divall heard rumours in Hamburg of a new group anxious to buy weapons, and learned that a former partner, Gunther Leinhauser, had been approached to carry a consignment to Ireland on the SS *Claudia*, the tramp steamer named after his eldest daughter which was registered to the Giromar Shipping Company in Nicosia, Cyprus, and part-owned by Peter Mulak, a former Wehrmacht paratrooper. This news proved to be of exceptional interest to his SIS handler, Donald G., who encouraged Divall to find out more, and Leinhauser confided that the Provisional IRA had already invested $70,000 for an arms purchase through a dealer in Geneva named Simoni, but that he had spent the money paying off his substantial debts. The Provisionals were now pressing Leinhauser for completion of the contact, and Gustav Haller from Cork and David O'Connell – who represented the Provisional Army Council – were due to arrive in Hamburg to oversee the remainder of the transaction. Divall solved Leinhauser's dilemma by flying him to Heathrow where he met Donald G. and arranged the financing of a voyage, via Tunis and Malta, to Tripoli where the *Claudia* was to load a cargo of weapons. Back in Hamburg Haller, whose father Adolf had liaised between the Abwehr and the IRA before the Second World War, went aboard the *Claudia* to protect the PIRA's investment and remained until the ship sailed for Tunis to collect O'Connell and the PIRA's Chief of Staff, Joe Cahill.

Upon her departure the ship's progress was monitored by an RAF Nimrod, and the Irish authorities were alerted to the operation. When the *Claudia* approached County Waterford's coast near Helvick Head it was shadowed by two Irish minesweepers and the *Deidre*, an Irish fishery patrol vessel. However, Leinhauser's German skipper, Hans-Ludwig Flugel, had spotted it on his radar as he was about to rendezvous with a smaller fishing boat manned by two local men, Donald Whelan and Gerard Murphy, and had ordered the crew – a Yugoslav, Bogdan Kessler, a Belgian, Armand Timmermann, and a German cook, Manfred Swoboda – to jettison the cargo. When the *Claudia* was eventually boarded by the Gardai on 28 March 1973, some of the contraband had been dropped overboard, but five tons of arms, including 250 7.65mm Soviet sub-machine guns, 246 bayonets and scabbards, 245 Webley revolvers, 100 anti-tank mines, 24,000 rounds of ammunition, 850 magazines and 500 grenades, plus 300 kilos of gelignite and 48lb of high explosives were recovered. Six men were arrested, including Joe Cahill, who was found aboard the *Claudia* accompanied by Sean Garvey and Gerard Murphy. Cahill was later sentenced to three years' imprisonment for illegal importation of weapons, while Denis McInerney and Sean Garvey received two years each. Charges against the sixth man, a plumber named Gerard Walsh from Dungarvon, were dismissed, and the crew were quietly released – as had been prearranged with Donald G. by Divall and Leinhauser, who had monitored the operation from the safety of a hotel room in London. Mysteriously, David O'Connell, who also had been on board, succeeded in slipping away.

Well-established as an international arms-dealer, with a

string of highly sensitive but successful SIS operations to his credit, in 1975 Divall participated in a deniable operation to supply the UNITA rebels in Angola (led by Jonas Savimbi) with the weapons they had been refused officially. His task was to create a route through Zaire and Zambia into Angola where the guerrillas were operating under the indirect sponsorship of the CIA, the Agency's direct involvement having been inhibited by the terms of the Clarke Amendment. Divall's contact was Jorge Sangumba, UNITA's Swiss-educated foreign minister-designate based in Lusaka, who handled the logistical details and made the reception arrangements in Silva Porto, Angola. The transport was an ex-New Zealand Airways Viscount 807 flown by Dieter Reinhardt and configured to carry up to ten tons of freight, provided by Pearl Air (named after Pearl Airport, Grenada, where it was registered), and the entire arrangement, moving the hardware through Kinshasa and the Grootfontein Rundu airstrip on the South African border with Angola, was completed without any leaks. This was in stark contrast to the media attention given to another scheme, masterminded by the Bulgarians, to provide logistical support to UNITA through South Africa, for use against the Cubans. The principal in this lucrative deal was President Todor Zhivkov's enterprising son-in-law, Ivan Slawkoff, who had negotiated the contract through his mistress, Vera Kelemer, in Vienna. Once exposed in the press, the illicit support for UNITA dried up, and Divall returned to the routine of occasionally passing on items of interest to Century House from the international arms trade. Although Slawkoff emerged from this affair apparently unscathed, his wife, Ludmilla Zhivkova, died soon afterwards in mysterious circumstances.

Soon after alerting SIS to some recruiting in Hamburg for mercenaries to assist in a *coup d'état* in the Maldives, Divall and his wife took a holiday on the Algarve, only to be called to London by Alan Rudgwick for an urgent assignment which was to be supervised by another officer, Tony Baynham. Although Divall had followed the progress of the Falklands conflict with interest, he had never contemplated his own involvement or the crucial role now offered him. Described as a former SAS officer who had served in the Gulf and was now running all Falklands operations, Baynham proposed that Carlos Corti should be enticed into a deal, or a series of deals, that would ensure Argentina failed to acquire any further Exocets. The scheme was not unlike those that had worked so well on the Provisional IRA in the recent past, and SIS proposed to pit the same operational teams against the Argentines. Quite how Divall was to accomplish this was left to his discretion but – very unusually for SIS – it was made clear that on this occasion money was no object and that a stand-by credit amounting to £16m, but rising to £30m, was immediately available, as confirmed in a letter handed over by Baynham in the Waldorf Hotel in London and signed by E. A. M. Lee, Assistant General Manager of the Holt's Whitehall branch of Williams & Glyn's Bank. In effect, Divall was given a free hand and a long pocket to do whatever was necessary to ensure that Argentina received no more Exocets.

His future contact with SIS would be directly to Baynham, who was Alastair S.'s subordinate, in charge of all SIS's Falklands operations. By the end of the meeting Divall's grasp of what had been happening in the South Atlantic was transformed. Having been entirely reliant on the BBC's World Service broadcasts, he had listened with dismay to the news bulletins announcing the growing naval losses, and in particular the sinking of HMS *Sheffield*. However, at the time he had not fully appreciated the terrible significance of the Exocet *vis-à-vis* the Task Force.

Sombre with the burden of his new responsibility, Divall flew home to Hamburg and immediately called Milan to speak to John Dutcher, a tough ex-US Marine of Irish and native American parentage who had seen combat in Korea and Vietnam, and had acted as his partner in several arms contracts – the most recent a consignment of ammunition bought in Taiwan and flown to Sirte in Libya the previous year. That episode had gone unreported, but among Dutcher's closest associates were the former CIA contract officers Frank Terpil and Edwin P. Wilson, who later were to be indicted on charges of the illegal supply of *matériel* to Colonel Qaddafi. Before being hired by Wilson, Dutcher had been running a karate school in Washington DC, but he was to fall out with his employers. Initially hired as Wilson's bodyguard, he later set up a training camp instructing Libyan commandos in the martial arts. Most recently, Dutcher's services had been bought by a Haitian, Roland Magliore, to recruit mercenaries for a coup he intended to mount against Jean-Claude 'Baby Doc' Duvalier. A former lieutenant in Haiti's army, Magliore's uncle had been president of Haiti between 1950 and 1956, and this was not the first time he had schemed to rid the island of the Duvaliers, but the plot collapsed anyway. Although Dutcher's past connection with Wilson made him a sensitive member of an SIS operation, and caused Divall's SIS handlers some disquiet, the need to have Divall operational in Paris outweighed the reservations. As Divall pointed out, he was a technician, not an actor, and he required Dutcher to adopt an entirely authentic role, that of an apparently neutral entrepreneur whose background and credentials could be verified without any elaborate charade.

After a short flight from Italy Dutcher was briefed by Divall at the Sheraton Hotel in Frankfurt, and it was agreed that the American should make contact with Carlos Corti without delay. Initially it was hoped that Dutcher, as a *bona fide* arms dealer with authentic credentials from a reputable firm in Milan, might interfere with whatever scheme Marcus S. Stone had prepared, but at their first meeting in Corti's offices in Paris, it became clear that Stone had disappeared without trace and his telephone and telex in Los Angeles had been disconnected. Dutcher strongly suspected that part of the vanishing act had been the removal of a large deposit paid for some non-existent Exocets, apparently to a bank in Amsterdam, because it was evident that Corti had taken on the role of a victim and was now willing to pay an even greater premium for AM-39s. His quoted offer, of $1m for the immediate delivery of each missile, was more than double the retail value of the weapon, itself a sign of his desperation. Having gained Corti's confidence, Dutcher undertook to test the market for him and see what might be available on the international black, white and 'grey' arms market which he knew so well. Apparently Corti, stung once by a con-man, was now very willing to take on the more experienced Dutcher as an intermediary, and the American immediately instructed his firm in Milan to circulate his list of contacts on Corti's behalf, expressing an interest in air-launched Exocets. Delighted with what had been accomplished in such a short time, Divall reported Dutcher's progress to Baynham over a celebratory lunch at the Waterside Inn at Bray, and then returned to Hamburg. The following day he flew to Frankfurt to meet Tony Baynham at the airport's Sheraton Hotel and introduce him to Dutcher. At this conference Divall obtained Baynham's consent to a strategy of buying in any available AM-39s, ostensibly for further sale to Corti but actually to ensure they were diverted elsewhere at the critical moment. The tactics were agreed with a bottle of champagne, Dutcher and Baynham arranging to meet again in Milan. In the meantime, to guarantee the transport and exercise complete control over the delivery of any purchases, Divall hired Wolfgang Wohlmuth, a German ex-Pearl Air manager based in Frankfurt with an unrivalled knowledge of air traffic regulations and ways of circumventing them, with whom he had worked in Angola. With Wohlmuth's approval, Divall took an

option on chartering a freight-configured Caravelle from
his Liberian registered airline, Coastal Airways, to shift
the Exocets at short notice to England if circumstances
dictated, or to be used as bluff should Corti need any
persuasion that Dutcher was not operating another sting.

The Milan firm was an entirely legitimate company
owned by an Italian aristocrat, and as soon as the news
flashed across the arms market the offers started pouring
in, the first being one from Lisbon, where an airline pilot
with good contacts in the Gulf suggested Qatar might have
four Exocets available for $500,000 each. A second came
from the Centro Studi Transporti Missilistici, a vehicle
for the Rome-based dealer Glauco Partel, an engineer
who had specialised in rocket technology and acquired
a reputation for putting together interesting arms deals
with a Syrian, Henry Arsan. Their association dated back
to 1977, when Arsan's company, Stibam SA, had rented
office accommodation in the Banco Ambrosiano building
in Milan, and more recently they had benefited from the
large number of arms transactions which followed the
Soviet invasion of Afghanistan and the Iran–Iraq war.
By 1982 Stibam SA had opened branches in Chiasso,
Frankfurt, Barcelona, New York and, most significantly
for SIS, Buenos Aires. Thus Dutcher was satisfied that
any approach from Partel was likely to be connected
with Stibam's interests, which were known to be linked
to the Argentine Junta. He was also aware of a slight
complication, that Arsan was widely believed to operate
under a measure of protection from some American federal
agency, possibly the Drug Enforcement Agency, which in
turn co-operated closely with the CIA.

While Dutcher screened the proposals, Divall recruited
another agent, Gunther Leinhauser, the Franco-German
who had participated in the *Claudia* coup, and had
good connections with the French DST and with Colonel
Massimo Pugliese, the head of the Italian Security Service,
SID. Following the *Claudia* affair Leinhauser had moved

to Paris and acquired a new ship, the *Natalya*, registered in Panama, which enabled him to keep in contact with the arms-dealing market, and maintain his links with SISMI, the DGSE and the DST, which provided him with a rent-free apartment. As soon as Leinhauser was indoctrinated into the project, he extracted a tentative tender from a contact he identified only as 'Alex' who could lay his hands on six AM-39s at a price of $1.3m each. Simultaneously another of Divall's friends, the veteran journalist Anthony Terry, rang to alert him to the latest rumour circulating in the nether-world of the international arms dealers. Terry had worked for years as a staff reporter for the *Sunday Times*, and served in Germany for SIS after his release from a wartime prison camp where he was sent following his capture on the St Nazaire raid in March 1942. According to Terry, who was awarded the Military Cross for his part in the St Nazaire operation, up to twenty Exocets had disappeared while in transit between France and Spain. Terry's tip – which had come from a former Free French *résistant* judged to be dependable – was promptly relayed to Baynham by Divall, as Terry had temporarily given up his direct link with SIS because of some disagreement. Nevertheless, Terry was held in high regard at Century House, where it was acknowledged that his range of contacts, which included Jacques Mitterrand of Aerospatiale and the French arms dealer Georges Starkmann, was both impressive and reliable.[7]

Apart from a few vague feelers from dealers holding assorted aircraft and Mirage and Skyhawk parts, the first positive offer made by Dutcher to Corti originated from Baghdad through an unnamed Iraqi sheikh and General Kadry Osman Badr. As Dutcher told the story, between twenty and twenty-five AM-39s were available for $1m each. Dutcher was sufficiently convincing to ensure that Corti was kept in a state of constant anticipation.

When General Badr's pitch appeared to lapse, the Partel offer looked the most promising, for he had a reputation for procuring the impossible. Most recently, in 1982, he had despatched a Swiss associate, Richard Aeschbach, to Baghdad with a proposal to supply the government with a quantity of Plutonium, Uranium-2328 and Uranium-239, but the sale had never materialised. His regular partner in Zurich was a Swiss, Gerhard Hallauer, and together they operated through a bank in Lugano which was to broker an arrangement in which thirty Exocets, allegedly stored in a warehouse in France, could be purchased for $30m upon presentation of a $10m performance bond. Although the suspicion was that Partel's Exocets were the Aerospatiale production allocated to Peru, the front-men handling the negotiating were a pair of Australians, H. Eugene Bartholomeusz and Ed Williams. Although little was known about Williams, his partner had a chequered past. In 1975 he was convicted of smuggling 1.5 kilos of 97 per cent pure Thai heroin into Hawaii and sentenced to three years' imprisonment. Later he was implicated in a scheme to sell three nuclear weapons to Syria, and was also associated with the 1980 collapse of the Nugen Hand Bank in Sydney, a scandal that was still under investigation but appeared to show that the bank had been deeply involved in laundering drug money in the Far East.

Knowing Bartholomeusz's unpromising past, Dutcher demanded inspection facilities to verify the existence of the weapons and have them tested, but while the negotiations continued a difficulty arose regarding the vital end-user certificate required to move the hardware out of France. The complication was the introduction of Carlo Villaviencio, a well-known end-user trickster, so a meeting of all the parties, including Baynham masquerading as an Irishman, was arranged in the Hilton Hotel at Orly.

The gathering proved inconclusive, partly because Hallauer seemed reluctant to allow the inspection to proceed, but also because Leinhauser revealed a previously unknown dimension to the affair: the DST had learned of an illicit plan to remove thirty Exocets from the Aerospatiale factory and had decided to mount a surveillance operation to monitor events and to arrest those involved. Nevertheless Corti continued to believe that the deal was proceeding, and was still negotiating as the news from his naval colleagues about the situation in the Falklands looked more bleak. Indeed, Corti was still attempting to rescue the deal on the day of the final surrender, on 14 June.

Chapter 9

HAMBURG

Hamburg quickly became the unlikely focus for one part of the intelligence war for the Falklands, partly because the Argentine Navy had ten ships awaiting completion and SIS was anxious to monitor their progress, but mainly because the Argentine Purchasing Commission had moved from its office in Vauxhall Bridge Road, conveniently close to the anonymous block which accommodated SIS's London Station and telephone intercept centre, to a building directly opposite the Blohm & Voss shipyard. One of Divall's tasks had been to acquire details of the property so that listening devices could be inserted into the rooms where conversations of a sensitive nature were likely to be held. Since the agents responsible for building management were British, Divall was able to complete this task with relative ease.

Rather more complicated was the effort made to monitor the Argentine attempt to buy Exocets through Lima. Although the French had prevaricated about completing the Peruvian order, the situation had become entangled with the financial disaster which overtook the Banco Andino, whose directors were facing increasingly skilful inquisitions from inspectors appointed by the Bank of Italy. Publicly, the Ambrosiano collapse had led to the bank being put into administration and the appointment of the respected auditors Coopers & Lybrand to prepare all future accounts. However, behind the scenes there was turmoil, with huge sums borrowed by the Banco Ambrosiano being channelled through Monte Carlo to the Banco Andino, which in turn had made loans to a web of companies, the largest being Nordeurop Establishment in Liechtenstein and Astolfine SA in Panama. In just eight months in 1980 sixteen loan transactions amounting to $348m had been approved by Andino and, according to the Vatican Bank in a document lodged in August 1981, these companies were under the control of the IOR. However, despite this 'letter of comfort', the financial position of the companies was dire; debts totalled £907m, of which Andino had supplied $852m, with an additional $55m funded directly by Ambrosiano from Milan. In reality, the Banco Andino was nothing more than a conduit for Ambrosiano's siphoned cash, and its ownership was concealed behind a complex series of share transactions. For example, far from being a significant stockholder, the Peruvian Banco de la Nación had acquired 2 per cent of Andino, but had paid for it with a loan financed by a deposit from Andino. Indeed, although superficially Andino's loan portfolio looked impressive, the majority of the deals were with front companies registered in Panama, which were also part of the same network of 'ghost' corporations ultimately under the control of Licio Gelli. Thus the books of each component looked sufficiently legitimate to meet the minimal standards required for offshore businesses operating outside the jurisdiction in which they were supposed to be regulated. To compound the challenge to auditors, Andino held its board meetings abroad, the first having been convened in Lausanne in November 1979.[1]

The Banco Andino's first appearance in October 1979 coincided with the fall of Anastasio Somoza, the Nicaraguan dictator whose family owned a quarter of the country's real estate. Calvi's Banco Comercial had operated in Managua since October 1977 under the management of Anastasio's cousin, Joaquin Sacasa, and had made numerous loans to

Somoza and his family, but the real business operated out of Nassau. As well as his home in the Bahamas, Calvi acquired a ranch in Nicaragua, and two passports, one of them diplomatic. Although Calvi had shrewdly arranged loans to Somoza's political opponents, and the Sandinistas made no effort to revoke the Banco Comercial's licence, it is likely that Andino's principal function was to take over Managua's role as a convenient conduit for siphoning Ambrosiano cash. Andino's Peruvian licence was granted by the superintendent of banking, who happened to be President Terry's brother-in-law, and among its directors was Alvaro Menese Diaz, the president of the Banco de la Nación. As for the original funding for the bank, its capital of $12.5m had been provided by Banco Ambrosiano Holdings, the main bank's offshore investment company registered in Luxembourg. By the end of October 1979 virtually all of the Banco Comercial's business, mainly loans to companies that were technically insolvent, had been switched into Andino's books. However, Calvi's skill in moving assets around by share purchases and back-to-back loans ensured that outwardly Andino looked respectable, and certainly not the ticking time-bomb waiting to detonate that it really was.

Although the Banco Andino had no overt Argentine connection, even through the web of Ambrosiano's Nicaraguan and Panamanian corporations, in 1980 Roberto Calvi had opened another subsidiary, the Banco Ambrosiano de America del Sud, with impressive headquarters in Buenos Aires. Also accommodated in the same building was Gelli's close friend Admiral Emilio Massera, formerly the head of the Argentine Navy and only recently resigned from the ruling military Junta. Gelli's relationship with the navy dated back to his friendship with Juan Perón, when the deposed leader was exiled temporarily to Spain, and to the sale of six frigates in 1976, purchased from the Cantieri Navali Riunita, the Italian state-owned shipbuilder. The significance of Ambrosiano's expansion into South America was that the market was relatively unregulated, and what made the strategy unusual was that Ambrosiano was by then one of the largest banks in Italy, but without a branch in either New York or London which would have brought the organisation under the scrutiny of the local regulators. Instead Calvi preferred to operate in the Caribbean, working from a home on the Lyford Cay estate in the Bahamas, where he had permanent resident status, running the locally registered Banco Ambrosiano Overseas, and through Panama, then acquiring notoriety as a money-laundering playground. Quite possibly Calvi's preference for the Banco Andino as a suitable replacement for the Banco Comercial in Managua was the initial reluctance of the authorities in Buenos Aires, perhaps his first choice, to scrutinise his choice of directors and reject some of his Argentine nominees on the grounds that they had insufficient banking experience.

Calvi, arrested in May 1981 and sentenced in July to four years' imprisonment and a fine of 16 billion lire, was released on bail pending an appeal, his position as Ambrosiano's chairman unchanged. Licio Gelli had vanished to South America in March, having abandoned a treasure trove of compromising documents in his office at Castiglion Fibochi to be found by the *Guardia di Finanzia*. Among them were the membership records of the notorious Propaganda 2 masonic lodge known as P-2, listing 962 names which were to hold Italy spellbound for years afterwards and initiate dozens of investigations. P-2's tentacles included much of the hierarchy of the Italian establishment, not to mention businessmen, diplomats, politicians and civil servants, among them forty-three Members of Parliament and three cabinet ministers. Also compromised were some of the most senior members of the security and intelligence establishment, such as General Guilio Grassini, head of the civilian security service SISDE, and his military intelligence counterpart, General Giuseppe Santovito, director of SISMI. Indeed, according to evidence submitted to one of the official P-2 inquiries, Gelli was regarded as a valued asset by SISDE, which appeared to have given him a measure of protection in the past. Even without SISDE's assistance, Gelli's papers revealed him to be extraordinarily well-connected, with fifty-two Carabinieri officers shown as affiliated to P-2, together with thirty-seven from the supposedly incorruptible *Guardia di Finanzia*.

The impact of Calvi's arrest undermined confidence inside the Banco Ambrosiano and its Latin American subsidiaries, even though the outside world continued to be impressed by the bank's reported performance. Three senior directors all based in Ambrosiano's Via Clerici headquarters in Milan – Filippo Leoni, Giacomo Botta and Carlo Costa – resigned from their posts in the South American banks, and the general manager of the Banco Andino, Giorgio Nassano, flew to Milan from Lima to confer with Calvi and demand assurances that Andino's Panamanian loans, which now amounted to nearly $1 billion, could and would be repaid. Nassano threatened to resign unless he received some guarantees, and was to be satisfied with one of IOR's 'letters of comfort', dated 1 September 1981. Since then Andino's situation had deteriorated markedly, although the true position was masked from external regulation and supervision by its offshore status. The Bank of Italy could not exercise any audit responsibility over an institution incorporated overseas, and Ambrosiano's control was managed through a supposedly entirely separate entity, Banco Ambrosiano Holdings, based in Luxembourg. Thus as Andino went into a downward spiral towards bankruptcy, accelerated by the mounting dollar interest incurred by the dubious Panamanian debts, only a handful of people realised what was really happening, for in January 1982 the Banco Ambrosiano published excellent trading results for the previous year. However, these did not deter Nassano from making a further visit to Calvi at the end of January, in which he set a deadline of 13 June for repayment of the Panamanian debt, the date on which the IOR's letters of comfort expired. Calvi undertook to honour the commitment, but he had run out of money and the pressure was escalating. In February Bank of Italy inspectors arrived in Lima and tried in vain to gain access to Andino's books, but received no co-operation from the local authorities. Another anxiety was the appointment by the Milan stock exchange of the international accountants Coopers & Lybrand to conduct an audit, in compliance with the much stricter regulations of the open market on which the bank's shares were to be traded. Hitherto the stock had been traded on the so-called 'restricted market' which had allowed Calvi and his predecessors to manipulate the share price, with the bank currently engaged in an illicit support scheme, buying its own stock, that was to cost $40m. With full listing scheduled for May, the bank was heading for much greater external supervision and compliance.

Gelli's disappearance as a fugitive and the revelations concerning P-2 were only part of the unfolding crisis. On 27 April Calvi's deputy chairman, Roberto Rosone, was the target of attempted murder when he was shot in the legs outside his apartment in Milan, but his putative assassin – subsequently identified as Danilo Abbruciati, a very well-known figure in Rome's leading crime family – was shot dead by security guards. Quite why Abbruciati, who was more used to hiring gunmen than handling weapons himself, should have tried to kill Rosone remains a mystery, but the dead man was closely associated with businessmen who had been recipients of Ambrosiano's largesse. Rumours began to circulate that perhaps Calvi had orchestrated the elimination of his own deputy to conceal the deepening crisis.[2]

Calvi's solution to Ambrosiano's financial decline was the bank's flotation on the Milan stock exchange in May, Andino's status having been enhanced by brokering the Exocet deal. However, the crisis of confidence in Calvi led to a collapse in Ambrosiano's share price as soon as trading opened. As the stock plunged, the Bank of Italy delivered an ultimatum to the directors, in a letter addressed to each individually dated 31 May. It contained a demand for details of all loans made by the Ambrosiano subsidiaries in Lima, Nassau and Nicaragua, and the threat to make the directors personally liable for compliance. Calvi received his letter on Friday, 4 June, having sent his wife and son to Washington DC and his daughter to Switzerland, and on the following Monday faced fourteen members of the Ambrosiano board who confronted him with the contents of a dossier compiled by the Bank of Italy in which it was alleged that the bank was imperilled by undeclared debts of $1,800m incurred by the foreign subsidiaries. Dismayed by the lack of support from his fellow directors, but still clinging to his post, Calvi flew to Rome in a private plane on Thursday afternoon and was dropped by his driver at his apartment on the Via Collegio Capranica, in the city centre. When the same driver arrived to collect him as arranged early on Friday morning to take him to a meeting at the Vatican, Calvi had disappeared. In fact he had stayed the night at a friend's home, taken Alitalia's scheduled midday flight from Fiumicino to Venice and then rented a car for the journey to Trieste.

Later the same evening, having met friends at the Hotel Savoy Excelsior, he slipped across the border to Klagenfurt using a forged Italian passport giving his first name as 'Gian', with his surname altered to 'Calvini' by the addition of two extra letters. After the weekend, spent at the home of friends, he moved on to a hotel at Innsbruck and then to one in Bregenz, close to the Swiss frontier. On 15 June, soon after the news of the formal Argentine surrender in the Falklands was announced, he flew in a chartered jet to Gatwick accompanied by his bodyguard, Silvano Vittor, having told the British pilot that they were Fiat executives. During the crucial period Calvi spent in Austria, between his arrival in the early hours of Saturday 12 June and his flight to Gatwick three days later, he made dozens of telephone calls across the world and held an important meeting at Bregenz with a well-known Swiss arms dealer, Hans Kunz.

Once in London Calvi checked into a rather shabby service flat, 881 Chelsea Cloisters, Sloane Avenue, organised by the same businessman, Kunz, who had also arranged the flight to England. He shaved off his moustache and apparently started to raise $1,000m over the telephone by selling shares in Ambrosiano owned by a Panamanian holding company.

In Calvi's absence Andino's deputy chairman, Angelo de Bernardi, flew to Milan to explain the bank's indebtedness, but it was clear that the IOR's 'letter of comfort' he produced was rather less than a legally enforceable indemnity, which meant the end for Ambrosiano, a conclusion compounded by Giacomo Botta's revelation that Andino could not avoid defaulting on a loan of $15m due for repayment by the end of the month. Archbishop Paul Marcinkus of the IOR declined to acknowledge the Vatican's responsibility for Andino's predicament, and resigned his Nassau directorship of Banco Ambrosiano Overseas, and on Thursday 17 June ten of the bank's board of fifteen directors met and voted to go into liquidation immediately, admitting a deficit of $1,200m. The bank's stock, already plummeting by the hour, was suspended and a temporary commissioner from the Bank of Italy was appointed to take control. That evening, as word of the bank's failure spread within the hour among the 4,200 employees, Graziella Corrocher, Calvi's devoted 55-year-old spinster secretary, threw herself out of a fourth-floor window.

Precisely what happened in London meanwhile remains unclear, but Calvi's body was found hanging from a yard of nylon rope attached to scaffolding under the northern span of Blackfriars Bridge at dawn on Friday, 18 June, his bodyguard having taken the first flight of the morning to Vienna. By mid-morning details of the corpse with the passport of Gian Roberto Calvini had been circulated by Interpol telex, and later the same day the Italian police responded with the suggestion that Calvini might be Calvi. Certainly the passport was a counterfeit, the authentic original bearing the same serial number having been issued to a resident of Naples. This transformed what hitherto had been regarded as an unsuspicious death into a matter for the CID. The detective inspector on duty that evening at the City of London station at Bishopsgate was John White, so he took charge of the investigation at Snow Hill and arranged for the Italian police to formally identify the body the next day.

Once the body was confirmed as that of the fugitive banker Roberto Calvi, speculation about the bizarre circumstances of his death began. In his pockets were £47 in sterling, $7,400 in cash and 58,000 lire, together with two Patek Philippe watches . . . and ten pounds of bricks. But how had the dead man got to the bridge in the middle of the night, and where were the possessions, such as his briefcase and address book, from which he was never parted? What had happened to Calvi's most treasured possessions, his two Nicaraguan passports, one of which gave him diplomatic status? Why had the rather stout banker, aged sixty-two, chosen such an inaccessible spot to kill himself? Was there any significance in the selection of Blackfriars Bridge, given the strong masonic connections of Blackfriars, which was also the name of a British masonic lodge? Was there any symbolic significance in the bricks found in Calvi's pockets and down the front of his trousers, or the immersion of his feet in the Thames as the tide rose? If the death had not been suicide, why had his murderers taken such extraordinary risks to commit the crime in so public a place?

A detective with more than a dozen years of experience in the City of London CID, John White conducted a meticulous investigation. Although the City Police have no need for a permanent murder squad, but maintain a large company fraud department and specialise in white-collar crime, White had participated in other murder inquiries including the major investigation that followed the shooting of a security guard at the *Daily Mirror* building in Holborn. At the outset of a case that was to last for the rest of his career, White supervised a thorough forensic examination and matched the bricks found on Calvi's body with similar rubble on a derelict site 300 metres from Blackfriars Bridge. Analysis of soil found in Calvi's handkerchief and grit taken from inside his shoes suggested that the businessman had visited the unfenced open area, and had scuffed and split the soles of his leather shoes on the uneven ground. Medical evidence gathered during the autopsy, including the characteristic 'PK' damage to the blood vessels of the retina, was consistent with asphyxiation, and microscopic examination of the nylon rope revealed it to be about four or five years old, and covered with algae. On a subsequent tide further lengths of similar rope were found tangled on the scaffolding, having been washed downstream.

Unusually, despite the widespread publicity and appeals made in the London taxi newspapers, no witnesses came forward to explain how Calvi had reached Blackfriars Bridge, but a reconstruction demonstrated that it would have been difficult to approach the scaffolding from the river by boat. Accordingly, the police concluded that Calvi, who knew his way around London from his frequent visits, had probably strolled along the Embankment from Chelsea to the City, had reached the empty site and then walked back to where his body was eventually found. This suicide scenario depended upon Calvi's state of mind at the time, but unfortunately the police were unable to establish precisely who he had spoken to before he died. The old-fashioned central switchboard at Chelsea Cloisters had kept no log of incoming calls put through to his flat by the operator, and there was only a meter to record the number of telephone units dialled. The total of 463 indicated that Calvi had placed at least one long-distance call before he left the flat for the last time, sometime around midnight on Thursday 17 June, and perhaps this had enabled him to learn of the catastrophe that had befallen his bank, and of the death of his secretary. According to the witnesses questioned by White, Calvi was not seen after a brief visit to meet friends at the Queen's Arms, a pub in nearby Draycott Avenue. Allegedly he had been depressed and anxious to find better accommodation, but no exact time could be put on his disappearance from Chelsea Cloisters.

The circumstances of Calvi's strange death were the subject of an inquest which, influenced by the lack of any forensic evidence indicating the use of drugs or violence, returned a verdict of suicide on 23 July. The distinguished Home Office pathologist, Professor Keith Simpson, had examined the body and estimated the time of death at within two or three hours of 2 a.m., concluding that this had been a case of 'deliberate self-suspension' – the second most common method of male suicide, after drug overdose. Given the fact that Calvi had once attempted to slash his wrists while in gaol in Italy, it seemed not improbable that, notwithstanding the absence of a suicide note, he had made a more determined effort to kill himself as he faced the certainty of financial ruin and a long prison sentence. However, the jury's decision was quashed the following year after lengthy investigation conducted by the international security consultants Kroll Associates and on an appeal launched by the dead man's family. A second inquest, held in June 1983, reconsidered much of the forensic and other evidence and gave an open verdict, making the mystery as baffling as ever but leaving plenty of room to reconstruct some of what had happened. According to Calvi's wife and daughter, to whom he frequently spoke by telephone during the last days of his life, the banker felt threatened but also expressed the view that he was on the brink of pulling off a deal big enough to transform the bank's fortunes. As the Banco Andino was at the very heart of Ambrosiano's troubles, and was also the lynchpin to the Argentine Exocet purchase, it is not unreasonable to link the two and suggest that Calvi may have done the same. The question that arises concerns the extent to which SIS exercised any influence over these events.

There is a perfectly credible scenario in which the British authorities – whose determination to prevent any more Exocets falling into Argentine hands cannot be doubted – intervened on two levels to ensure the transaction never took place. The first was through the City of London to derail Ambrosiano's refinancing and to undermine the group of international banks put in place to keep Ambrosiano afloat. There was a sizeable British participation in the consortium, not least a $40m loan from the Midland Bank in 1980 to Banco Ambrosiano Holdings in Luxembourg, and SIS has always enjoyed considerable influence in the City by virtue of the very large number of SIS officers who retire at the age of fifty-five and pursue a second career in merchant banking. There is scarcely a bank within the square mile which does not employ a 'former diplomat' whose *curriculum vitae*, upon closer examination, identifies him as having been one of 'the Friends', and the drift from Century House to the City was at its height during the late 1970s and early 1980s, sponsored by men such as George Young, the SIS Vice-Chief who joined Kleinwort Benson in 1961, and Frank Steele, a legendary figure from the Cold War who followed in 1975. In subsequent years their subordinates joined Hambro's, Morgan Grenfell, Lazards, Barings and Samuel Montagu. In addition, SIS has actively assisted its retirees to find jobs in the security departments of the larger institutions, and has been so successful that it almost has a monopoly among the larger multinationals based in London. SIS business connections have always been strong, and date back to the Second World War when SOE's senior management was drawn almost exclusively from City institutions. Thereafter numerous senior City figures such as Sir Kenneth (later Lord) Keith of Hill Samuel maintained a close relationship with SIS, into which SOE was absorbed in 1945, thus enabling 'the Friends' to protect what subsequently has been described as the nation's 'economic well-being' and to be particularly well informed about British trade interests overseas.

This manifested itself in the equivalent of the CIA's famous 'directed traveller' programme, in which business-men visiting target countries were invited to undertake clandestine tasks while on trips abroad, or to attend debriefing sessions upon their return. Greville Wynne, who acted as a courier for the GRU spy Colonel Oleg Penkovsky in 1962, maintained his cover as an innocent businessman until his release from prison in Moscow in 1964. His more modern successor, Paul Henderson of Matrix Churchill, supplied invaluable information from Eastern Europe and latterly Iraq until his exposure during a misconceived criminal prosecution in 1992. Throughout the Cold War almost every British traveller who made regular journeys behind the Iron Curtain acquired a contact with either SIS, which operated for many years from a front office accommodated in a suite in Artillery Mansions, Victoria Street, or the Security Service's physical security branch. The rule was that each approach to a member of staff had to be approved by the company's chairman, and the actual recruitment of an individual often occurred under the guise of a security briefing arranged to warn businessmen of the potential hazards of working in Eastern Bloc countries. The system proved extremely useful and was facilitated by the circulation of two booklets published by MI5, entitled *Their Trade is Treachery* and an updated version, *Treach-ery is Still Their Trade*, in which case histories of Soviet 'honey-traps' are described for the benefit of those who might merit the attention of the KGB and its surrogates. A large proportion of firms trading abroad have a liaison with MI5, and every organisation engaged in classified contracts has a permanent relationship which extends to advice concerning physical security and the screening of employees. Whilst this is intended to strengthen security procedures within particular companies, it also provides a useful opportunity for agent handlers to cultivate potential sources. Similarly, the CIA maintains a large 'domestic contacts' branch for the sole purpose of building a network of sources along the lines so well established by the French DGSE's structure of 'honourable correspondents'.

It was also common practice for both SIS and the CIA to place their own personnel under commercial cover consciously provided by companies trading abroad, the salaries of those nominees being reimbursed in full by the relevant agency. The CIA maintains a large Central Cover Staff within the Directorate of Operations to supply its officers with authentic posts overseas, within legitimate companies, from which they can work undetected as intelligence officers.

Bearing in mind SIS's many interests in the City and its traditionally close but confidential relationship with the Bank of England, it is highly likely that at the very least 'the Friends' were in a position to bring the Banco Andino's troubled balance sheet to the attention of the Italian authorities. Certainly it would have been far from abnormal for the Governor of the Bank of England, as chairman of the Committee of London Clearing Banks, to offer the chairman of Britain's largest bank some guidance regarding a dubious credit risk abroad. Given SIS's past association with consortium banks, institutions created by other banks like the Orion Bank, it may have had a hand in obstacles Ambrosiano experienced while trying to obtain new financial support. The question of whether the pressure was applied elsewhere is a moot one. Certainly SIS has had a marked Roman Catholic influence, with several SIS directors being senior members of the church, a characteristic which can be seen among the disproportionately high number of SIS officers in the

Knights of Malta, a club drawn exclusively from the upper social echelons of the Catholic laity. SIS has also enjoyed considerable leverage with the Vatican, dating back to a discreet but highly successful investigation of KGB penetration of the cardinals conducted by the late Nicholas Elliott. Could SIS have played a role in the IOR's decision not to revalidate the 'letters of comfort' granted to the Banco Andino, which proved to be the catalyst for the collapse of the Banco Ambrosiano? If so, one can be certain that the paper-trail, if any, would have been concealed very swiftly.

Conspiracy theorists might be tempted to draw conclusions from the withdrawal of the Midland Bank from a consortium intended to inject funds into the Banco Ambrosiano, an event which in retrospect can be seen to have been a catalyst for the final collapse. Accepting SIS's long-standing relationship with the City's merchant banks, could the organisation have influenced a major clearing bank like the Midland? Certainly there is a temptation to make the inference, especially as the Midland has a preference for appointing senior Establishment figures; the most recent Chairman, the retired head of the Home Civil Service, Lord Armstrong, is a prominent example. However, the proposition comes unstuck when one examines how inter-bank trading is conducted. At the relevant time, at the end of 1981, loans to projects where the lead syndicating bank was Italian were the subject of enormous care because the country was regarded as bankrupt, and known in banking circles as 'off cover', with even the state bank experiencing difficulty in meeting its obligations. No loan for the purpose of propping up a single institution would have been contemplated in 1982, and especially not a bank with Ambrosiano's reputation, unless it was accompanied by the appropriate security or collateral.

The Midland, of course, is known as 'the bankers' bank', and has an unrivalled international reputation which is supported by more than 12,000 individual accounts held by other banks. Ambrosiano was just such a bank, but deals in excess of its day-to-day inter-bank trades, honouring letters of credit and other instruments, would have required the sanction of two separate internal credit committees before being agreed. Ambrosiano's actual limit remains a commercial secret but is unlikely to have exceeded $7m, so the consortium in which Calvi had placed so much faith would have been the subject of intense scrutiny from the Midland's regional general manager, the ten or twelve members of the International Credit Committee and finally the Domestic Credit Committee before achieving the required 'following fair wind' sanction. Altogether, Ambrosiano's application would have undergone five or six different screenings before reaching the credit committees, which suggests that it offered back-to-back support from deposits to have had any hope of success, for the Midland would never have made an open loan to Ambrosiano. In short the Midland, then headed by the oil-man Sir David Barren, would have rejected the Ambrosiano on purely commercial grounds without any encouragement from Century House. While SIS is not averse to promoting its ubiquitous image, there was never any need to nudge the Midland, which had an exposure, together with sixteen other banks, on the 1980 loan. The scheduled repayment, of $5.7m plus $3m in interest, was due in July 1982, and it was normal business practice for the Midland to discuss a potential default with its consortium partners. Naturally these talks would have had an influence on the participants of a further loan of $75m to Banco Ambrosiano Holdings, negotiated in 1981 with the National Westminster Bank and twenty-eight others.

Another unanswered question centres on precisely what SIS knew of Calvi's movements after his disappearance from Rome. The circumstances of his clandestine entry into the UK at Gatwick, by private charter and with a false passport, suggest that the banker was anxious to avoid detection, and there is no evidence that he came under surveillance by any official agency while he was holed up in Chelsea. Indeed, during the City of London CID enquiries, neither MI5, SIS nor Special Branch intervened to the knowledge of the detectives running the case. On the other hand, he was the key player in Argentina's efforts to acquire Exocet reloads and represented the Junta's last chance to change the course of the Falklands conflict, so he unquestionably qualified on those grounds alone as a target for the kind of covert sabotage that so effectively had prevented Carlos Corti from fulfilling his mandate in Paris. Certainly his relationship with Hans Kunz, who facilitated Calvi's final journey and his accommodation in London, would have been the subject of scrutiny by the British authorities because the arms-dealer had participated in several previous transactions that had come to SIS's attention.

However, despite the widespread but mistaken belief outside the intelligence community that SIS has engaged in assassination, or what the CIA once euphemistically termed 'termination with extreme prejudice', it is most unlikely that any British security or intelligence service played any part in Calvi's bizarre death. Of course, that is not to rule out participation by some other agency and, considering the high stakes involved and the byzantine qualities of the P-2's organisation, which extended to an affiliated freemasonry lodge in Buenos Aires, intervention by Calvi's business associates seems not improbable. It might be thought that, with the catastrophe that had befallen his bank, combined with the Argentine surrender in Stanley which he must have realised would have put paid to the Peruvian Exocet deal, Calvi would have had ample reason to succumb to depression, or perhaps be pushed over the edge by the suicide of his most loyal secretary, but his family remain adamant that he gave no hint of self-destruction.

The possibility that Calvi was murdered by professionals hired by members of P-2 who feared the banker was planning to disclose the lodge's secrets, or negotiate some kind of an immunity with the Italian authorities from the safety of London, cannot be overlooked. There may also have been individuals connected with the Argentine Exocet purchase who, in the light of the defeat in the Falklands, feared details of the abortive transaction emerging. Huge sums of money were at stake, and the accompanying commissions themselves might have been enough to motivate homicide. As for conspirators willing to participate in a murder, the Argentine military establishment had fostered an entire culture in which torture and denial of human rights was routinely acceptable, and indulgence in secret executions was far from unusual.

Chapter 10

STANLEY

While the British concentrated their efforts in Europe on denying Carlos Corti access to further air-launched missiles, the Argentine forces on the Falklands pursued an alternative strategy which was intended to make use of the Exocet's lethal firepower in a way which no one, least of all the Royal Navy, could have anticipated.

The arrival of Admiral Edgardo Otero in Port Stanley on 26 April was not considered important at the time. He was the senior naval officer on the islands, but there were no naval warships of any size participating in the defence of the Falklands. However, when he experienced the Royal Navy's first bombardment of the Stanley area on the afternoon of 1 May, from the destroyer *Glamorgan* and the frigates *Alacrity* and *Arrow*, which went unchallenged, he was quickly on the radio to Bahia Blanca to demand action, and in particular the deployment of two motor torpedo-boats to harass the enemy and deter further shelling. Armed with wire-guided AEG SST-4 torpedoes, the small craft would have been ideal for the task he had in mind, and the Argentine Navy possessed a total of four German-built PR-71s. Otero knew there was nothing more demoralising for the beleaguered troops than to submit to an artillery barrage without the means of replying in kind. Even when the gunners of the 3rd Artillery Regiment had responded, with 155mm howitzers hurling shells twenty kilometres, the British warships had simply moved out of range and continued firing. To add insult to injury, the Royal Navy had made the first attack in broad daylight, with accurate 4.5-inch gunfire directed by helicopter spotters which also had escaped unscathed. *Glamorgan*, accompanied by *Alacrity* and *Arrow*, had come close inshore, south of Stanley, and had fired on Argentine troops dug in on Sapper Hill and Mount William. It was a bold show of force by the Royal Navy, but perhaps also an opportunity not to be missed by the defenders.

Those who were present when Otero made his views known to the Navy staff on the mainland recall that his language became so heated that there was a danger of the signals equipment melting, but his effort was in vain – his demand was firmly rejected. Undaunted, the diminutive admiral – who had participated in the original naval preparations for AZUL in Puerto Belgrano back at the end of February – put through a call to his old friend Captain Julio Perez, the engineer in charge of the Exocet workshops in Puerto Belgrano. His request was simple. Would it be possible to fire a surface-launched MM-40 Exocet from the land? If the Navy was unwilling to defend the islands with ships, could some missiles be transferred from the ships and set up on a coastal site? A naval engineer by profession, Perez had received the huge Exocet computer system from Aerospatiale in March, and although he had only minimal experience with the sophisticated equipment, he was captivated by Otero's idea and undertook to investigate the possibility and report back urgently. Hitherto he had concentrated on mastering the art of linking the AM-39s to the Super Etendards at the Naval Aviation headquarters at Base Espora, just thirty kilometres away. He and his team of six at each end had risen to that challenge in the very shortest time, and now Otero had confronted him with a new one.

Perez, who had spent ten months in Paris studying the complexities of the Exocet, did not underestimate the task ahead of him, and after five days of intensive consultations with his technical colleagues he concluded that to dismantle an MM-40 launcher, perhaps from one of the obsolete American Summer-class destroyers *Segui* or *Comodoro Py* presently docked in Puerto Belgrano, was entirely possible, but it would take around two months to rig up the inertial platform which supplied the missile's computer with the guidance data necessary for flight. For the missile to be launched successfully, its internal system had to be fed with a mass of technical data from the main computer. To improvise this synchronisation would require the duplication of the platform's processors, thereby deceiving the missile into believing that it had received all the authentic information necessary to select a target, determine the range and programme the active homing memory in the nose with the final instructions for a launch.

Once Otero had explained the disadvantages of enduring a nightly bombardment, Perez became enchanted with the prospect of building what amounted to an entirely new surface-to-surface missile system, and he started work on removing an Exocet from the *Segui*. Dismantling the launchers proved relatively straightforward, but three serious obstacles were encountered in the development of the new inertial platform. Firstly, there was the question of power. The Exocet required an electrical source of 440 volts at 60 cycles, an almost unique combination and, just when Perez was close to despairing of ever finding a substitute, Lieutenant-Commander Benjamin Davila remembered a Siemens generator which had been purchased from the Nazis in 1938 as part of a searchlight battery. Consigned to a storage depot on the base twenty years earlier, the huge Siemens unit, weighing six tons, was wheeled out and found to be in near perfect working condition, producing precisely the desired current.

Perez's second problem was the physical platform for the new Exocet. The wheeled flatbed unit on which the *Segui*'s two launchers were eventually fitted was an unwieldy vehicle weighing five tons. The base had to be sufficiently robust to withstand the pressure of two launches, but still retain enough mobility to be manhandled into position. Finally, there was the substitute radar system to acquire the target, but Perez was confident that one could be found in the Islands. Using an improvised wooden control box to reproduce the digital dialogue between the missile and the inertial guidance system, Perez and his technicians succeeded in simulating ten apparently faultless launches.

This was an extraordinary breakthrough, because the military situation was deteriorating rapidly for both sides, although neither realised the other's true situation. The Argentines, dismayed by the apparent ease with which a beach-head had been established at San Carlos, were convinced that the large ship struck by one or both AM-39s launched on Argentina's National Day, 25 May, had hit the *Invincible*. When the British revealed the loss of the *Atlantic Conveyor*, its true significance was not fully appreciated. Naturally the elimination of the Chinooks had not been announced, nor the impact the disaster was likely to have on the British timetable for moving the ground troops away from the landing area towards Port Stanley. Sinking the *Atlantic Conveyor* had turned a high-risk strategy into a definite gamble, but the Argentine intelligence apparatus had failed to realise the very precarious position of the troops already landed, and of the Task Force which was paying a high price to the bombs dropped on the vulnerable ships gathered in San Carlos Water. Nevertheless, the prospect of offering the Islands surface-to-surface missile protection against the Royal Navy looked exceptionally attractive, if only the MM-40 could be made to work in such an unconventional manner.

The biggest hurdle, of marrying the computer system to the missile's guidance memory, had been overcome, so the generator and the flatbed were loaded on to two Hercules for a night-flight to Port Stanley on 1 June. According to Perez, who accompanied the generator on the second aircraft, he took up smoking again when the plane made a total of four approaches to the runway, having been warned off three times by hostile radar and enemy combat air patrols.

The extraordinary secrecy that had surrounded the development of the improvised Exocet did not end after the system's safe arrival in Stanley. The flatbed and the generator were hauled into the town and hidden in a convenient shed to shield them from prying eyes, while an attempt was made to develop a radar system capable of acquiring a target and providing the data to the Exocet. The only suitable unit was the French RASIT, designed for use in combat by infantry to detect surface movement up to thirty kilometres away, which had been the subject of some experiments by Carlos Ries, a young Argentine television journalist more used to filming wildlife documentaries for Channel 13 in Buenos Aires than tinkering with radar. Nevertheless, he was the holder of an amateur radio licence and had shared Otero's frustration at the artillery's impotence to respond to the nightly bombardment. Formerly a marines officer, having been invalided out of the service after a car crash in 1973, Ries had approached the Argentine military authorities in Port Stanley and volunteered to use the RASIT, with an extended range over the sea of 3,700 metres, as an early-warning system to give notice of British bombardments. He had been listened to politely, but instead of taking him up on his offer Admiral Otero asked him to collaborate with Perez's project. Together the two men found that the principal obstacle to synchronising the incompatible systems was that the RASIT collected target data in metres and mils, requiring a complex conversion to the Exocet's computer which could only handle degrees of azimuth and a range in kilometres. By using an improvised conversion table and a pocket calculator, one of Perez's engineers, Mario Abadal, succeeded in entering the RASIT data into the Exocet command computer. Satisfied that at least in theory the Exocet could be made to work, Perez judged the launchers ready on the night of 5 June, and the hardware was hauled the four kilometres to the launch site, overlooking a stretch of water used by British warships to transit to and from their bombardment positions.

Ries assembled the RASIT's antenna on a sandbank overlooking the shore and powered the radar from the 24-volt battery on his jeep, while Perez supervised a crane to lift the two launchers on to the flatbed. Protected by a SAM-7 battery to defend the site against a British helicopter attack, the crew of five settled down to wait for an enemy ship to move into range.

A few hours before dawn, the army's big Westinghouse radar reported an unidentified surface vessel on the horizon, heading out into the Atlantic after a night of pouring fire on to Argentine positions. The RASIT radar locked on to the target and the launch initiator was pressed, but the missile malfunctioned. Disappointed, Perez disconnected the first launcher and prepared the second tube, but he failed to take account of the improvised capacitor which required a full twenty minutes to warm up and absorb the telemetry data. In his enthusiasm he fired after just eight minutes. The second missile launched, but missed the target, which steamed to safety apparently oblivious to its very close call.

This was a huge disappointment for Perez and Otero, for although they had now proved that an MM-40 could be fired from land, neither of the two missiles off the *Segui* had worked. Furthermore, the British remained unaware of the threat, so the project had lost the advantage of its deterrent value. Nevertheless, what had been achieved in technical terms was impressive, and the prize remained sufficiently attractive for another flight to be made to bring in more missiles.

A further attempt was made with a second pair of launchers flown in under cover of darkness on the night of 7/8 June, the offending capacitor having been replaced. Almost by accident, Ries's videotape editor had spotted two connections on the improvised equipment that had been inverted. The television technician had studied the tape of the entire launching sequence and noted that the mid-flight course adjustment made by Perez was 8 degrees right, whereas the video evidence suggested the missile had swung about the same angle *left*. Once the cables on the equipment had been reversed the crew began a series of vigils for a warship to present itself in front of the flatbed's axis, and patience was rewarded, after a curious rain-dance performed by Corporal Edgardo Rodriguez, on the night of 11/12 June.

On that particular night *Yarmouth*, *Avenger* and *Glamorgan* had been operating close inshore on what was known as the Stanley gunline, giving supporting fire to 45 Commando's attack on the hills of Two Sisters. Just before dawn HMS *Glamorgan* made a belated dash across a short cut for the open sea after the long bombardment and, when the 500-foot destroyer was moments away from the Exocet's maximum range of 24,000 metres, she passed over the 180-degree bearing of the Exocet.[1] The missile fired successfully and an 'Ashtray!' warning was given by the ship's operations room, enabling the captain to execute a sharp turn to present the weapon with the narrowest profile. A Sea Cat was fired, but a few seconds later the Exocet ploughed into the stern of the ship, still heeling over from the sharp change in course, and detonated in the Wessex helicopter hangar, killing eight of the crew instantly. Fuel then flooded through the gaping hole in the deck, into the galley, where a steward and four cooks died of burns.[2]

The *Glamorgan*'s last-minute manoeuvre undoubtedly saved the ship, for if she had been hit amidships like HMS *Sheffield* she would certainly have been lost. However, she was able to limp away from the scene under her own power, but would not take any further part in the campaign. To date she had led something of a charmed existence, having been bombed and strafed by Daggers during a short attack on the afternoon of the first land bombardment. *Glamorgan* fired a Sea Cat on that occasion, but had not been hit, and a fortnight later she participated in the successful SAS raid on Pebble Island, laying down covering shellfire while two Sea Kings deposited the men from 'G' Squadron beside the grass airstrip.

The Exocet that hit *Glamorgan* was the last to be fired in the South Atlantic, the final surrender following just over forty-eight hours later, thereby denying Perez the chance to capitalise further on his extraordinary invention. His flatbed platform and the ancilliary equipment were captured intact by astonished British paratroopers who, understandably, had never seen a land-based Exocet. In retrospect the efforts made by Perez and his team did little to alter the course of the conflict but, in such a tight-run situation, they might have tipped the balance in Argentina's favour by creating the kind of delay that the British simply could not afford.

Chapter 11

WHITEHALL

'My time in the Falkland Islands had taught me that tri-service command is a peculiar art, difficult to manage until one is used to it. The Army, Navy and Air Force all have their own procedures and ways of doing things; it therefore needs a combination of tact and firmness to make them work together in harmony. Rather than issue sweeping orders and directives, one has to bring all three services into line by gentle yet firm manipulation'

Sir Peter de la Billière, *Storm Command*

The Franks Report, formally entitled the *Falkland Islands Review*, which was handed to Mrs Thatcher on 31 December 1982 and released to the public on 18 January 1983, came to the convenient conclusion that the Argentine decision to invade the Falklands had been taken so late that it would have been impossible to foresee or prevent, and accordingly 'we would not be justified in attaching any criticism or blame to the present Government'.[1] As a verdict on her administration's handling of the crisis, Mrs Thatcher seized on these final words of the Report and maintained that her administration had been exonerated, claiming in the first volume of her memoirs that 'the invasion could not have been foreseen or prevented' and that 'this was the main conclusion of the Franks Report'.[2]

The exercise conducted by the venerable 77-year-old

Lord Franks was unusual by any standards, and amounted to a re-examination of the intelligence background to the conflict. The Committee explained that it had been provided with

> every report from the intelligence agencies relating to the Falkland Islands from the beginning of 1981 until 2 April 1982, and a large number of reports from previous years, including all those circulated in 1976 and 1977, and every assessment on Argentina and the Falkland Islands made by the Joint Intelligence Organisation since 1965, together with any relevant minutes of meetings.[3]

In addition, the Committee asked for 'reports from the intelligence agencies received after 2 April that threw light on the events leading up to the invasion'.[4] Precisely how much this material amounted to is unknown, but if the Prime Minister is right in her assertion that 'we had no intelligence until almost the last moment'[5] it could not have taken the six members of the Committee long to read it all. This particular observation of hers has drawn very little comment, which is surprising when one considers the volume of intelligence material that reaches the Foreign Office. Remarkably, Mrs Thatcher's successor gave evidence on this point to Lord Justice Scott and declared, in support of his proposition that ministers cannot read everything, that annually some 40,000 separate items of intelligence are delivered to the Foreign Office by SIS and GCHQ, with the latter agency supplying about two-thirds. This was an important disclosure because, for the very first time, a Prime Minister revealed the huge scale of Britain's intelligence collection effort. On a daily basis these statistics break down to rather more than seventy GCHQ intercept summaries and thirty SIS reports, excluding material from the Security Service. Admittedly John Major's assertion was in the context of the events of 1986, four years after the

Falklands conflict, but on the reasonable assumption that his figures were not the subject of significant fluctuation during the intervening period (when expenditure on both organisations increased markedly), it would be surprising if none of the data concerned Argentina. Recalling Ted Rowlands' embarrassing gaffe in the Commons debate on the Falklands, in which he confirmed GCHQ's success in solving Argentina's diplomatic ciphers during his period as a minister at the Foreign Office, one wonders what happened in the previous three years to choke off Cheltenham. Or was Mrs Thatcher implying that there was intelligence available, but none had come the way of ministers?

Whether the Prime Minister's interpretation of the Committee's conclusions is really justified is open to considerable question,[6] and certainly Sir Nicholas Henderson, the British Ambassador in Washington DC throughout the conflict, has pointed out that apart from anything else, Franks mistakenly identified the Junta's fateful decision as having been taken on 31 March 1982, whereas it is now conceded by all concerned that the correct date is five days earlier, on 26 March, when the Junta had assembled at the Army headquarters in the Libertador Building. However, even this cannot really be described as the moment when the Junta agreed to seize the Islands. In fact, as has been seen, the planning started in earnest in November 1981, and by January 1982 many of the details had been drawn up by the various staffs of the three services. According to the Rattenbach Commission, which performed a similar role to the Franks Committee, on 5 January the Junta had formally authorised the preparation of 'a contingency plan for the employment of military power' in the Islands, and on 26 January had issued National Strategy Document 1/82 which

> resolved to analyse the possibility of the use of military power to obtain the political objective. This resolution must be kept in strict secrecy and should be

circulated only to the heads of the respective military departments.[7]

The meeting held on 26 January is highly significant, because this was the first occasion when a timetable had been agreed by the Junta, with mid-March specified for the planning deadline. Thereafter the Junta met weekly, and discussed the growing crisis on 23 March, when it was arranged that they would gather on a daily basis. Certainly those involved in the preliminary work had exercised considerable secrecy, but in a country given to military coups, isolated watertight planning cells are not exceptional. Thus the fact remains that *if* the tentacles of British intelligence could have known where to reach, there *were* plans to be seen, planners to be suborned. What the Franks Committee did not explore was the reason why the relevant agencies failed to spot any of the tell-tale signs which had alerted a sizeable proportion of the Argentine intelligence establishment to the fact that something unusual had been under way since January. A rather smaller proportion of the *cognoscenti* guessed what was in the wind.

To the lay reader it would appear that Franks really believed that an operation the size of the invasion could be assembled and mounted in just a matter of days, supposedly on the Junta's unexpected whim. In reality, of course, the planning had been under way for the best part of six months, with troops and hardware being moved across the country. There were plenty of tea-leaves to be read, signs to be interpreted, sources to be cultivated, but there were insufficient assets on the ground to do the required legwork. Surprisingly, Franks makes no mention of any of this, nor even attempts an analysis of the chronology of events on the Argentine side. Even the most superficial scrutiny would have undermined the Committee's belief that the Junta's 'final' decision was taken on Friday, 26 March.[8]

It must be questioned whether the Franks judgment also applied to the authentic 'final' date of 26 March. Franks cast doubt on the validity of Mrs Thatcher's assertion that the invasion could not have been anticipated because the intelligence coverage was inadequate or, in her words, 'we had no intelligence until almost the last moment'. In Henderson's view more attention should have been paid to the Argentine reactions to numerous British decisions, such as the closure of the Antarctic Survey base at Grytviken, the failure to grant full British citizenship to the Falkland Islanders in the British Nationality Bill and the refusal to extend the runway at Stanley. In these circumstances, given the dress rehearsal alleged to have been undertaken as recently as 1977, it would have been reasonable to conclude that rather more than a single Spanish-speaking SIS officer was required to provide intelligence cover for the whole of South America. However, even in these unfortunate circumstances, the Franks Report did not really absolve the government of blame. What it actually said was that because the Junta had acted so quickly, it was impossible to determine whether the invasion could have been prevented. Of course, this is hardly the same as insisting that the Government had been cleared, but the Committee was 'convinced that the invasion on 2 April 1982 could not have been foreseen' even though it had accepted that 'there is no simple answer' to the question of whether the invasion could have been prevented. Although no empiric solution to the conundrum can be offered, one can at least take a step in the right direction by analysing the various parts of the intelligence jigsaw available at the relevant time, and look at the top of the political pyramid where the JIC's advice was intended to be read.

After her election triumph in May 1979 Mrs Thatcher arrived in Downing Street with virtually no experience of intelligence, apart from a couple of private briefings – given while she was leader of the Opposition with the consent of the Prime Minister – by Sir Maurice Oldfield shortly before his departure from SIS in 1978. She relied primarily upon her trusted adviser and parliamentary colleague Airey Neave, himself a former SIS officer who had served in the wartime escape and evasion service, MI9, and it was Lord de Lisle who introduced her to Brian Crozier, another SIS officer who was to give her a grasp of the intelligence scene. As Crozier later observed, 'her experience of the outside world, of foreign affairs, of secret intelligence and security, was virtually nil'.[9]

Crozier had retained a close relationship with SIS after his contractual relationship had ended, whereas Mrs Thatcher's other main sources – Harry Sporborg, Sir Stephen Hastings MP and Nicholas Elliott – had been out of the business for some years. Hastings had left SIS, having been based in Cyprus, to fight the Mid-Bedfordshire by-election in November 1960, and Elliott, who was infuriated by Crozier's disclosure of his advisory role, had moved to Lonhro in 1969 from his post as SIS's Director of Requirements. Sporborg, a director of Hambro's Bank, had not been involved in the clandestine world since his role as vice-chief of the wartime Special Operations Executive, the sabotage organisation which was wound up in 1946. Unfortunately the focus of this illustrious group was firmly concentrated on Moscow, so although her eyes were opened to the KGB's machinations and to the very real threat of home-grown subversion, she remained a novice in the art of appreciating what weight should be given to particular types of intelligence, and how to call for collateral evidence from other clandestine agencies. According to Hastings, the advice she received was limited to 'the subversive menace to this country presented by the Soviet Union and the Communist Party'.

It was a serious exercise. The work took nearly a year. I began with a guide to historical materialism and an attempt to define how the Communist mind worked, for it was impossible to appreciate the diabolical nature of the Soviet communist conspiracy without some idea of the twisted philosophy from which it was devised and practised. My report sought to describe the enemy's resources and methods, followed by a review of our own security services, their strengths and weaknesses as we had known them.[10]

While Hastings and Crozier were well-informed about the true nature and scale of Soviet hegemony and the KGB's penetration and manipulation of the Labour movement, they had nothing practical to suggest regarding the long-overdue reforms required to make the JIC responsive to non-Warsaw Pact threats. Indecd, it is now widely acknowledged that in 1982 Britain's defence posture was entirely dictated by the British Army of the Rhine, at the expense of attention to threats from outside the NATO area.

Deprived of Airey Neave by an INLA car-bomb before she could establish herself properly in Downing Street, Mrs Thatcher's first major encounter with Whitehall's security and intelligence structure occurred after she had been in office just eight months, when the Director-General of the Security Service, Sir Howard Smith, urged her not to compromise Professor Sir Anthony Blunt. He insisted that if the distinguished art historian's role as a Soviet spy was exposed, the value to MI5 of the immunity from prosecution granted to him, and other traitors like him, would be diminished if not destroyed completely. If he was to be revealed and humiliated, what chance was there of tempting another of his ilk to collaborate? Smith argued that Blunt's co-operation had been vital, and had only been achieved with the Attorney-General's formal immunity, but the current Attorney, Sir Michael Havers, pointed out that as a barrister the Prime Minister could not stand aside while Blunt perjured himself in a libel action in the High Court. Mrs Thatcher's dilemma was whether to accept MI5's advice or her Attorney's. In the end she opted for Blunt's disgrace, with a statement to the Commons accompanied by an announcement from Buckingham Palace stripping the Queen's art adviser of his knighthood, and thereby opened a veritable Pandora's box of mischief which led directly to the *Spycatcher* fiasco and numerous other security-related crises that were to dog her administration for nearly a decade.

Suffice to say that prior to March 1982 Mrs Thatcher had scarcely encountered the intelligence professionals and had been more preoccupied with domestic considerations, such as the economy and Britain's membership of the European Community. During this early period of her administration overseas policy was dominated by the settlement achieved in Rhodesia, the unexpected imposition of martial law in Poland and the sudden Soviet invasion of Afghanistan. While SIS had played a peripheral role in monitoring the internecine politics of the various rival groups in what was to become Zimbabwe, it failed entirely to predict the highly efficient KGB-executed coup of December 1979 in Kabul, and gave no warning of General Jaruzelski's swift seizure of power almost exactly two years later. Worse, as Jaruzelski's tanks rolled unexpectedly through Warsaw, GCHQ's efforts to monitor developments were handicapped by industrial action taken by the civil service unions. None of these events reflected much credit on Whitehall's intelligence establishment, and for all the apparent success accomplished in Rhodesia, the final result was the legitimation and installation of a regime led by an avowed Marxist, which was precisely what Mrs Thatcher, her Cabinet and her party had hoped to avoid.

Mrs Thatcher's relative inexperience in the intelligence field during the early stages of her tenure in Downing Street manifested itself in her appointment, in September 1979, of Sir Maurice Oldfield to the post of Co-ordinator of Security and Intelligence in Northern Ireland, to supervise the competing roles of MI5, SIS, GCHQ, the military and the RUC. She had not been informed of a problem in his private life which was to prompt his retirement nine months later in circumstances that, when disclosed publicly, were later to cause severe embarrassment to both her and SIS. It was yet another episode where, in the absence of Airey Neave, she lacked sound professional advice, and thus it is hardly surprising that during the spring of 1982 Mrs Thatcher was ill-equipped to read such signs regarding Argentine intentions as were available. Indeed, during the conflict itself she co-opted the outgoing Permanent Secretary at the Foreign Office, Sir Michael Palliser, to be her special adviser at Number Ten, and thereafter retained a retired senior diplomat to assist her with foreign policy.

While she may have failed to read the danger signals, and been slow to tackle Whitehall inertia, she responded with ruthless alacrity once the Falklands crisis was upon her, as can be seen by her creation of the War Cabinet, her selection of its membership – from which she excluded the Chancellor of the Exchequer, Sir Geoffrey Howe – and her determination to circumvent John Nott's team of ministers at the Ministry of Defence. In these decisions her consultation was minimal, but her instinct for political survival prevailed.

Certainly another important influence upon the Prime Minister, and the prosecution of the Falklands campaign, was the SAS's skilful handling of the Iranian embassy siege in April 1980, when her official car pulled over en route between Chequers and Downing Street for her to give permission for the regiment's famous intervention. The vital decision having been passed to her by the Home Secretary, Willie Whitelaw, she had risen to the occasion. There was no hesitation, no procrastination at a potentially hazardous moment full of international ramifications, in granting authority for British troops to force an entry into a foreign embassy. Later the same day she drove to the SAS's tactical headquarters in Regent's Park barracks to convey her personal congratulations and thanks to the troops who had performed as required.

In her memoirs Mrs Thatcher readily concedes that 'the significance of the Falklands War was enormous, both for Britain's self-confidence and our standing in the world', and she acknowledges frequently the tremendous importance for her administration of the eleven weeks the campaign lasted. What is remarkable, however, is her description of HMS *Endurance* as 'a military irrelevance', an odd term for the sole Royal Naval unit in the region which could provide intelligence. Noting that Franks had enjoyed 'unprecedented access to government papers, including those of the intelligence services' she says that as late as Wednesday, 31 March,

> the advice we received from intelligence was that the Argentine Government were exploring our reactions, but that they had not contrived the landing on South Georgia and that any escalation they might make would stop short of full-scale invasion.

Later that same evening, Mrs Thatcher recalls a visit from her Defence Secretary, John Nott:

> He had just received intelligence that the Argentine Fleet, already at sea, looked as if they were going to invade the islands on Friday 2 April. There was no ground to question the intelligence.

Nott's decisive information was the intercept which arrived over the secure teleprinter at teatime, and so dismayed the JIC assessment staff. This is the same item that was transmitted instantly to Sir Nicholas Henderson at the British embassy in Washington DC and prompted him to deliver it immediately to General Haig at the State Department, on his own initiative, without seeking the Foreign Office's sanction for the dissemination. Whilst the provenance of the intercept is well-established, the origins of the other more reassuring assessment, upon which Mrs

Thatcher allegedly had relied earlier in the day, is more difficult to trace. Did it come from the JIC, and was it examined by Lord Franks and his committee?

The principal political victim of the Falklands War in Britain was, of course, Lord Carrington, who resigned together with his team of Foreign Office ministers, Humphrey Atkins and Richard Luce, after experiencing a roasting by Conservative back-bench MPs. Carrington insisted that

> throughout the first months of 1982 we had continuing Intelligence reports that an Argentine attempt to invade the Falklands was unlikely in the near future, despite the cold diplomatic climate, the sense that there was a volatile situation in Argentina and hints (clearly inspired) in the Argentine newspapers that if negotiations 'failed' a military solution might be inevitable. We had throughout the previous years had a good deal of this sort of thing and there was no particular reason to suppose the situation might not still be contained or defused.

Like his Prime Minister, Lord Carrington believes that the Franks Committee was set up to find out 'exactly what had happened, on who knew what when, and on whether they might have done something more or different about it' and he asserts that when the report 'was published, it set out all the events, developments and reactions in exact detail . . . We knew the situation was dangerous but our Intelligence reports gave no indication of any basic change,' apparently overlooking the crucial flaw in Franks relating to the date of the Junta's decision to invade. Carrington deals with this point obliquely, recording that 'our advice was that if there were a decision for invasion we might get very little actual warning of the decision and the hour; but that there would be preliminary indicators, in the sense of a deteriorating situation over a period. With this we had to be content . . .' Thus, while Mrs Thatcher felt 'the

invasion could not have been foreseen or prevented' her
Foreign Secretary seems to be rather more cautious in his
analysis, reaching the slightly different conclusion that the
invasion was not foreseen or prevented. A distinction, of
course, founded on two rather different perceptions of
what intelligence was available, and exactly how it had
been interpreted.

Mrs Thatcher has called the first Falklands debate in
the Commons, on Saturday 3 April, 'the most difficult
I ever had to face', and says that her 'first task was
to defend us against the charge of unpreparedness'. On
that occasion she received the support of the House,
but anxiety was expressed on both sides about how the
situation had been allowed to happen. The announcement,
in July 1982, that a committee of Privy Counsellors would
look into the background of the war, and report its findings
to Parliament, effectively defused a potentially explosive
political time-bomb.

Undoubtedly the Franks Committee undertook an impossible task, with minimal staff, interviewing forty-six named
witnesses, an unknown number of 'members of the intelligence community' and receiving written submissions from
124 other individuals or organisations, as diverse as the
Astronomer Royal, Sir Martin Ryle, and the National
Union of Seamen, all in the space of six months. Precisely how many members of the intelligence community
appeared before Franks is unknown, the Whitehall cult
of secrecy being so pervasive that even thirteen years
later witnesses remain reluctant to admit they gave evidence. Indeed, the committee itself exercised extraordinary
restraint by limiting its description of the JIC assessment
machinery to three short paragraphs in Annex 'B', and of
the secret agencies to just half a dozen lines of anodyne text.
Neither GCHQ nor SIS are mentioned anywhere, and none
of the key personalities, such as the Chairman of the JIC, his
deputy, the Intelligence Co-ordinator or the head of the JIC
Assessment Staff, are identified by name, thus conforming

to the convention that very little should ever be disclosed
about the JIC or Whitehall's innermost sanctums. Actually
it was not until 1993 that an official document, entitled
Central Intelligence Machinery, was released to inform the
public about how ministers receive intelligence advice. Just
twenty-seven pages long, it identified by name the then
current JIC Chairman, Sir Roderic Braithwaite, and the
Intelligence Co-ordinator, Gerald Warner, but nowhere
described the American, New Zealand and Australian
participation in the assessment processes.

In comparison with the painstaking investigation by Sir
Richard Scott into the Matrix Churchill affair, which
started in December 1992 and lasted more than three years
– taking written evidence from 200 witnesses, with more
than 60 appearing in 80 days – Franks looks indecently
swift. The comparison is quite compelling, particularly
when one considers that some 800 employees in the
Midlands lost their jobs when Matrix Churchill collapsed,
but nobody died, whereas 255 British servicemen died in
the Falklands and nearly 800 were wounded. Scott sat
in public for over 430 hours, and in private for 60,
contrasting with the Franks Committee which never sat
in open session. At the heart of the Matrix Churchill
inquiry was the somewhat esoteric issue of whether British
government guidelines relating to the export of arms to the
Middle East had been breached following the August 1988
ceasefire in the Iran–Iraq war. To assist his investigation,
Scott conducted his cross-examination with a senior QC
and a barrister from the Attorney-General's chambers,
backed up by a staff of thirteen experienced officials
seconded from departments of Whitehall, complete with
a press secretary. Lord Franks was obliged to rely on three
officials and a typist.

Despite being handicapped in their inability to research
in depth, Lord Franks and his five Privy Counsellors
did uncover some awkward embarrassments, such as the
admission that until the Falklands were put on the agenda

of the Cabinet's Oversea and Defence Policy Committee on the day before the invasion, the topic had not come up for discussion since January 1981. Equally surprising was the revelation that the Foreign Secretary, Lord Carrington, had not been told of Operation JOURNEYMAN – the secret deployment of HMS *Dreadnought* and two frigates, in November 1977 – until 5 March 1982. Significantly, his officials even then had omitted to mention that news of the deployment had been leaked deliberately by SIS in Buenos Aires,[11] so he had discounted the deterrent value of what had occurred and rejected its relevance to the current crisis then unfolding. With more resources and more time, Lord Franks and his colleagues might have discovered rather more in the same vein.

Curiously, Franks did not pursue two important matters, both highly germane to the intelligence background to the conflict. Having learned that the Foreign Secretary had been kept in the dark over precisely what had occurred in 1977, very little effort was made to establish whether James Callaghan's recollection, disclosed to the Commons on 30 March 1982, that the news of *Dreadnought*'s deployment had been allowed to become known 'without fuss or publicity'[12] was in accordance with what had really happened. Perhaps significantly, in his 1987 memoirs, *Time and Chance*, Callaghan retracted his original claim that the task group had become known, but offered a slightly different version in which he gave a hint, rather than an explicit order, to Oldfield to leak news of the deployment to the Argentines: 'I informed the Head of MI6 of our plans before the ships sailed and it is possible that, as I hoped, some information reached the Argentine Armed Forces.'[13] Since then Callaghan has gone further:

> I told Maurice Oldfield of our plans to send a naval force to stand off the Falklands at a discreet distance, but I did not make a direct request to him to inform the Argentinians of our purpose. We discussed the

future prospects against the background of possible hostile action by Argentina, and I am clear that he understood that I would not be unhappy if the news of our deployment reached the Argentinian Armed Forces. I did not question Maurice Oldfield subsequently about what action he had taken so that remains speculative . . .[14]

Since Oldfield had died in March 1981, and apparently taken this secret to the grave, SIS's Chief Sir Colin Figures was asked by Franks to confirm the sequence of events, but the station commander in Buenos Aires at the time, Simon C.-L., had not been the channel used to convey the information, or the implied threat, to the Argentines. There the matter was allowed to remain, unresolved, despite the reservations of the then Foreign Secretary, David Owen, who gave evidence to Franks and had some trenchant observations to make about the 1977 episode.

Intelligence can play a crucial role in defence decision-making, which is literally a life-or-death affair. But Ministers need to understand how to use intelligence, whether military, diplomatic or obtained by covert means, through MI6 or GCHQ. In both 1977 and 1982 the factual evidence of a potential invasion of the Falklands was available to Ministers. The 1977 record shows that intelligence served as a tool for Ministerial decisions. The 1982 records show how intelligence was ignored.

Owen, of course, had played a key role in the 1977 drama, demanding that a nuclear submarine be detached from its patrol to join *Alacrity* and *Phoebe*, despite scepticism and resistance from the Naval Staff, and insisting that the US Navy not be informed of the task group because of its close links with the Argentines. As for whether SIS had acted as a conduit in the way suggested by Callaghan,

Owen is emphatic that the task group had performed as 'an insurance policy' and 'it did not of itself deter'.

> I do not believe that Maurice Oldfield, who was primarily answerable to me as Foreign Secretary as well as to the Prime Minister, would have disclosed the naval deployment as a result of a discussion with the Prime Minister, at least not without talking to me first. Although in some delicate areas he would be entitled to respond only to the Prime Minister I do not believe this was one of them.[15]

No further enquiries were initiated, although the JOURNEYMAN episode was regarded within the Royal Navy as the classic example of how a nuclear submarine could be used as a highly effective deterrent. Presumably this view was shared by others, because Lord Franks noticed that according to the Cabinet papers for February 1978, Callaghan had considered a repetition to coincide with the Anglo-Argentine talks held at that time in Lima. According to some of those who had been on the scene at the time of the original deployment, *Dreadnought*'s commander, Captain Hugh Michell, had been ordered to find an Argentine vessel and expose herself deliberately, thereby breaking the first rule of submarine operations, but also ensuring that there could be no doubt in the minds of the Argentines that a British submarine was on station to defend the Falklands against any attempt to invade.

Neither Michell nor JOURNEYMAN's task group commander, Hugh Balfour, were invited to give evidence to Lord Franks to clarify precisely what had happened in 1977. If they had, they would have confirmed that the modernised Type-12 frigate *Phoebe* had led *Dreadnought*, and *Alacrity*, commanded by Captain Robert Mortlock, down to the South Atlantic in the most unusual conditions of total secrecy, under complete radio silence. The rest of the fleet was led to believe that the task group, which included the fleet tanker *Olwen*, carrying a full complement of four Sea King helicopters, and the RFA *Resource*, had been sent to the Caribbean, ostensibly to guard Belize. The two anti-submarine warfare frigates *Phoebe* and the new Type-21 *Alacrity* were selected because they had been fitted with the very latest satellite communications equipment and were armed with Exocet missiles, making them formidable opponents in any confrontation with an Argentine invasion force. Essential signals to Northwood were restricted to the satellite channel which reduced the possibility of hostile interception. Balfour's orders were to avoid all shipping, protect the covert nature of JOURNEYMAN's mission and take up a holding position north of the Falklands while *Dreadnought* continued south to approach the islands. Undetected, the ships were kept on station for two weeks, re-supplied several times by air, but whether *Dreadnought* received instructions to expose herself remains unclear, although her periscope was spotted on one occasion by a sharp-eyed look-out on the bridge of the RFA *Cherry Leaf* en route to Stanley. Having been trained at Portland, where the *Cherry Leaf* had recently participated in an anti-submarine exercise, he was quite convinced of what he had seen, but was persuaded that he had made an error in order to prevent word from spreading.

The question of whether *Dreadnought* deliberately exposed herself to the Argentines has been the subject of much discreet discussion among submariners. The rather ancient and noisy nuclear hunter-killer, then seventeen years old, represented a powerful deterrent, but only if a potential opponent knew she was likely to be in the area. Although *Dreadnought* was under the command of Michell, he was unwell for much of the mission so operations were managed by the next most senior officer aboard, Lieutenant Martin Macpherson. Those aboard recall the embarrassment of the *Cherry Leaf* incident, which occurred during a slightly over-ambitious mock intelligence-gathering approach on the RFA, but there is general agreement that no Argentine vessel was sighted. Experienced submariners point out that to be properly identified, *Dreadnought* would have had to surface completely, a manoeuvre that would have been complete anathema to a service whose entire ethos is stealth, and to a submarine working under combat conditions with special rules of engagement. Furthermore, only a very well-informed Argentine naval officer would have been able to ascertain the submarine's true nationality. Although built by Vickers Armstrong at Barrow-in-Furness, much of the stern was American designed and, despite the lack of characteristic diving planes on the sail, could easily be confused with a US boat, which was far more likely to be in the area. As for recognition of a submarine's masts, only specialists trained to NATO standards could be expected to distinguish between the very different types of periscopes, radar, high-frequency communications and electronic support measure structures which so characterised British, American and Russian boats. Accordingly, it is far from clear that the Argentines ever learned of the task group before the Callaghan disclosure. Indeed, some submariners have suggested that they would have been angered to know that their presence had been compromised through a calculated leak, and were astonished by the former Prime Minister's claim.

Certainly HMS *Endurance*, also on patrol in the area, was informed of the task group's existence, but even after Operation JOURNEYMAN had been terminated the whole episode stayed classified to avoid any accusation of provocative behaviour. Upon their return *Phoebe* and *Alacrity* spent a weekend on a courtesy call on Madeira, the crews' cover story being that both ships had been engaged in trials in the Atlantic. Until James Callaghan made the astonishing disclosure which revealed the existence of the task group, no word ever leaked, and the First Sea Lord had complimented those involved for executing the assignment with efficiency and discretion. Following the Whitehall convention that no administration can be privy to its predecessor's papers, Mrs Thatcher's Cabinet was never indoctrinated into the events of 1977, and Lord Carrington was informed of JOURNEYMAN only at a very advanced stage, much too late for the exercise to be repeated.

For such a key point, about whether a deterrent had worked in 1977, when an exhaustive probe by the Franks Committee undoubtedly was merited, perhaps justifying enquiries being made in Argentina, the omission seems quite bizarre. Officially it is denied by the Argentines that there was any plan to invade the Islands in November 1977, and the closest anyone is willing to come is to acknowledge the possibility that there might have been a deliberate leak of a false Argentine plan in order to provide deceptive cover for an attack on Chile which, at the time, was the Junta's main preoccupation. Alternatively, a more Machiavellian scheme has been proposed, with Britain deploying the Task Force to the South Atlantic to assist Chile and deter an amphibious landing on Tierra del Fuego. Neither seems entirely credible, but as to why the Franks Committee chose to overlook the episode, David (now Lord) Owen has an explanation. He believes that because Callaghan was mistaken in 1982, when he alleged that SIS had deliberately leaked news of the task group to Buenos Aires, the membership of the Franks Committee effectively conspired to conceal the truth. According to his scenario, the two Opposition nominees, Merlyn Rees and Harold Lever, wanted to avoid embarrassing Callaghan, while the two Conservatives, Harold Watkinson and Anthony Barber, were equally anxious not to draw a comparison between what Callaghan had accomplished in 1977 and what his successor failed to achieve five years later. As for the two Whitehall independents, Sir Patrick Nairne and Lord Franks, neither was particularly keen to explore why the 1982 Cabinet had not been advised of what had happened in similar circumstances in 1977. Thus, in Owen's interpretation of the omission in the Franks Report, Callaghan was allowed to slip off the hook on which he had so nearly impaled himself because it was judged to be in everyone's interests that the full story should not emerge.

The second topic, perhaps overlooked deliberately, was what the Argentines saw as the pivotal strategic significance of HMS *Endurance*, and the Argentine appreciation of the ship's true function. In fact Franks took no evidence on this from anyone outside the British intelligence community, so *Endurance*'s contribution to the overall scenario was greatly underestimated.

The full text of the Franks Report and the evidence submitted is unlikely to be published for many years, if ever, but it is evident that the Falklands War will be included in that long list of intelligence failures which allowed aggressors to seize the initiative. Pearl Harbor in December 1941; the invasion of South Korea in June 1950; the Soviet invasion of Czechoslovakia in September 1968; the Tet Offensive in October 1968; Yom Kippur in October 1973 and the occupation of Kuwait by Iraq in 1990 are all easily identifiable examples of disasters that might have been avoided if the appropriate political or military action had been taken in time to deter the attacker. Certainly a swift deployment can prevent bloodshed, and the proof is to be seen in the arrival of HMS *Bulwark*'s Royal Marines in Kuwait in 1966, and the secret mission undertaken by HMS *Ark Royal* in January 1972 when British Honduras (now Belize) was under imminent threat from Guatemala. On that occasion the aircraft carrier steamed at full speed across the Atlantic in time to launch two Buccaneer aircraft at maximum range, with mid-air refuelling from another pair, for a flight over the colony. The unexpected sight of the Fleet Air Arm fighter-bombers was enough to change the minds of the Guatemalans, as was the public announcement a few years later of the transfer of RAF Harriers. Doubtless there are many other hitherto undisclosed cases of clandestine dissuasion, but did the Falklands experience really change anything?

All of the failures cited above were quickly acknowledged as grievous lapses in the chain that links the component parts of the overall intelligence jigsaw to the politicians who take responsibility for any ensuing catastrophe. The Congressional inquiries into the origins of Pearl Harbor, which highlighted America's lack of a unified system of intelligence collection, collation and distribution, led to the creation of the Central Intelligence Agency in 1947; when Saigon was unexpectedly nearly overrun by North Vietnamese regulars, the Pentagon's intelligence assessment machine was overhauled; after Israel was suddenly attacked on three fronts at Yom Kippur, a greater emphasis was placed on technical sources of intelligence; and following the West's failure to predict the collapse of the Warsaw Pact there was a renewed effort to tilt the balance in favour of recruiting human sources.

The main conclusion of the Franks Report, apart from the very doubtful verdict 'that the Government had no reason to believe before 31 March that an invasion of the Falkland Islands would take place at the beginning of April', was the need for a restructuring of the Joint Intelligence Assessment Staff, taking the appointment of the JIC's Chairman away from the Foreign Office and moving it into the Cabinet Office, thereby making the post and the Assessment Staff more independent. This led to the appointment of Sir Antony Duff, the Intelligence Co-ordinator, to take on the additional role of JIC Chairman, but behind the scenes two further, unannounced changes were made: the Prime Minister's foreign affairs adviser, latterly Sir Anthony Parsons, was drafted in to attend meetings of the JIC, and Duff instituted a regular weekly conference of all the CIG chairmen where views could be expressed on an informal basis. In Duff's opinion this innovation allowed him direct access to a lower echelon before the Whitehall committee system had distilled reports to a point where a potential crisis could be overlooked by the anodyne presentation of the report. He also demanded sight of all the intelligence product, a hugely time-consuming burden for one individual working alone but clearly an essential lesson of the pre-invasion crisis.

Duff's reforms went far beyond the rather superficial analysis made by Franks, and owed much to a critique of the JIC written in 1980 by an experienced and senior intelligence officer, Douglas Nicoll, in which he coined the word 'perseveration' – the determination to cling to an opinion in the face of evidence to the contrary. Nicoll claimed that such perversity was institutionalised in the JIC and the absence of any safety valve, in the form of external criticism, undermined the JIC's perceived validity. Just because everyone agreed with the content of a JIC assessment did not automatically make it right. At the time Nicoll circulated his paper it was considered akin to heresy, but in the light of the Falklands experience it looked remarkably prescient. After all, the JIC's assessments of the threat from Argentina had scarcely changed from the early 1970s, and had been characterised by inertia. Overlaying Nicoll's commentary on to the sequence of events prior to April 1982 proved an interesting exercise, almost an object lesson in 'perseveration', with the JIC clinging doggedly to the view that as Argentina's past sabre-rattling had been so inconsequential, there was no reason to believe that matters had become more serious. As a convert and advocate of the dangers of perseveration, Duff's mandate in his post-Falklands role was to prevent history from repeating itself.

Duff's enlightened approach to managing the JIC retained the uniquely British analytical style, allowing each Whitehall department to contribute to a commonly agreed assessment, but had the advantage of giving him an insight into the development process at a much earlier stage. Combined with his new status, independent of the Foreign Office, the Chairman gave his staff much greater

confidence and encouraged them to take the initiative, in
contrast to the previous arrangement which had inhibited
the Assessment Staff's ability to do anything other than
respond to the requirements articulated by the JIC. This,
of course, was an implied criticism of the *ancien régime*
which had operated at too elevated a level and obviously
lost sight of the Falklands as an escalating crisis. In the
aftermath of the war, the JIC's composition remained
the same, with a preponderence of very senior military
figures, such as General Glover, who had commanded the
Land Forces in Northern Ireland; Admiral Halliday, who
had been retained on the JIC as Deputy Chairman after
being succeeded in the MoD by Glover; and Air Marshal
Armitage, a postwar graduate of Cranwell who had been
Deputy Commander of the RAF in Germany. Acting as
Glover's deputy throughout the Falklands crisis, Armitage
took his place in 1983, and in 1985 was appointed Chief of
Defence Intelligence in the new MoD hierarchy reorganised
by Michael Heseltine. Having won a DSO in February
1944, when he commanded the submarine HMS *Stubborn*,
Duff was respected by all the JIC's membership and was
probably able to accomplish rather more than another,
perhaps more conventional mandarin. He had joined the
10th Submarine Flotilla in 1940, serving aboard HMS
Unique in the Mediterranean, and had a particular grasp
of submarine operations. Having survived a prolonged
and harrowing period under enemy depth-charge attack
in a Norwegian fjord, he knew what it was like to be
fired on.

At the Foreign Office, which largely escaped unscathed
in the Franks Report, there were few obvious signs of con-
cessions to any acknowledgment of a failure of intelligence.
However, the new appointee to head the South America
Department was Adrian Sindall, recently returned from
Jordan, who had spent four years in Lima during the
1970s. His career had been unaffected back in October
1971 when Kim Philby denounced him incorrectly in an

interview published in the Estonian magazine *Kodumaa* ('Homeland') as the current SIS station commander in Beirut. In fact Sindall had never been one of 'the Friends', and his move to Peru was unconnected with Philby's mischievous intervention. Actually the SIS representative in Amman at the end of 1982 was David Spedding, later to be SIS's Chief.

Aside from the almost imperceptible structural changes made in Whitehall for the handling and evaluation of intelligence, the organisation most affected by the Falklands War has been the 22nd Special Air Service Regiment. Immediately after the conflict several members of 'B' Squadron re-established contact with John Moss and let him know that they were fully in support of the candour with which he had expressed his reservations to the Director. In their view he had, quite literally, saved their lives.

The question of whether the raid on Rio Grande could have succeeded without massive loss of life is still a subject for much debate. Although the defenders were not equipped with a single portable missile system, their light flak units remained effective despite their age. As for the dispersal of aircraft, they never took advantage of all the options available, which included an auxiliary airstrip thirty metres wide, five miles north of the main airfield. Built for the 1977 Chilean crisis, it was one of a series of hardened 2,500–3,500-metre strips integrated into the road system, not unlike those frequently found in Switzerland and Sweden. The existence of this strip, although well outside the perimeter of the main base, was never discovered by the British and would have been a good site to which some of the Super Etendards could have been dispersed safely.

The Argentines admit they had not anticipated such a bold stroke by the SAS, but insist that their troops were kept at a high state of readiness and would have responded instantly to pursue the British troops, into Chile if necessary. The Chileans, on the other hand, insist they would have protected their territorial integrity and made every effort to allow the SAS to take advantage of Chile's neutrality. As for the War Cabinet, it was willing to change the rules of engagement at the request of the forces, but preferred to avoid decisions of a military nature. Certainly Sir John Nott, bruised by his own earlier budget confrontations with the Royal Navy, and having already tendered his resignation to the Prime Minister, was determined to apply the need-to-know principle to issues of strategy, aware nonetheless that the Task Force had developed some imaginative missions for the SAS to perform.

Apart from the *Falkland Islands Review*, the Ministry of Defence commissioned an after-action report, written by Colonel David Parker of the Parachute Regiment, to document the lessons learned during the campaign. Although still classified, it is believed to be the most candid account of just how close to failure the entire campaign had been, amounting to a catalogue of wrong decisions at every critical moment. It is quite chilling to learn that some units on the front line outside Stanley were down to their last six rounds of ammunition on the day of the surrender, with no prospect of new supplies. Its conclusion was, quite simply, that the Task Force was lucky not to have been confronted by opponents meeting Warsaw Pact standards, a damning indictment of both staff and hardware.

POSTSCRIPT

The campaign in the South Atlantic affected all those who participated, and since the Argentine surrender some have fared better than others. This is particularly true of what might be termed the intelligence dimension:

Air Marshal Armitage was knighted in 1983 and went on to be Chief of Defence Intelligence; at the time of his retirement in 1989 he was Commandant of the Royal College of Defence Studies.

Captain Nicholas Barker, the commander of HMS *Endurance*, was prevented from publishing his account of the Falklands crisis, which he first gave at a Cambridge seminar in 1983, and now lives in Northumberland. He is currently preparing his memoirs, *Beyond Endurance*.

Sir Peter de la Billière was appointed Commander of the British forces in the Falklands in 1983, and in 1991 commanded the British troops in the Gulf War. During the annual 'crossbrief' at the SAS headquarters shortly before Christmas 1982 he expressed his disappointment at 'B' Squadron's performance during the Falklands, and received a rough reception from his audience of all ranks. His rather pointed story of an SAS officer who, during the Second World War in France, had driven deliberately into a German ambush to reach his men and had been killed, was greeted with derision by the assembled regiment. His two volumes of memoirs, *Looking for Trouble* and *Storm Command*, were written with Duff Hart-Davis. De la Billière now works for the bankers Robert Fleming in the City. To discourage other SAS personnel from capitalising on their experiences, a committee has been set up under the chairmanship of Colonel David Lyon to give advice to the regiment's potential authors.

Vinx Blocker has left the CIA and now runs his own trading organisation in Virginia. His deputy in Buenos Aires is now an Assistant Deputy Director in the CIA's Directorate of Operations.

Dewey Clarridge became embroiled in the Iran/Contra scandal, but received a pardon from President Bush in December 1993. He has retired from the CIA and now lives in San Diego.

Carlos Corti returned to Buenos Aires in September 1982 and now works in an electronics business. He remains philosophical about his encounter with SIS: 'Mr Dutcher got to be, how you say, a cupid? I have no problems with that. He was a professional, like me, but he was on one side of the war and I was on the other. You know, I never really thought we would get any missiles. When my government told me to find Exocets, I said to my chief that it was impossible, absolutely impossible. But I was ordered to try at any price. For me it was impossible to refuse.'

Tony Divall remains in Hamburg, having engaged in a public row with SIS to recover some of the expenses he incurred while running the Exocet denial programme.

In addition to his role as Intelligence Co-ordinator, Sir Antony Duff was appointed Chairman of the JIC in the wake of the Franks Report, and in 1985 became Director-General of the Security Service, a post he kept for two years before retiring to Hampshire.

Robin Fearn received a knighthood in 1991, while British Ambassador in Madrid, and is now retired.

Colin Figures received a knighthood in 1983 and two years later was appointed Intelligence Co-ordinator to the Cabinet in succession to Antony Duff. He retired in 1989.

Alexis Forter was decorated with the CMG in 1982, but retired from SIS because of ill-health soon afterwards and died in July the following year.

Licio Gelli was arrested in Geneva in September 1982 as he attempted to withdraw $55m from a Swiss bank using a false Argentine passport, but escaped from Champ-Dollon prison in August the following year. He subsequently gave himself up to the Swiss authorities in September 1987 and was eventually extradited to Italy in February 1988 to face charges relating to the Banco Ambrosiano, but was released on grounds of ill-health ten weeks later. He has since written his autobiography, *The Truth*, and now lives at his villa outside Arezzo in Tuscany.

General Sir James Glover commanded UK Land Forces until 1987, when he retired from the Army and was appointed a director of British Petroleum.

Oleg Gordievsky, the SIS mole inside the KGB's First Chief Directorate, was recalled to Moscow from London in May 1985 for interrogation, having been betrayed by the CIA traitor Aldrich Ames. He was exfiltrated into Finland by SIS in July 1985 and, divorced from his wife Leila, he now resides in Surrey under a new identity.

Brian Gorman, the Australian SIS representative in London, returned home the following year, having bought a racehorse in Ireland, and in 1994 was serving in Bangkok.

Arkadi Gouk, the KGB *rezident* in London, was expelled in April 1984, having been the recipient of secret documents deposited through his front door in Holland Park Avenue on Easter Sunday 1983 by the MI5 traitor Michael Bettaney. He returned to Moscow where he now lives in poor health, his career blighted by his inability to produce accurate assessments of the British political scene, and also by his close association with Oleg Gordievsky, whom he never suspected as a long-term agent for the British. According to Gordievsky, Gouk was guilty of 'failing to foresee that the British were prepared to go to war with Argentina over the Falklands' and had not raised the issue with Moscow Centre until two days after the Argentine invasion. Thereafter he reported to the KGB twice a day, but predicted a British defeat.

Brigadier Gurdon completed his secondment to the JIC and now manages the affairs of his son-in-law, Sir Andrew Lloyd Webber.

Elizabeth Halliday remained in London until 1985, when she was transferred to Washington DC. She then returned home to New Zealand to resume her NZSIS career.

Admiral Sir Roy Halliday retired as Director-General of Intelligence in 1984, and now lives in the New Forest.

Unusually, John Heath was asked to remain on in Chile as Ambassador beyond his official retirement age. He now lives in Bath.

Mark Heathcote spent five years supervising the Latin America desk at SIS's headquarters and then served as station commander in Islamabad, before moving to an international oil company where he now works as a political risks adviser.

Stephen Love gave evidence to the Franks Committee and retired to his farm near Brixham in Devon, where he took a leading part in local Conservative politics and was elected a county councillor.

John Moss served with his regiment in the Falklands in 1983 and soon afterwards was appointed deputy commander of the Sultan of Oman's forces. He is now based in London, working in the security industry.

Robin O'Neill, formerly head of the JIC's Assessment Staff, retired from the Diplomatic Service in 1992, having served as British Ambassador to Belgium, and now lives in London.

Alastair S. became Oleg Gordievsky's escort on several courtesy visits to allied security and intelligence services, and retired from SIS in April 1995 to work for British Aerospace.

Harry Schlaudemann has retired from the State Department and lives in Washington DC.

Jonathan Tod was decorated with the CBE in 1982, has since commanded the destroyer HMS *Fife* and the cruiser HMS *Illustrious*, and is now a Vice-Admiral and the Deputy Commander, Fleet, based at Northwood.

Anthony W. remained in Washington DC until 1986 and retired from SIS in 1993 to live near Lowestoft in Norfolk.

Caspar Weinberger, the US Secretary for Defense, received an honorary knighthood from the Queen and remarked in his autobiography, *Fighting for Peace*, that 'Former Secretary Haig said he spent some time at his negotiating sessions with the Argentinians telling them we had refused to fulfil British requests for arms. If he did tell them that, it was simply wrong.'

Anthony Williams was knighted upon his retirement in 1983 and moved to his farm in Salehurst, Sussex where he died in May 1990.

Alan Wolfe later served as the CIA's Chief of Station in Rome and has retired to Virginia.

Perhaps the most unfortunate postscript to the Falklands War was the offer made by Philip Aldridge, a nineteen-year-old lance-corporal in the Intelligence Corps, to sell a classified seventeen-page JIC assessment relating to the Islands to the Soviets. Aldridge had been seconded to the Defence Intelligence Staff at the Ministry of Defence for a fortnight in August 1982, and at the end of his assignment had smuggled the document out of the Metropole Building instead of destroying it as he had been ordered.

His attempt to contact the KGB was intercepted by the Security Service, which conducted a swift operation to identify Aldridge. He confessed and was imprisoned in January 1983 for four years.

APPENDIX I

Colonel Stephen Love's Report,
2 March 1982

SECRET

050/492/1   2 March, 1982

His Excellency
H' R M Hunt CMG
PORT STANLEY

THE ARGENTINE MILITARY THREAT TO THE FALKLANDS

Although most recent Argentine statements
have discounted the use of force there has also
been an increase in hard line articles in the
Argentine press on the subject of the Falkland
Islands. (I enclose: form DI 4 copies of two
examples by Iglesias Rouco in "La Prensa", which
this post has already sent to South America
Department).

2.   The notable feature in most of these is the
mention of the use of military force as a natural
follow-on from any breakdown in the current
negotiations. While the Government does not itself
dictate what we read, it would be easy enough for it
— or any of its members — to inspire sentiments of
this kind on a discreet basis in order to see what
reactions they provoke (and not surprisingly to
date no criticism has been voiced); and those I have
talked to in the Military recently stress that this
year is an important one indeed for Anglo—Argentine
relations.

SECRET

3. Putting the worst possible interpretation on
things this could mean an Army President, who has
already demonstrated his lack of patience when
frustrated over such issues (Chilean frontier closure
April 1981) giving orders to the military to solve the
Malvinas problem once and for all in the latter half
of this year, and in so doing aiming to secure at least
one invitingly easy looking point at a time when it
may quite possibly seem most attractive to him to do
something popular.

4. Following my recent private visit to the Islands,
we have been giving this problem some thought here
and feel it would be useful to record what the
military options might be, and to look briefly at the
intelligence problems they pose. This paper does not
address itself to non-aggressive measures.

"Shots across the bows"

5. Until and unless the talks break down the most
likely threat is posed by *the Navy*. Possibilities
for action by them are legion, but might include for
example,

    i.   the establishment of a Naval "research
           station" on an outlying island,
    ii.   the helicopter landing of marines on one of
           the islands for a 24-hour exercise coupled
           perhaps with low level overflights of Port
           Stanley, or
    iii. the denial of access to supply ships.

Such measures would be designed to demonstrate to
the Islanders how the Argentine claim to sovereignty
could be backed by strength whilst our own forces
could guarantee no effective protection. Successfully
carried out they would not result in bloodshed, would
therefore be unlikely to be condemned too harshly by

SECRET

others and would help to convince the United Kingdom
of both the seriousness and the urgency of the
problem. The Navy moreover would be politically keen
to flex their muscles in an area they regard as their
own and these sort of pranks would not need the support
of either of the other Services — an attractive
feature when the practice of joint operations is not
the norm. They would not moreover be overly dependent
on good weather.

"Invasion"

6.   The new danger is perhaps that the Argentines
might in days to come no longer believe a negotiated
settlement of any sort to be possible, and therefore
a military plan designed to prod Britain into talking
more seriously (in however changed an atmosphere)
might at that point seem to them outdated. A straight
seizure of the Islands is an obvious alternative.

7.   Although Navy and Marines could of course still
be used in any number of ways to land a force and take
Port Stanley, surprise could not be assured and the
possibility would exist of quite numerous casualties
being suffered by both sides. This consideration
might be overriding and cause them to think instead
(or additionally) of airborne delivery of a smaller
specialist force at Port Stanley followed by air or
sea landing of marines. One has to remember that the
military coup is a fairly well practised art here in
Argentina and it is also a fact that the Army study and
admire *coup de main* operations of all sorts. Of course
such a plan would carry high risks but the follow-on
force would be available for early committal if things
went wrong.

8.   The obvious first task in such an assault would be
the neutralisation of NP 8901's capability to react

SECRET

(destruction of arms, telephones, vehicles?), the capture of government, communications facilities, seizure of the FIDF armoury; next would come the securing of air field and jetties. The capture of Governor and key personnel would follow and Argentine military replacements would move in.

9. Our ally in this scenario is the Falkland Island weather with its capability for rapid and unforecast changes particularly in cloud base and wind speed. Although parachute operations should not be ruled out, once the decision was taken, troops would have to be prepared to spend several days waiting for good conditions, preferably as close to the Islands as possible to reduce the possibility of still having to abort on account of changed conditions after launch. Of course accurate and timely intelligence from Port Stanley itself to the mainland presents no problem to the Argentines; our own ability to give early warning would depend upon any coverage of airfield activity in Córdoba, home of the airborne brigade, and possibly Rio Gallegos, nearest field to the Islands. With present arrangements we could not realistically hope to get any information at all. Otherwise any warning would depend on NP 8901's ability to watch the western approaches to the Islands particularly during first light on days when conditions were judged good.

10. A further conclusion which the Argentines might have drawn is that the clandestine delivery of an assault party, possibly in plain clothes and with weapons concealed on their persons, could be a simpler (and cheaper) alternative. The easiest way for the group to arrive would be piecemeal week by week by the scheduled LADE F 28 under the guise of tourists or technical personnel or by special flight made under different cover (eg in one of the Argentine Air Force C130s which occasionally make freight deliveries).

SECRET

Their approach to the primary objectives (paragraph
8 above) could then be made at their convenience any
time after arrival. The only intelligence which could
be gained that such an attempt was being undertaken
would be through the Port Stanley airport Immigration
authorities' records of Argentines arriving in the
Colony.

Conclusions

11.   From a Buenos Aires perspective then the
following conclusions can be drawn:

    a.   it would be difficult to see any operation
        mounted at the present stage or in the future
        which did not involve the Navy — and very
        probably the Marines;

    b.   an airborne or clandestinely-mounted *coup
        de main* attempt against Port Stanley would
        have definite appeal to a force planning the
        seizure of the Islands;

    c.   special arrangements could enhance our
        chance of providing early warning from
        Argentina, but at present we could not
        realistically expect to be able to detect
        any moves;

    d.   important dividends can be gained by
        constant vigilance in the Colony itself
        and over its surrounding waters, as the
        knowledge that surprise would be hard
        to obtain is in itself a deterrent to a
        potential enemy aiming for an easy and
        clean win.

12.   I apologise if on the basis of an all too short
private visit I might have worked with incomplete
knowledge on territory which is theoretically
outside my area of concern (and possibly arriving at
conclusions contrary to official views to which I am
not privy). However, I am sure that as the diplomatic

SECRET

exchanges reach the crunch point, we, the intelligence
machine, should be clearing our minds as far as is
possible on what realistically the military threat
comprises (at the same time considering how we could
keep ourselves better informed upon it) — and the
forces which pose this threat are very definitely of
my concern.

13.   We should be glad to hear any comments which you
might have on all of this.

Sincerely, S. Dunlove

cc: DI 4   Stephen Love (Colonel)
       Ministry of Defence   Defence Attaché
       Dept
       P C C

APPENDIX II

British Defence Attaché's Telegram,
24 March 1982

CONFIDENTIAL

GRS 273
CONFIDENTIAL
DESKBY FCO 251920Z
FM BUENOS AIRES 24/2030Z MAR 82
TO IMMEDIATE MODUK
TELEGRAM NUMBER 24/2030Z OF 24 MARCH 1982
AND TO IMMEDIATE FCO
INFO IMMEDIATE PORT STANLEY (PERSONAL FOR GOVERNOR)

24/2030Z
CONFID
FROM BRITDEFAT BUENOS AIRES.
TO MODUK
SIC U2C/U2C
FOR DIA

RED IN MOD FORM 102 BOOK
................27..............
No. ....644..............

THE ARGENTINE MILITARY THREAT TO THE FALKLAND ISLANDS

1.   YOU MIGHT WELCOME A SHORT UPDATE ON OUR ASSESSMENT OF THE
MILITARY THREAT TO THE FALKLAND ISLANDS IN THE LIGHT OF CURRENT
EVENTS IN SOUTH GEORGIA. YOU ALREADY HAVE A NOTE ON WHAT WE SEE
AS THE ARGENTINE MILITARY OPTIONS: WHAT CAN NOW BE ADDED IS A
VIEW AS TO HOW THESE MIGHT BE EXERCISED IN A DEVELOPMENT OF THE
PRESENT SITUATION.

2.   IF THE ARGENTINES FAIL TO REMOVE THE WORK PARTY FROM LEITH
HARBOUR AND HMS ENDURANCE WERE TASKED TO DO THE JOB, THERE WOULD
BE THE STERNEST OF REACTIONS (ARGENTINE NATIONALS TAKEN ON BOARD
BRITISH WARSHIP IN ARGENTINE WATERS, ETC). ONE UPSHOT MIGHT WELL
BE AN ENCOUNTER WITH AN ARA WARSHIP. AN ALTERNATIVE WHICH MIGHT
WELL ATTRACT THE ARGENTINES COULD BE TO AWAIT THE ARRIVAL OF THE
PARTY AT PORT STANLEY AND THEN TO MOUNT QUOTE A RESCUE MISSION
UNQUOTE WHICH ON ENCOUNTERING RESISTANCE COULD BE ESCALATED INTO
AN OCCUPATION.

3.   THERE IS A HAWK FACTION IN THE FFAA WHOM WE MAY SEE PRESSING
THE LEADERSHIP THUS TO TAKE ADVANTAGE OF THE HEIGHTENED BLOOD
PRESSURE OF RECENT DAYS AT A TIME WHEN MILITARY MEASURES MIGHT
ATTRACT LESS CENSURE AND BE MORE EASILY JUSTIFIED ABROAD.

4.   WE MUST THEREFORE BE AWARE THAT IF HMS ENDURANCE IS COMMITTED
WE WOULD BE FACING NOT ONLY THE OBVIOUS RISK OF THE OPERATION ITSELF
MEETING RESISTANCE BUT ALSO AN INCREASE IN THE THREAT TO PORT
STANLEY — AND THAT AT A TIME WHEN NP 8901 ARE HALF EMBARKED AND
HANDOVER IMMINENT.

5.   DR HEAP, OF SAMD HERE FOR TALKS ON ANTARCTIC, ADDITIONALLY
POINTS OUT THAT TRADITIONALLY THE RESPONSE TO SUCH AN OPERATION
IS FOR THE OTHER SIDE TO REMOVE A LIKE NUMBER OF THE OPPOSITION
(EG DECEPTION ISLAND 1952). IN THIS CASE THIS COULD INVOLVE ARA
TAKING THE BAS DETACHMENT OFF FROM GRYTVIKEN.
WILLIAMS
STANDARD

CGS SENT TO

APPENDIX III

Anthony Divall's Letter of Credit, issued by Williams & Glyn's Bank

WILLIAMS & GLYN'S BANK LIMITED   000078

HOLT'S WHITEHALL BRANCH

KIRKLAND HOUSE
WHITEHALL LONDON SW1A 2EB

TELEPHONE
01-930 1701
01-930 5256

TELEGRAMS
MENSARIUS LONDON SW1

ARMY & ROYAL AIR FORCE AGENTS

EAML/DB   24th June, 1982.

Dear Sirs,

We write to advise you that £16,000,000 Sterling will be
available to Mr. Anthony Divall, Account No. 15467923, on
satisfactory receipt of a Performance Bond for US$10,000,000
and on condition that the goods subject to contract are tested
and inspected and approved on behalf of our Principal, and on
the basis of a contract to be drawn up between the Principals.

This letter does not constitute a commitment by Williams &
Glyn's Bank Ltd. unless the above conditions are completed to
our and our Principal's satisfaction, and we are issuing this
letter on the instructions of our Principal.

Yours faithfully,
for WILLIAMS & GLYN'S BANK LIMITED

E.A.M. Lee
(Assistant General Manager)

Julius Baer International Ltd.,
Bankers,
3 Lombard Street,
London, E.C.3.

Registered in England   Registration No. 952374   Registered Office: 20 Birchin Lane London EC3P 3DP

A MEMBER OF THE ROYAL BANK OF SCOTLAND GROUP

NOTES

Further publication details are provided in the Bibliography. The place of publication is London unless specified.

PREFACE

1 Sandy Woodward, *One Hundred Days*, p. 330.
2 Woodward, op. cit., p. 331.

CHAPTER 1: 'HANDBRAKE!'

1 See Sharkey Ward's account in *Sea Harrier Over the Falklands*, p. 83.
2 Martin Middlebrook, *The Fight for the 'Malvinas'*, p. 125.
3 Woodward, op. cit., p. 103.

CHAPTER 2: OPERACIÓN AZUL

1 Lord Franks, *Falkland Islands Review*, pp 26–7.
2 *Daily Express*, 29 March 1982, according to Mrs Thatcher, (see *The Downing Street Years*, p. 178), but actually 'Atom sub alert for Falklands' by John Miller in the *Daily Telegraph*, 29 March 1982.
3 Jeffrey Richelson and Desmond Ball, *The Ties That Bind*, p. 77.
4 Middlebrook, op. cit. p. 23.
5 For Gordievsky's account of his defection, ghosted by Duff Hart-Davis, see *Next Stop: Execution*.

6 For Casey's career, see Joseph Persico's *Casey: From the OSS to the CIA* (Penguin, 1990).
7 Stephen Love to Rex Hunt, 2 March 1982.
8 Ibid.
9 Ibid.

CHAPTER 3: LACIG

1 For an account of Operation JONATHAN, see *Israel's Secret Wars* by Ian Black and Benny Morris (Hamish Hamilton, 1991), *Spec Ops* by William H. McRaven, and *The Imperfect Spies* by Yossi Melman and Dan Raviv. The only previous comparable operation was an attack on three Romanian airfields in August 1944, executed by the Paratroop Battalion of the Brandenberger Division. The troops were flown into Tandarei and Boteni by two pairs of Junkers 52s, but surrendered soon after their arrival, having failed in their objective to sabotage the Romanian aircraft parked on the apron.

2 President Reagan's recollection of the US role in the Falklands is not entirely reliable. For instance, he claimed that 'in late March 1982 . . . our intelligence indicated Argentina was preparing to invade the Falklands'; whereas the CIA certainly was unaware of the invasion until the very last moment. He also asserted that his administration's policy was one of a 'genuine as well as an official neutrality' and to provide 'military help to neither adversary' (Ronald Reagan, *An American Life*, p. 358); whereas in fact Caspar Weinberger had authorised the transfer to Britain of Side-winder missiles without which, according to Mrs Thatcher, the entire enterprise would have failed.

3 Duncan Campbell, *The Unsinkable Aircraft Carrier*, p. 144.

4 Mrs Thatcher confirms Henderson's recollection, identifying the USS *Eisenhower* as the American carrier on offer (*The Downing Street Years*, p. 227). Another contingency plan for the loss of *Hermes* or *Invincible* involved the preparation of HMS *Illustrious*, then still under construction but approaching completion. Following the loss of HMS *Sheffield*, two Phallanx close defence systems, previously

rejected by the MoD on grounds of cost, were purchased, installed and tested with live rounds, in record time.

CHAPTER 4: PARIS

1 See Alexandre de Marenches in Marenches and Ockrent, *The Evil Empire.*
2 For details of the Marcovic affair, see *La Piscine* by Roger Faligot and Pascal Krop.
3 Vetrov's name was first disclosed in the French edition of *KGB: The Inside Story* by Oleg Gordievsky and Christopher Andrew (Hodder & Stoughton, 1990).
4 *Buenos Aires Herald,* 12 January 1979 and 18 September 1982.

CHAPTER 5: BUENOS AIRES

1 Britain's efforts to persuade the Americans that the Argentines were receiving Soviet intelligence were surprisingly successful, as demonstrated by President Reagan: 'As the Royal Navy sailed towards the Falklands, we learned that Soviet ships were trailing the British vessels and providing intelligence information about the fleet to Argentina via Cuba. We also learned that the Soviets offered to supply low-cost arms to Argentina if war broke out – an offer which, to its credit (and with encouragement from us), the Junta refused' (*An American Life*, p. 359).
2 The extent of American intelligence surveillance of Argentina's military capability in the last weeks of March 1982 has been consistently exaggerated. For a representative example, see Philip Knightley in *The Second Oldest Profession* (André Deutsch, 1986): 'The intelligence on the Argentine invasion of the Falklands in 1982 was voluminous. NSA/GCHQ was reading Argentinian military and diplomatic traffic, two American reconnaissance aircraft satellites were passing over the Argentine coast once a day (the ports were free of cloud so there were photographs of the build-up of the fleet), the American navy had spy satellites reporting on the Argentinian electronic emissions, and an American air

force spy plane, an SR-71, was making flights in the area' (p. 379).

3 See Max Knight, *US Satellite Reconnaissance During the Falklands Conflict*.

4 See William E. Burrows, *Deep Black*.

CHAPTER 6: SANTIAGO

1 See John Dinges and Saul Landau, *Assassination on Embassy Row*.

2 See 'The Chile Connection' in the *New Statesman*, 25 January 1985, in which Duncan Campbell alleged that six Canberra PR-9 aircraft were flown from Chilean bases throughout the conflict, and that SAS troops had infiltrated into Argentina from Chile and mounted an attack on Rio Grande.

3 For an account of Operation GLADIO see *The Puppet Masters* by Philip Willan; see also the Swiss Parliamentary Enquiry, 17 November 1990.

CHAPTER 7: STIRLING LINES

1 The SAS's reputation for ruthless efficiency in an undercover role in Northern Ireland is not entirely justified. Much of the clandestine activity attributed to the SAS has been the work of the 14th Intelligence Company, a wholly separate military unit which trained at Hereford but was based at Portadown. Charges of involvement in assassination, as alleged for example by 'Paul Bruce' in *The Nemesis File*, are completely fictional. The book was written by the former *Daily Mirror* journalist Nick Davies and prompted a police investigation which found no evidence to support the author's claims.

2 See Tony Geraghty, *Who Dares Wins*.

3 See Martin Dillon, *The Dirty War*.

4 Michael Paul Kennedy, *Soldier I, SAS*, p. 250. The author incorrectly identifies the target airfield as Port Stanley.

5 Sir Peter de la Billière, *Looking for Trouble*, p. 346. The manuscript, ghosted by Duff Hart-Davis, was the subject of

over 300 deletions imposed by the MoD prior to publication, and John Moss is not identified by name.

6 Harry McAllion, *Killing Zone*, p. 176.
7 Speculation about the Sea King's mission has not abated. A recent example is G. M. Dillon, *The Falklands: Politics and War*, in which the author cited the Buenos Aires *Clarion* and referred to 'the appearance of the Sea King helicopter in Punta Arenas, rapidly hidden from view by the gendarmes when the first reporters arrived on the spot. The Argentine Navy maintains that this helicopter could not have come from the British Fleet, situated as it was to the north of the Falklands, because it lacked the range to fly such long distances. One is inclined to think, on the other hand, that some British ship, perhaps winked at by the Chileans, was sailing in the Pacific and used such helicopters to carry out espionage tasks. Finally, it must not be forgotten, Argentine air operations of heavy transport were executed invariably from the mainland. Nevertheless, one version has it that the appearance of the Sea King on trans-Andean soil was in reality the advance party of a hazardous mission by eight members of the Special Air Service (SAS) into Argentine territory. The purpose of such a mission would be to obtain information about planned air manoeuvres' (p. 221).
8 The single surviving Chinook flew a total of 109 hours in combat without spares or ground support. See *The Falklands Campaign: The Lessons*, p. 20.

CHAPTER 8: HEATHROW

1 See Patrick Seale and Maureen McConville, *The Hilton Assignment*. The authors concealed the identities of George Strakaty ('Gregor Jirasek'), SIS's source in Omnipol; his partner Mirko Melich ('Stefan Vlcek'); and his SIS contact Harry Briggs ('Frank Higgins'). 'James Kent' was really Denys Rowley.
2 Charles Haughey was charged with conspiring to import guns and ammunition, together with James Kelly, who was described as a 'retired intelligence officer', and two others, but they were acquitted at the Dublin High Court on 23 October 1970. Kelly had worked undercover as a customs

officer on the Ulster border before his arrest. See James Kelly, *Orders for the Captain?*.

3 For further details of Otto Schluter's career, see Erwan Bergot, *Le Dossier Rouge*.

4 For an account of the Dublin arms trial, see Tom McIntyre, *Through the Bridewell Gate*.

5 The Felsted School raid was led by Cathal Goulding, a future IRA Chief of Staff, with Stephenson and Manus Canning. All three were caught immediately and sentenced to eight years' imprisonment. Goulding was released from Wormwood Scrubs in 1959 and returned to Dublin.

6 David O'Connell represented the PIRA at the summit with William Whitelaw in London, July 1972. After less than a year in the PIRA McGuire defected and described her experiences in *To Take Arms: A Year in the Provisional IRA*.

7 For further information regarding Georges Starkmann, see John Cooley, *Libyan Sandstorm*.

CHAPTER 9: HAMBURG

1 See Rupert Cornwell, *God's Banker*.

2 See Larry Gurwin, *The Calvi Affair*; David Yallop, *In God's Name*; and John Cornwell, *A Thief in the Night*.

CHAPTER 10: STANLEY

1 Middlebrook, op. cit., p. 247.

2 Woodward, op. cit., p. 327.

CHAPTER 11: WHITEHALL

1 Lord Franks, op. cit., p. 90.

2 Thatcher, op. cit. p. 177.

3 Lord Franks, op. cit. p. 2.

4 Ibid.

5 Thatcher, op. cit., p. 176.

6 The final exoneration in Franks seemed unsupported by the evidence contained in the rest of the Report. As G. M. Dillon commented: 'The Franks Report ... was

intellectually dishonest in making *every* political allowance for each mitigating factor. Its conclusion provided a quite unwarranted apologia for Thatcher and Carrington, totally unsupported by the evidence on which the report itself was based' (*The Falklands: Politics and War*).

7 Rattenbach, *The Rattenbach Commission*.

8 Lord Franks, op. cit.

9 Brian Crozier, *Free Agent*, p. 89.

10 Stephen Hastings, *The Drums of Memory*, p. 237.

11 The issue of whether the Argentine Navy learned of the 1977 task group is unresolved. All the published references postdate the Franks Report, including *La Guerra Inaudita* by Ruben Moro, which records that 'towards the end of that year, in secret form Great Britain sent a nuclear submarine and two frigates to the South Atlantic which remained close to those islands, alleging hypothetical Argentine manoeuvres' (p. 26). According to F. I. & D. M. Hoffman's *Las Malvinas Falklands 1493–1982: Soberania en Disputa*, 'Britain chose to deploy a military presence in the area at the time of the December talks, and it consisted of a nuclear-powered submarine in the proximity of the islands and two frigates at 1,000 miles distance . . .' (p. 145). This latter item is interesting because the detail of HMS *Dreadnought*'s detachment from the 1977 task group was never disclosed, which suggests that the Argentine Navy did discover the submarine independently. However, no Argentine naval officer has admitted knowing about the 1977 episode until Mr Callaghan's revelation in March 1982, and officers of the Argentine Navy's submarine surveillance squadron are emphatic that their aircraft were not operational in the area during the critical period. Guillermo Montenegro, the commander of the *Salta*, a Type-209 submarine, insists 'the presence of the British Task Force went unnoticed by the Argentine Navy', and suggests that Argentine naval activity directed against Soviet fishing fleets inside Argentina's economic exclusion zone may have been the cause of the misinterpretation.

12 *Hansard*, 30 March 1982, Col. 168.

13 Denis Healey has confirmed Callaghan's version of 'a small naval task force . . . including a nuclear submarine' (*The*

Time of My Life, p. 494) and asserts: 'This deterrent was sufficient. There was no invasion.' However, he adds rather unconvincingly that 'if Mrs Thatcher had begun to assemble these ships into a task force as soon as the Joint Intelligence Committee reported in 1981 that there was a risk of invasion, and made the task force's existence known when firm intelligence of Galtieri's intention began to accumulate from the beginning of 1982, the invasion would not have taken place'. Doubtless a task force would have had a deterrent effect, but there was no intelligence accumulating in 'the beginning of 1982' as he suggests.

14 James Callaghan, *Time and Chance*, p. 375.
15 David Owen, *Time to Declare*, p. 350.

BIBLIOGRAPHY

The place of publication is London unless specified.

Bergot, Erwan, *Le Dossier Rouge* (Paris: Editions Grasset, 1976)

Bilton, Michael, and Kosminsky, Peter, *Speaking Out* (André Deutsch, 1989)

Bishop, Patrick, and Witherow, John, *The Winter War* (Quartet, 1982)

Branch, Taylor, and Propper, Eugene, *Labyrinth* (Viking, 1982)

Brown, David, *The Royal Navy and the Falklands War* (Leo Cooper, 1987)

Bruce, Paul, *The Nemesis File* (Blake Publishing, 1995)

Burrows, William E., *Deep Black* (Random House, 1986)

Callaghan, James, *Time and Chance* (Collins, 1987)

Calvert, Peter, *The Falklands Crisis: The Rights and the Wrongs* (Pinter, 1982)

Campbell, Duncan, *The Unsinkable Aircraft Carrier* (Michael Joseph, 1984)

Cardoso, Oscar, Kirshbaum, Ricardo, and Van der Kooy, Eduardo, *Falklands: The Secret Plot* (Preston Editions, 1987)

Carrington, Peter, *Reflect on Things Past* (Collins, 1988)

Central Office of Information, *Their Trade is Treachery* (1964)
———, *Treachery is Still Their Trade* (1973)

Charlton, Michael, *The Little Platoon* (Oxford: Basil Blackwell, 1989)

Clayton, Anthony, *Forearmed* (Brassey's, 1993)

Cooley, John, *Libyan Sandstorm* (Sidgwick & Jackson, 1982)

Cornwell, Rupert, *God's Banker* (Victor Gollancz, 1983)

Crozier, Brian, *Free Agent* (HarperCollins, 1993)

Dalyell, Tam, *One Man's War* (Cecil Woolf, 1982)

Danchev, Alex, *International Perspectives on the Falklands Conflict* (New York: St Martin's Press, 1992)

de la Billière, Sir Peter, *Storm Command* (HarperCollins, 1992)

————, *Looking for Trouble* (HarperCollins, 1994)

de Marenches, Alexandre, and Ockrent, Christine, *The Evil Empire* (Sidgwick & Jackson, 1988)

Dillon, G. M., *The Falklands: Politics and War* (Macmillan, 1989)

Dillon, Martin, *The Dirty War* (Arrow, 1991)

Dinges, John, and Landau, Saul, *Assassination on Embassy Row* (New York: McGraw-Hill, 1980)

Dobson, Christopher, *The Falklands Conflict* (Coronet, 1982)

Ethell, Jeffrey, and Price, Alfred, *Air War: South Atlantic* (Sidgwick & Jackson, 1983)

Faligot, Roger, and Krop, Pascal, *La Piscine* (Oxford: Basil Blackwell, 1988)

Fox, Robert, *Eyewitness Falklands* (HMSO, 1983)

Freedman, Lawrence, and Gamba-Stonehouse, Virginia, *Signals of War* (Faber & Faber, 1990)

Gavshon, Arthur, and Rice, Desmond, *The Sinking of the Belgrano* (Secker & Warburg, 1984)

Geraghty, Tony, *Who Dares Wins* (Warner Books, 1992)

Gordievsky, Oleg, *Next Stop: Execution* (Macmillan, 1995)

Gurwin, Larry, *The Calvi Affair* (Macmillan, 1983)

Haig, Alexander, *Caveat* (Weidenfeld & Nicolson, 1984)

Harris, Robert, *Gotcha! The Media, the Government and the Falklands Crisis* (Faber & Faber, 1983, reprinted in Harris, *The Media Trilogy*, Faber & Faber, 1994)

Hastings, Max, and Jenkins, Simon, *The Battle for the Falklands* (Michael Joseph, 1984)

Hastings, Stephen, *The Drums of Memory* (Leo Cooper, 1994)

Healey, Denis, *The Time of My Life* (Michael Joseph, 1989)

Hervey, John, *Submarines* (Brassey's, 1994)

Hoffman, F. I. and D. M., *Las Malvinas Falklands 1493–1982: Soberania en Disputa* (Buenos Aires: Instituto de Publicaciones Navales, 1992)

Kelly, James, *Orders for the Captain?* (Co. Cavan: Kelly Kane 1971)

Kennedy, Michael Paul, *Soldier I, SAS: Eighteen Years in the Elite Force* (Bloomsbury, 1989)

Knight, Max, *US Satellite Reconnaissance During the Falklands Conflict* (Aston University)

Koburger, Charles, *Sea Power in the Falklands* (Praeger, 1983)

Laffin, John, *Fight for the Falklands* (Sphere, 1982)

McCallion, Harry, *Killing Zone* (Bloomsbury, 1995)

McGuire, Maria, *To Take Arms: A Year in the Provisional IRA* (Macmillan, 1973)

McIntyre, Tom, *Through the Bridewell Gate* (Faber & Faber, 1971)

McRaven, William H., *Spec Ops* (Presidio, 1995)

Melman, Yossi, and Raviv, Dan, *The Imperfect Spies* (Sidgwick & Jackson, 1989)

Middlebrook, Martin, *Operation Corporate: The Story of the Falklands War 1982* (Viking, 1985)

———, *The Fight for the 'Malvinas'* (Viking, 1989)

Moro, Ruben, *La Guerra Inaudita* (Buenos Aires: Editorial Pleamar, 1985)

Owen, David, *Time to Declare* (Michael Joseph, 1991)

Perkins, Roger, *Operation Paraquat* (Picton Publishing, 1986)

Raw, Charles, *The Moneychangers* (HarperCollins, 1992)

Reagan, Ronald, *An American Life* (Hutchinson, 1990)

Richelson, Jeffrey, and Ball, Desmond, *The Ties That Bind* (Allen & Unwin, 1986)

Speed, Keith, *Sea Change* (Ashgrove Press, 1982)

Stockwell, John, *In Search of Enemies: A CIA Story* (New York: W.W. Norton & Co., 1978)

Sunday Times Insight Team, *The Falklands War* (Sphere, 1982)

Thatcher, Margaret, *The Downing Street Years* (HarperCollins, 1993)

Thompson, Julian, *No Picnic* (Leo Cooper, 1985)

Ward, Sharkey, *Sea Harrier Over the Falklands* (Leo Cooper, 1993)

Willan, Philip, *The Puppet Masters* (Constable, 1991)

Woodward, Sandy, *One Hundred Days* (Fontana, 1992)

Wright, Peter, *Spycatcher* (Viking, 1987)

OFFICIAL REPORTS

Franks, Lord (chair), *Falkland Islands Review: Report of a Committee of Privy Counsellors* (Cmnd 8787, HMSO, 1983)

Government of the United Kingdom, *Falkland Islands: Negotiations for a Peaceful Settlement* (HMSO, 21 May 1982)

——, *The British Army in the Falklands* (HMSO, 1982)

House of Commons, *The Falklands Campaign: A Digest of Debates in the House of Commons, 2 April to 15 June 1982* (HMSO, 1982)

——, First Report of the Defence Committee, Session 1982–83, *Handling of Press and Public Information During the Falklands Conflict* (two volumes, HMSO, 1982)

——, *Minutes of the Proceedings of the Foreign Affairs Committee, Session 1982–83* (HMSO, 11 May 1983)

——, Third Report of the Foreign Affairs Committee, Session 1984–85, *Events of the Weekend of 1st and 2nd May 1982* (HMSO, 1985)

——, Fourth Report of the Defence Committee, Session 1986–87, *Implementing the Lessons of the Falklands Campaign* (two volumes, HMSO, 1987)

Rattenbach, Benjamin, *The Rattenbach Commission* (Buenos Aires, 1983)

Secretary of State for Defence (chair), *The Falklands Campaign: The Lessons* (Cmnd 8738, HMSO, 1982)

Supplement to the *London Gazette* (HMSO, 8 October 1982)

Swiss Parliamentary Report, 1 November 1990

INDEX